Roman Catholic Political Philosophy

D1570356

Roman Catholic Political Philosophy

James V. Schall

LEXINGTON BOOKS
Lanham • Boulder • New York • Toronto • Oxford

LEXINGTON BOOKS

A division of Rowman & Littlefield Publishers, Inc.
A wholly owned subsidiary of The Rowman & Littlefield Publishing Group, Inc.
4501 Forbes Boulevard, Suite 200
Lanham, MD 20706

PO Box 317
Oxford
OX2 9RU, UK

British Library Cataloguing in Publication Information Available

The hardback edition of this book was previously cataloged by the Library of Congress as
follows:

Schall, James V.
    Roman Catholic political philosophy / James V. Schall.
        p. cm.
    Includes bibliographical references and index.
    1. Christianity and politics—Catholic Church. 2. Political science—Philosophy.
I. Title.

BR115.P7S2685 2004
320'.01—dc22   2003028188
ISBN-13: 978-0-7391-0745-4 (cloth: alk. paper)
ISBN-10: 0-7391-0745-3 (cloth : alk. paper)
ISBN-13: 978-0-7391-1703-3 (pbk : alk. paper)
ISBN-10: 0-7391-1703-3 (pbk : alk. paper)

Printed in the United States of America

♾™ The paper used in this publication meets the minimum requirements of American
National Standard for Information Sciences—Permanence of Paper for Printed Library
Materials, ANSI/NISO Z39.48–1992.

By political theology we understand political teachings which are based on divine revelation. Political philosophy is limited to what is accessible to the unassisted human mind. . . . Political philosophy is the attempt to understand the nature of political things. Before one can even think of attempting to understand the nature of political things, one must know political things: one must possess political knowledge. At least every sane adult possesses political knowledge in some degree. Everyone knows something of taxes, police, law, jails, war, peace, armistice.

> —Leo Strauss, "What Is Political Philosophy?"
> *What Is Political Philosophy? and Other Studies* (Glencoe, Ill.:
> The Free Press, 1959), 13–14

Man is not made for justice from his fellows, but for love, which is greater than justice, and by including supercedes justice. *Mere* justice is an impossibility, a fiction of analysis. . . . Justice to be justice must be much more than justice. Love is the law of our condition, without which we can no more render justice than a man can keep a straight line, walking in the dark.

> —*George MacDonald: An Anthology*, no. 51.
> Edited by C. S. Lewis (New York: Macmillian, [1947] 1974)

Render to Caesar the things that are Caesar's, and to God, the things that are God's.

> —Matthew, 22:22

Many would even go so far as to hold that statesmen have got to do things that virtuous persons hate to do, so that power should better be in the hands of men not too particular about the morality of their means. This goes directly against the doctrine of the Greek philosophers who founded political science and philosophy. It is often said that Aristotle's ethics is political and that his politics is ethical; this nicely balanced proposition happens to express the case with perfect accuracy.

—Yves Simon, *A General Theory of Authority*
(Notre Dame, Ind.: University of Notre Dame Press, 1980), 139–40)

A science which is free in the highest degree cannot be a possession of that nature which is servile and subordinate in many respects. But human nature is servile "in many respects," i.e., in many ways. Therefore this science (metaphysics) is not a human possession. Now human nature is said to be servile insofar as it stands in need of many things. . . . But that science which is sought for itself alone, man cannot use freely, since he is often kept from it because of the necessities of life. Nor again is it subject to man's command, because man cannot acquire it perfectly. Yet that very small part of it which he does have outweighs all the things known through the other sciences.

—Thomas Aquinas, *Commentary on the Metaphysics* of Aristotle, no. 60
(982b29; 1178a1–2)

Contents

~

Acknowledgments

The following sources are to be thanked for permission to use an essay originally appearing in their pages: chapter 2, *Perspectives in Political Science*; 4, *The American Catholic Philosophic Quarterly*; 5, Center for Economic and Policy Education, St. Vincent's College, Latrobe, Pennsylvania; 6, *Angelicum*; 7, in *Faith & the Life of the Intellect*, edited by Curtis Hancock and Brendan Sweetman, Catholic University of America Press; 8, *Homiletic and Pastoral Review*; 11, *The Review of Politics*. These chapters are modified for this book.

~

Introduction

"Whoever does not appreciate the fact that Catholic political philosophy lives in the cosmos—this is its true meaning—of Christian Catholic life, will come to strange conclusions. . . ."

—Heinrich Rommen,
The State in Catholic Thought: A Treatise in Political Philosophy (1945)[1]

No doubt, any endeavor to "introduce" what I shall call, with deliberate paradox, "Roman Catholic Political Philosophy" or "Catholic Christian Political Philosophy" will seem to not a few like proposing a contradiction in terms or squaring a circle. Or to cite from my learned mentor, Heinrich Rommen's well-known and massive book, the topic itself will seem to be full of "strange conclusions." The purpose of this book, both to those belonging to a "Christian Catholic life," as Rommen rather quaintly put it, and to those who do not, is that they will, in the end, come to see that the "conclusions" about political philosophy and Roman Catholicism will, on consideration, hopefully appear less "strange." The argument, as it develops, is meant to be cautious, irenic, something that needed to be, at least once, thought out at some length.

In fact, I have been thinking and writing on the relation of reason and revelation to political things for many years now. Something more is present here than, at first sight, meets the eye, both for philosophy itself and for revelation. What has continually struck me as "odd" is, as I argue, the curious "incompleteness" of both political philosophy and revelation, a mutual incompleteness that portends, for that very reason, some relationship. Or perhaps "incompleteness" is not the right word, as both revelation and political philosophy are what they are, each in its own order. I do not want either revelation or political philosophy to be something other than it is. I claim neither more nor less than what is properly due to each. Political philosophy, by being itself, however, points beyond itself, to philosophy. Philosophy, in turn, leaves a certain abiding unsettlement in our souls because of the paucity or lack of firmness of the ultimate answers it does provide to its own legitimate questions. The inability of philosophy satisfactorily to answer many of philosophy's own questions constitutes its own sense of mystery about itself. It is almost as if its seeming "incompleteness" were "intended," or at least related to the structure of things.

Philosophy is the search for the knowledge of the whole. It is the "love" of wisdom, the "quest" for the meaning of reality, not yet its complete possession, even when, as it must, it seeks the possession that is true knowledge. But, in spite of our best efforts, philosophy does not leave us with this complete knowledge of the whole, or, following Aristotle and Aquinas, not much of it, worthy as it is that which we can and do know. Nonetheless, I am someone who thinks that the questions that philosophy deigns to raise from its own sources do require answers. But answers are not properly "answers" until questions are formulated as questions. The idea that the purpose of philosophy is exclusively to "raise" questions is itself questionable.

Indeed, this opinion that there are only questions can be a form of skepticism, itself a philosophical position that holds in principle and as certain that there can be no answers. This latter is a position that famously contradicts itself in its very formulation, the certainty of uncertainty, the uncertainty of certainty. Questions, however, are raised in order to find, establish, or receive answers. Questions are not designed to reach just any answer. They are structured to conclude to the truth, to affirm of *what is*, that it is. Not every "philosophy" is a bearer of the truth, though any false or erroneous position usually possesses, when sorted out, some valid elements that need to be affirmed. No "error," in other words, is completely "in error." Evil always resides in what is good; error always resides in or is related to in what is true.

Let me immediately establish what this book is not:

1) This is not a book on the constitutional or legislative legalities of "church and state" in any given nation or political system.
2) It is not a handbook for voters and politicians.
3) It is not a book in comparative religion or philosophy contrasting Catholicism with Protestantism, Buddhism, Islam, Chinese Communism, or contemporary liberalism, conservatism, or socialism.

4) Nor is this a book on what is called "the social doctrines of the Church."[2] Whatever these "social doctrines" might be, and I have no problem with most of them, they are not, as such, "political philosophy." Political philosophy and theology are different disciplines, though each is aware of each other. Both exist in the ordered—or, if such be one's philosophy, "disordered"—world *that is*.

5) Likewise, this book is not an effort to "reconcile" the positions of modern liberalism *or* conservatism with Catholicism or with some "third way" related to neither. The dichotomy "liberal or conservative" whenever used to analyze political things is too narrow and is itself part of the problem in understanding both revelation and political philosophy.

6) Nor do we have here a book on what sorts of regimes or institutions within a regime would be closest to Catholic opinions on politics.

7) This book is not a history or summary of the views of classic or modern Catholic thinkers on politics and the state found in such representative and excellent Catholic thinkers as, say, Ambrose, Augustine, Aquinas, Suarez, Maritain, Rommen, Murray, Simon, Finnis, Molnar, or a host of others.

While I presuppose and respect such traditions from whatever philosophic or religious source, this book is rather an extended, non-polemic essay or consideration about political philosophy itself as it relates to a particular account of revelation, namely, that found in Roman Catholicism. Such a concentrated reflection has not, as such, I think, been attempted before in quite this manner. Both for political philosophy and for revelation, as well as for philosophy itself, it is worth doing. This book is, in the French sense, an "essay," an "effort," a relaxed, literate "attempt" to present from various angles a rarely heard argument about how the highest things of philosophy, politics, and revelation relate to each other. My purpose here is to suggest that there *is* an argument and to indicate its general outlines. Whether or not anyone might finally agree with that argument is quite another issue. It is enough that it be formulated after the manner of that "serious play" in which, as Plato said in *The Laws* (803), we are to consider what it is that we are about in the very being in which we exist.

Obviously, I am aware of the classic retort that we find no such thing as a "Roman Catholic" or any other religious mathematics. There is just mathematics, though I grant that certain philosophical presuppositions would make even mathematics impossible. Likewise, certain philosophical presuppositions would make Roman Catholicism impossible—one that denied, for example, the existence of the real world, or one that found nothing outside the mind. Such positions would have a terrible time with the Incarnation, one of the two central doctrines of Roman Catholicism. Roman Catholic "social thought," to be sure, does contain significant considerations from philosophy, but, as such, it takes its starting point from what is found in revelation. The New Testament, however, is not a handbook in politics. In fact, it has very little to say about politics at all, even though what little it does say is rather provocative. I will argue that, on its own grounds, for its own integrity, political philosophy itself has to reckon with revelation, but after the manner of each. Unlike "Catholic social thought," political philosophy does not begin with revelation, but it does not unilaterally ignore its presence at least to the extent that it must account for all things that in fact appear in the public world, among which are the things said to occur because of revelation.

Insofar then as Roman Catholicism is interested in genuine philosophy as a direct result of its own concern about what it does maintain through revelation, it must examine philosophical positions that would make what it holds to be contradictory or unlikely or impossible. Because of its own understanding of revelation, Roman Catholicism itself cannot avoid attending to philosophy. Therefore, it must be philosophically critical, open to any truth *that is*. Already here, we have intimations of Aquinas's position that faith builds upon and presupposes nature, a knowledge of which is itself a good and, as such, has nothing to do with revelation.

As far as its own particular manifestation in the world, Catholicism appeared at a definite time and place, in the reign of Caesar Augustus, when the whole world was at peace (Matthew, 2:1–21). It presupposes a definite history, the Hebrew account of itself, but also it deals with or encounters both Athens and Rome in its very foundation. Christ is tried by a Roman governor in Jerusalem. Paul speaks to Athenians, appeals to Caesar, and writes a letter to the Romans. Though having the power of intelligence by nature, we begin to know from noting things outside the mind. We therefore require a philosophy that can defend an empirical starting point that does justice to both mind and world.

Here, moreover, I am not concerned with "Christianity" as if it were some alternate religion to Roman Catholicism. I acknowledge the existence of the Great Schism and of the Reformation, of subsequent sects and congregations within Protestantism. Each of these can be depended on to explain itself either through its own revelational or its own philosophical presuppositions. This capacity or responsibility to explicate itself is likewise true of Islam, Judaism itself, Buddhism, Hinduism, or other religions or intellectual systems.

I have no problem with the existence of other explanations of reality, but I do not grant that they are free to excuse themselves from the burden of philosophy and political philosophy as it relates to themselves.[3] There is a *philosophia perennis* that allows no position, especially Catholicism, to remain untested. Nor am I an Averröist who thinks that somehow political philosophy is superior to revelation and subsumes it into itself. Neither am I a fideist who thinks that there is nothing arising out of the world with which I have to reckon even in the name of revelation.

At the beginning of this book are found five citations, each of which needs to be considered in understanding the nature of this argument about Catholicism and political philosophy. The first citation is from Leo Strauss's famous essay, "What Is Political Philosophy?" I will often refer to this essay in these pages. Strauss begins by pointing out the common sense notion of political things. We do not have to begin from outside our experience, with formal science or social science, for example, to confront political things. By our very living, we all have some experience of political things. This raw material was initially what Aristotle knew and organized into the picture of the whole in his *Ethics*, *Politics*, and *Rhetoric*. Yves Simon was right that this corpus of Aristotle did reject the notion that immorality could somehow be the best form of political action, or at least that it was a useful tool available to the ruler when needed. At the heart of Greek thought lies Socrates' affirmation that "it is better to suffer injustice than to do it." Catholicism itself, from its own sources, not excluding its own reflections on Plato, is founded on the abiding truth of this Socratic principle.

However central justice is in political things, somehow it always remains incomplete, even experientially so. Justice is subsumed into something beyond it, as Aristotle already intimated in his great treatise on friendship and his understanding of *epichia* (equity, 1136a33–38a2). George MacDonald's remarks, that love and charity, are higher than justice are to the point. Aquinas had earlier affirmed that the world is not created in justice but in mercy (I, 21, 4). A world of pure justice would somehow be a terrible world— a theme that was the point of C. S. Lewis's great novel *Till We Have Faces*.[4] Perhaps a world of justice would look like Book Five of *The Republic*, a book that stands as a perennial warning to us about the consequences of creating pure justice in this world. It should not surprise us that Aristotle pointed out that man's nature was somehow held in bondage (982b29). There is a science beyond politics, even beyond metaphysics, as Aquinas maintained (I, 1, 1–4). If man were the highest being, Aristotle said in a passage I shall often repeat, politics would be the highest science (1141a20–22). But some science exists beyond politics. This fact is not intended to denigrate politics but to put it in its proper place and thereby to glorify it, in as much as something that is not itself a being, such as a "state," can be glorified.

Each of the eleven chapters of this book deals in one way or another with the interrelation of reason, revelation, and political philosophy. Common themes return in each new chapter. The beginning point is always political philosophy as a matrix discipline in the modern world because, almost alone of the academic disciplines, it recognizes its relation to the past of philosophy and at least reflects the impact of revelation on its very nature. I am much influenced by Leo Strauss and Eric Voegelin as modern thinkers who have enabled these considerations to reach maturity precisely as political philosophy.

To be sure, there will be some lightsome passages found in these pages. I consider Samuel Johnson and G. K. Chesterton to be original, delightful, minds of incomparable depth, never to be neglected even when they are neglected. I do not hesitate, from time to time, to cite Charles Schulz's *Peanuts* as an original philosophical source. Charlie Brown will have remarkable insights. Though this is hopefully a sober book, I do not consider humor and philosophy to be contradictory but to require each other, even in the highest things, especially in the highest things. I belong to a tradition in which the greatest of its poems was called, with philosophic exactness, "the Divine Comedy," not "the Divine Tragedy."

The uniqueness of this book, in my own mind at least, is that it takes the liberty, the genuine academic liberty, the freedom of research, to argue the possibility of a controversial position. To some contemporaries, an argument about the consistency and validity of reason and relation in a coherent relationship to each other will be rejected as impossible or at least implausible. I do not expect otherwise. But a certain confidence inclines me to think that most thinkers will be willing to reflect on the issue, even welcome it, if it is presented in its clearest terms. Thus, I do hope, at least once, that the argument can be made as a valid and coherent position to be considered on its own terms and not, a priori, rejected because we cannot allow ourselves to think that reason and revelation have any plausible relationship to each other. I do not maintain, be it noted, that political philosophy *must* lead to revelation, or even that revelation *must* make its relationship to reason and experience so evident that no one could doubt it. I do hold that some relationship is remarkably plausible, but not so intellectually compelling that the connections cannot be disputed or doubted.

What needs to be made clear, furthermore, is what I mean by "Catholicism." It is not a product of my imagination. Due to public scandals, to various internal issues of controversy and disagreement, what is in fact Catholicism will often look rather like a chaotic system. How disedifyingly certain clerics or Catholics live obscures what Catholicism holds about itself. However, if we grant, for the sake of argument, that Christ was sent precisely to save sinners, as revelation maintains, we should not be overly surprised to find sinners among us, even in high offices. It is not orthodox to hold, nor is it experientially verifiable, that believers are, on that ground alone, sinless. The "scandals" produced by Catholics themselves, in this sense, are not indications of the falsity of this faith and of its teachings but of its uncanny shrewdness in revealing ourselves to ourselves, even as sinners. What, as a working premise, I take to be Catholicism, as an outline and statement of what it is, is that central line of doctrine, morality, and practice that is found presented in, say, the *General Catechism of the Catholic Church*.[5]

No doubt, "Christians" and "Catholics" exist who maintain that Christ is not divine, that God is not Trinitarian, or that sundry moral commandments of the Decalogue need not be obeyed. I am not one of these. Nor is this the place to argue the truth of such questioned positions, though, in fact, I think that the core positions of what Catholicism does teach about itself can be maintained in an intelligent fashion. My argument here is based on the coherence and validity of the central position. I only ask anyone who does not hold these views to accept them at least as an hypothesis to be considered or examined as any other proposed truth. I do not think "unorthodox" views by whoever espouses them answer the basic human or transcendent questions that arise in philosophy and political philosophy; otherwise, I would follow them.

Again, I do not ask any reader to agree with any or all of these classic positions. But I do ask that they be understood as they are and are presented in their clearest and most coherent and authoritative form. I do not think that one needs to be a Catholic to understand any basic doctrine at least in its essential terms, just as I think I can understand a Marxist, or Confucian, or Buddhist, or Hegelian position without my being an advocate of any of these positions. I do think, however, that if anything is "owed" to Catholicism in academia, it is that it be understood for what is holds itself to be, not for what it itself rejects. If someone, speaking about the nature of society, rejects, for example, the Trinitarian notion of God on the grounds that there cannot be three gods, it seems only fair to point out that Catholicism agrees with him that there are not three gods.

Moreover, I do not think that Catholicism is simply a matter of "dogmas," though I think, with Chesterton, that the mind, as mind, is made to affirm dogmas, that is, to state what is true in the clearest and most tested way possible. But I also am conscious of what concerns Eric Voegelin, namely, that no doctrinal formulation will itself, as a verbal statement, be the object of the truth that it affirms. Through any formulation, the mind seeks to know the reality so indicated. The human mind is made to affirm the truth of things, including the truth of God, without that affirmation implying that our concepts exhaust the reality about which we know or that such concepts of God constitute the reality itself.[6] If a finite mind could fully know what God is, it would be God. Obviously, no Catholic mind confuses what it can strive to know with the reality known.

Each of the following chapters will approach the relation of reason, revelation, and political philosophy in a different manner, though abiding themes will be found in each chapter. Needless to say, what I have argued in previous books, especially in *Reason, Revelation, and the Foundations of Political Philosophy, At the Limits of Political Philosophy, What Is God Like?, Does Catholicism Still Exist?*, and *The Politics of Heaven and Hell*, will illuminate what is found here. What is presented here, however, is a different consideration of these relationships. In these pages, I have not gone into the substantial issues in any detail—such as Incarnation, Trinity, friendship, immortality, evil, leisure, play, or the structure of actual polities. In the chapter on "Worship and Political Philosophy" (X), I have come to see, to me in a surprising manner, in a more particular way, the real direction of classical political thought itself. Catherine Pickstock's phrase "The Liturgical Consummation of Philosophy" is of immense importance and, in my view, arises directly out of questions that properly arise within political philosophy.[7] This realization is, in fact, part of the reason that I think political philosophy is one of the fundamental paths (there are others) that the human intellect can begin to take to a knowledge of *all that is*.

Basically, I argue here that political philosophy, by being what it is, stands at the threshold of all practical and theoretical sciences. This position is the import of chapter 2. The political life, by itself, however, can tend to become all-absorbing and all-commanding, as I suggest in chapters 7 and 8, the problem of modernity. But the limits of political philosophy lead us to the things that cannot be otherwise, to the things that simply are for their own sake. The sobering questions of the dangers to the philosopher in the city, of the power of the Prince drastically to deal with any philosopher, are to be counterbalanced against the subtle dangers of sophistic corruption coming from the philosophers. Revelation, as I understand it, does address itself to human intellect, which, to be sure, remains free even on the hypothesis of revelation. Thus, anyone can fail or refuse to recognize that something is being directed to its own reality.

But before the human intellect can recognize that it is being so addressed in any full sense by an intelligence not its own, it must first formulate for itself the philosophic questions that most concern it, the questions about which somehow political philosophy cannot find its own answers, or at least answers that really resolve the issue so brought up by its own methods and experiences. I do not understand revelation to mean that believers are not also sinners. Indeed, I maintain that the real failure of classical political practice and thought is not that it did not understand what the human good was, but that it could not figure out, on its own resources, how to achieve it, especially for everyone. And while revelation with its teaching on the Fall and grace addresses this very problem, the fact remains that the teaching of revelation is both that we have free will and that we have here in this world "no lasting city." All questions have "answers," but not always political ones.

Once we realize, as an intellectual position, that revelation adds truths that, when lived, cause results in real cities that are positive for such cities, even in political terms, we are freed from the most corrupting of political temptations. That temptation, in essence, is to construct a "new man" by political or economic or biological means in this world. In other words, for political philosophy, the principal effect of revelation in politics is to free it to be itself. It thereby prevents politics from conceiving itself as a substitute metaphysics or an eschatological kingdom in this world. This freedom from the burden of constructing its own world is the liberty that grounds the effort to live and act in a real world. It is not the "unlimited" freedom of making "right" to be "wrong," but the freedom to follow what is right if we so choose. The ultimate things still need to be confronted. Man is a mortal being in this world in any of its polities. But his true being contains intimations of immortality and resurrection, both issues hinted at in the classical philosophers—immortality by Socrates, resurrection by Aristotle's tractate on friendship.

These chapters follow one another in a systematic order. They are intended to "interpret" or "illuminate" what happens when we realize that political philosophy, by being what it is, raises questions it cannot itself answer. They are directed to the satisfaction of the mind in its fundamental hope that the order of the world and the world itself are not "in vain." Political philosophy is not itself defective because it cannot itself do what is beyond its competence. Yet, if revelation is indeed addressed to such questions that political philosophy provides or formulates for us, we can expect that our understanding of things, political and philosophical, will be greater precisely because of our effort to understand this relationship. We did not, however, in advance, anticipate the manner in which political philosophy and revelation converge. Yet, it does, in fact, reveal a certain coherence or order in the universe that is not, after all, "in vain," again to cite Aristotle's worrisome phrase about an existence in the world that has no meaning (1094a21; 1253a4).

This is a book in political philosophy. Because it is, likewise it is a book that requires us to consider certain revelational positions as they relate to political philosophy, not only to understand revelation but also to understand political philosophy itself. We can, of course, take the position that "it is not *my* revelation and therefore I need not consider it." While this position may have much to be said for it, it is not my point here. If any claimed revelation gives a reasonable and consistent answer to questions in political philosophy, we cannot simply ignore that position on the grounds that it is not "ours." In principle, we cannot hold that there is any truth, after our own manner of knowing, that cannot potentially be "ours." We must remain open to the whole to retain intellectual integrity. What is presented here is not so much an argument about the truth of Catholicism as it relates to political philosophy, but a reminder that there is an argument that merits consideration on the grounds of political philosophy itself.

Notes

1. Heinrich A. Rommen, *The State in Catholic Thought: A Treatise in Political Philosophy* (St. Louis: B. Herder, 1945), 11.

2. See *The Social Agenda: A Collection of Magisterial Texts*, edited by R. Sirico (Vatican City: Pontifical Commission on Justice and Peace, Liberia Editrice Vaticana, 2000); Roger Heckel, *General Aspects of the Social Catechesis of John Paul II: The Use of the Expression 'Social Doctrine' of the Church* (Vatican City: Pontifical Commission on Justice and Peace, 1980); Rodger Charles, *The Social Teachings of Vatican II* (San Francisco: Ignatius Press, 1982).

3. See James V. Schall, S.J., "On the Uniqueness of Catholicism and the Diversity of Religions," *Homiletic and Pastoral Review* 97 (January 1997): 13–21.

4. "'Are the gods not just?' 'Oh no, child. What would become of us if they were?'" C. S. Lewis, *Till We Have Faces* (Grand Rapids, Mich.: Eerdmans, 1970), 297.

5. *General Catechism of the Catholic Church* (Vatican City: Liberia Editrice Vaticana, 1994). See also the *Documents of Vatican II*, edited by W. Abbott (New York: Guild Press, 1966); Denziger, *Enchiridion Symbolorum* (Friburg: Herder, 1955).

6. See Josef Pieper, *The Truth of All Things* (San Francisco: Ignatius, 1989).

7. In this regard, see James V. Schall, *On the Unseriousness of Human Affairs: Teaching, Writing, Playing, Believing, Lecturing, Philosophzing, Singing, Dancing* (Wilmington, Del.: ISI Books, 2001).

~

CHAPTER ONE

Why Is
Political Philosophy Different?

The political science that was created by Plato and Aristotle was established in opposition to the opinions held by the intellectuals of their time, by the sophists. And this conflict with the intellectuals, the revolt against the intellectuals, from which emerged our science, is monumentally commemorated to this day in the political dialogues of Plato's early and middle years. From its origins the science of politics is a militant enterprise, a defense of truth both political and practical. It is a defense of true knowledge about human existence in society against the untrue opinions dispensed by intellectuals; and it is a defense of true human being against the corruption of man perpetrated by the intellectuals.

—Eric Voegelin, "Political Science and the Intellectuals"[1]

In his indignation at the extravagance of Plato, and his sense of the significance of facts, he (Aristotle) became, against his will, the prophetic exponent of a limited and regenerated democracy. But the *Politics*, which, to the world of living men, is the most valuable of his works, acquired no influence on antiquity, and it was never quoted before the time of Cicero. Again it disappeared for many centuries; it was unknown to the Arabian commentators, and in Western Europe it was first brought to light by St. Thomas Aquinas, at the very time when an infusion of popular elements was modifying feudalism, and it helped to emancipate political philosophy from despotic theories and to confirm it in the ways of freedom.

—Lord Acton, "Review of Sir Erskine May's *Democracy in Europe*"[2]

Summary: The world is filled with many things worth examining. We must normally proceed one step at a time. The first step is to establish that political philosophy has its own realm, its own relative autonomy within which certain questions and certain answers about the nature of man and the world necessarily arise.

I

Why, we might ask, in the words of Lord Acton, does "political philosophy" need to be "emancipated" from "despotic theories"? Are not "despotic theories," a subject familiar to both classical and modern authors, an aspect of "political philosophy" itself? And why, in the words of Eric Voegelin, does "true human being" need to be defended "against the corruption of man perpetrated by the intellectuals"? Are "intellectuals" more dangerous than politicians?[3] What is clearly implied in both of these blunt observations is that despotism and human corruption are not accidents or happenstances but the result of "theories," of intellectual errors originating with and deliberately perpetrated by "intellectuals," "academics," or "sophists" who, in the modern world, sometimes also go by the noble name of "philosophers."

What has proved to be peculiarly dangerous about the modern world, especially the recent twentieth century, is that not a few of these latter "philosophers" and "intellectuals" became active politicians. These philosopher-politicians proved to be considerably more dangerous than the older tyrants, who were brutal men, no doubt, but they had no particular philosophical pretensions. The philosopher-politician is bent, hopefully unlike the philosopher, on universalizing his intellectual vision no matter what the consequences. By contrast, speaking of the "world of living men," Acton called Aristotle's *Politics* "the most valuable of his works," for it was a book that moderated politics and distinguished it from metaphysics, without denying the validity of either. Both politics and metaphysics had an ordered place in the understanding of *all that is*. Philosophy and politics both go wrong when they have no fixed place or theory within which to locate themselves. As Aristotle put it, "political expertise does not create human beings but makes use of them after receiving them from nature" (1257b22–23). The origin of human beings as such is not political, even though man is by nature a political animal.

A politics without a metaphysics, however, soon becomes itself a substitute metaphysics, something that Acton no doubt saw coming from the "extravagance of Plato." But to give Plato his due against all those ancients and moderns who see him as the origin of ideology, it was he who saw, in its classic form in the *Gorgias*, the dangers to the philosopher coming from a popular, intelligent, handsome young politician who himself contemptuously refuses to engage in philosophic discourse. He thereby, before acting on them, refuses to have his ideas put to the test of intelligence.

Political philosophy at its best is a dialogue with the politicians about the worth and validity of things that are not political, of things that are "not Caesar's," to use the scriptural phrase for it (Matthew, 22:22). It is the politicians who order the deaths of Socrates and Christ, though it is generally the theoretician, as Machiavelli sensed, who prepares the minds of both princes and potential philosophers to be able to carry out such orders. Political philosophy must consider the aberrations of the actual politicians as well as the reasons they give for these aberrations. Political philosophy must also be aware of the disorders of soul possible to philosophers themselves, something about which politicians can also know from an empirical observation of how philosophers live.

At first sight, this background, steeped in intellectual considerations from Western philosophy, does not even touch the whole Islamic world, so much in our attention. In this world, the state, unless it imitates Western notions, as few do, is identified with the religion and serves as its instrument. Voegelin, in fact, saw Islam as but an aspect of a broader movement in political philosophy that strove by force to put into effect the image of the world and man that it had conceived in theory. "Islam was primarily an ecumenic religion and only secondarily an empire," Voegelin wrote in the fourth volume of his *Order and History*. "Hence it reveals in its extreme form the danger which beset all of the religions of the Ecumenic Age, the danger of impairing their universality by letting their ecumenic mission slide over into the acquisition of world-immanent, pragmatic power over a multitude of men which, however numerous, could never be mankind past, present, and future."[4]

In other words, one cannot avoid the question of the truth of a theory and of its explanation of the world, whether that theory be from religion or philosophy, from ideology or intellectual system. And the instrument of this explanation cannot be yet another "theory" that holds that there is no truth. We cannot forget that there were metaphysicians in Islam. They tried to reconcile the absolute ungrounded will of Allah to which all must submit with some rational order in things. One can wonder with Stanley Jaki whether the theoretic impossibility of making this reconciliation is not at the roots of our present political turmoil.[5] It certainly was at the root of a similar line of thought in the West that led from Occam to Hobbes, Rousseau, and Hegel, a line that placed absolute will at the center both of the divinity and of the Leviathan in all its changing forms.[6]

II

How is political philosophy different? and what difference does its difference make? we ask. On hearing such questions asked, what first comes to mind is the further question: different from what? Let me first address the second question: what difference does it make? We are to call things *that are* by their right names. That identifying, that calling things by their right names, is the first and, in some sense, the most important theoretical act we can perform. It stands before all action, the truth of which, that is, the truth of action or in action, is itself to be known, affirmed, and judged. This putting the stamp of truth on action is what the virtue of prudence (*phronesis*) means (1139b24–40a30).

"Political philosophy" is not, however, a "thing." That is, it is not a substance having its own independent being (*esse*). Rather it is an activity of the mind in its actually knowing something not itself. What it knows is not exclusively of its own construction. That is, it does not just know itself and what it causes to be from itself, which latter position is essentially what "the modern project" or modernity is about.[7] What is known in politics is how human beings stand to one another in an orderly or disorderly way. This knowledge requires us to know distinctions between good and bad, just and unjust, in order accurately to describe what we in fact see or understand ourselves to do on the basis of what we are. Moreover, we need to "speak" this understanding. The polis, to be *what it is*, needs to be locked in conversation, in persuasion. The political man is the man who speaks.

Thus, the first step is a negative one. It is to grant that political philosophy is *not* itself the whole of philosophy; it is *not* theology, nor is it even political science or political or legal theory. It is not sociology or economics; nor is it a physical science or based on its methodology. It is not a branch of logic or psychology or anthropology. Though it has some articulated relation to all of these disciplines, they are not *what it is*. Phrases such as "the economics of politics," or the "sociology of politics," or the "psychology of politics," or even the "biology" or "genetics" or "theology" of politics may have some contribution to add. But, contrary to what is usually meant by such phrases, they do not explain what specifically political philosophy, in itself, is "really" about.

Initially, about political philosophy or anything else, something is to be said for getting the question it answers stated correctly. We do not always know if our questions can be answered, but that is no reason not to have the proper questions. The questions that political philosophy poses to itself, as Strauss affirmed in the first citation, arise out of "politics" and "ethics," that is, out of the experience of human living. They do not begin with some pre-existing theory, say of contract or state of nature or modern physics or linguistics, or with some "science" that stands between the knower and what is known. The possibility that some legitimate questions apparently are not or cannot be humanly answered is not necessarily a reason for not asking them. It is not a question of despair nor for thinking that the difficulty of their answer is itself a bad thing. Aristotle told us in a famous passage in his *Ethics*, that we must "strain every nerve to live in accordance with the best thing in us; for even if it is small in bulk, much more does it in power and worth surpass everything" (1177b34–78a1). Aristotle hints here that this "straining every nerve," this sense of the worth in what "surpasses everything," is the greatest delight that we naturally know.

In an old *Peanuts* cartoon, Linus runs up to Lucy with triumphant news, "Look, Lucy, I tied my own shoes." He instinctively knows that she figured that he would never learn how to tie them. Lucy bends down to have a closer look at this unexpected feat. She exclaims, "So you did . . . but you got 'em on the wrong feet." They both stand up straight with frowns on their faces, staring at the wrong-footed shoes. Linus replies, petulantly, "Waddya mean, the wrong feet?" In the last scene, defiantly to a Lucy sternly glaring at him, Linus shouts, "THESE *are* my feet!"[8] Linus is right, of course, the first of all questions is that of existence. *Is it? Is it not?* Right and wrong presuppose and follow from this first question. Right and wrong are not abstractions or mere ideas unrelated to reality. Lucy, after all, is also right; Linus does have his shoes on the wrong feet. Both answered different, but legitimate, questions.

III

In the introduction to his famous essay, "What Is Political Philosophy?" Leo Strauss began his lecture with these solemn words: "It is a great honor, and at the same time a challenge to accept a task of particular difficulty, to be asked to speak about political philosophy in Jerusalem. In this city, and in this land, the theme of political philosophy—'the city of righteousness, the faithful city'—has been taken more seriously than anywhere else on earth."[9] But this affirmation does not deny that in fact political philosophy is also taken seriously elsewhere on earth. The very fact that Strauss could juxtapose Jerusalem and political philosophy recalls, as he intended it to recall, the famous distinction between Jerusalem and Athens of the early Christian theologian, Tertullian, who rather thought that the two cities did not have anything to do with each other.[10]

In a sense, Strauss is almost equally as shocking as Tertullian. Strauss implies that the "theme" of political philosophy, as he calls it, is identified with the "city of righteousness." We are surprised to hear this clearly Old Testament theme, this Augustinian theme, identified with precisely "political philosophy." At first sight, we would not expect a pious Jew, even if he also be a philosopher, to make such a comparison. The things of God descend, after the manner of an unexpected gift. Man does not command the divinity. Strauss himself, in contra-distinction with Christian thinkers, was loathe to posit too much, if any, relationship between reason and revelation.[11] Still, the sense that, even if we choose to avoid its implication, some relationship between them exists, some consideration of which ultimately cannot be avoided.

St. Augustine made this connection between Jerusalem and Athens more easily but he made it as a Christian, for whom the Word was made flesh, something, as he tells us in his *Confessions*, that he "did not read in the Platonists" (Bk. VII, c. 9). Augustine had no trouble in calling his major work *The City of God*, a phrase from the Psalms (48, 87), but one that also clearly associates him with the project of Plato's *Republic*, his city in speech that always seemed to be searching for a more grounded home. And St. Thomas, also as a Christian who read Aristotle, made the connection between Athens and Jerusalem. For both Aristotle and for Aquinas, the body was a constituent part of what it is to be a human being. And unlike Aristotle's, Aquinas's God was Trinitarian. God was not lonely. Aristotle's "thought thinking itself" did, however, serve to illuminate the inner life of the Trinity, the Father, the Word, the Spirit in one nature, as we read also in Augustine's *De Trinitate*.[12]

Strauss wants to know how much we can know of this "faithful city" by our own powers. Implicitly, at least, he is rejecting, or at least avoiding, a consideration of how much we can learn of it, even philosophically, with the prod of revelation.[13] Here, Strauss does not appear to wonder about the curious paradox that considerations of the same "city" come up in both reason and revelation. He was concerned, however, that our politicians and judges are more influenced by "social sciences" than by the "Ten Commandments," an issue that remains as acute decades later as when he first raised it.[14] Strauss implies that the dubious grounding of "social sciences," inventions of modernity, may be one reason why the Ten Commandments did not need to be rejected. They might in fact indicate true norms. It is clear that the crisis of Western civilization, which it is his purpose to examine, does not arise from strict observance of the Ten Commandments but from failure to adhere to them. Strauss may be taken to hint indirectly that the crisis of the civilization might well be best met by teachings found in "the city of righteousness," of which the Ten Commandments stand, most obvious as the cornerstone.

Eric Voegelin, also recalling Plato and Aristotle, remarked that "the science of politics" was "militant." It was engaged in war against "untrue opinions" of "intellectuals," namely, sophists. The "True human being" needed defense against the constructs of the intellectuals. Intellectuals "perpetrated" something that was not the truth about men in society. Clearly, "intellectuals" were not equivalent to political philosophers. Voegelin identified intellectuals with the ancient sophists against whom Plato wrote. These were the speakers who came to our town and, for a fee, could tell us how to achieve what we wanted in our lives or in our regime. Themselves, they took no stand on such issues. They were neutral, "value free," as we have come to say following Max Weber.

Even Lord Acton in the last century said that Thomas Aquinas "emancipated" political philosophy from "despotic theories" and "confirmed it in the ways of freedom," evidently, along with "a true knowledge of human existence in society," its real vocation. Aristotle had said, however, that "it would be absurd for someone to think that political science or intelligence is the most excellent science, when the best thing in the universe is not man" (1141a20–21). Emancipation of political philosophy from "despotic theories" and a confirmation in "the ways of freedom" indicate why political science is not the "most excellent science." The ways of freedom lead not to "freedom" as such but to what is best in man.[15] The despotic theories claim a metaphysical power for politics, the power to change the very nature of what it is to be a human being.[16]

If political science is not the "highest science," it remains, nevertheless, the highest practical science, something worthy in itself. It is good that man exists. If man is not the best thing in the universe, he is still a good and worthy thing as such. The implication follows that if we know as much as we can about this political being and its political activities, we will reach the outlines of the "city of righteousness," the city of God. We will understand that, though we be political animals, we are also rational animals, animals who laugh. The political life is generally necessary to know and practice the virtues. But virtue, while practiced for its own sake, leads to what is able to be seen because of virtue. The one thing the un-virtuous cannot see is what is beyond virtue but not apart from it. And the virtuous or political life is a worthy life, as is the political life that strives to prevent the worst from gaining power.

IV

Classical political philosophy, in addition to Aristotle's discussion of wit and humor in Book Four of his *Ethics*, could be amusing. Take the question of whether philosophy itself is "useless." Of course, there are two meanings to the word "useless"—one would be that the thing is worth nothing at all, the other that something is beyond the criterion of "use" or utility. The example that Aristotle uses in Book One of the *Politics* has to do with Thales of Miletus. It seems this good man was chided for his poverty and general frumpiness. In a spirit of light vengeance, Thales decided to show the locals that philosophy was not useless after all. He would meet his critics on their own ground.

Because of his knowledge of astronomy, Thales figured that it would be a good season for olives and grapes. So in the off-season, he cornered the market on the presses needed to crush olives and grapes. When the season sure enough turned in a bountiful crop, the local growers suddenly found out that they had to pay a premium to Thales in order to get their produce crushed. Thales made a tidy sum. Thus, in retrospect, the locals realized that the philosopher was not poor because he had to be but because he wanted to be. He was busy about other, higher things. He could not be bothered with useful things like business and cornering the market to make a fortune. The conclusion evidently was that the philosopher, by choice and not by necessity, understood and delighted in the things beyond use (1259a1–25).

The city was a place of merchants and farmers selling produce, but these latter did not compose the essence of the city. Yet, even if we had the rulers and the ruled in a legitimate constitution, a citizenry leading virtuous lives, we still did not have philosophy. Philosophy existed only if we had philosophers. And politicians had the power to kill the philosophers, so it was necessary that the rulers knew the worth of philosophy, even while not themselves having time for philosophy. Philosophers did not have their own civil defense league to protect themselves.

Aristotle remarked in the *Rhetoric*, however, that "it is absurd to hold that a man ought to be ashamed of being unable to defend himself with his limbs, but not of being unable to defend himself with speech and reason, when the use of rational speech is more distinctive of a human being than the use of his limbs" (1355b1–3). But as the trials of Christ and Socrates showed, the effort to defend the philosopher against the politicians does not always succeed. But it is the first task of political philosopher, as Plato's *Gorgias* makes clear, at least to formulate an argument that would convince the politician not to kill the philosopher. But once it is agreed that the philosopher might live, he has to be free to philosophize. And one of his first efforts must be to understand the limits of the city so that what can become clear on the horizon is a city that is not, as it were, a polis that comes from man the political animal who is neither a god nor a beast.

Aristotle called political science an "architectonic" science (1094a7–17). This term meant that the polity might well be able to call, say, a mathematician into military service because it needed his skills. But it did not mean that the politician had the power to decide what mathematics is. For the good of the polis, the science had to remain what it is, even though the mathematician was serving the good of the polity in the employment of his knowledge. If one asks whether a priest or a philosopher might also be called upon to serve the public good, the traditional answer to this question was affirmative. Implicitly this meant that what a priest or a philosopher did remained what he was defined to be by the nature of his office or profession. The "common good" included that priests be priests and philosophers be philosophers. But the politician was not to be himself unintelligent or unaware of unworthy priests or philosophers.

Political philosophy, then, is distinct in two ways: it is a defense of the cause or need of the philosopher before the politician who himself is aware of, though not especially proficient in, philosophical things. It is also a defense of virtue in the city as a prerequisite for a philosophy that, in its turn, is able to look to and state the truth of things. A city must know of itself that it is not despotic. It must know that the human good is itself a real good that must be chosen and habituated in customs and laws. Finally, it must know that the things beyond politics are worthy things, of more ultimate moment than the polis itself, however necessary it may be. The philosopher knows that most human lives are not themselves devoted to philosophy, even though they may be aware of and indeed interested in philosophy. No ultimate end is said to be different for the philosopher and the nonphilosopher.

Yet, it seems unjust that those who are not in practice philosophers do not have a hope of achieving the higher ends of which philosophy makes us aware in an acute fashion. Revelation, in fact, addresses itself not merely to virtue but also to happiness and to contemplation as its end, to a way to the highest good not just for philosophers but for everyone and not just in this passing life (I–II, 91, 4). Revelation articulates a more clear and defined end than even the philosopher could envision by his own powers (I–II, 91, 4). Yet, the efforts of the philosopher to envision this end were themselves needed to understand why revelational answers were answers to real questions that did not arise only from revelation.[17]

After Thales proved he could make a minor fortune by cornering the olive and wine presses, he returned to philosophy, to the pursuit of the highest things. When Socrates was executed, he reminded Crito to offer a cock to Asclepias, the god of healing, from whence he passed to the Isles of the Blessed to speak, as he suggested at the end of The Apology, with Homer and Rhadamnathus and the other philosophers. In preparing to die, in dying, Socrates was healed. When Christ died, He did speak about authority to a politician, a Roman governor (John, 19, 8–11), but not to a philosopher. He did speak to ordinary thieves. One blasphemed Him. Christ remained silent. The other acknowledged that he himself was justly executed and asked to be remembered in His Kingdom (Luke, 23:19–43). The city that killed Christ and the outlines of the city in speech converge. Political philosophy is different because it can, if it will, consider these cities—Athens, Jerusalem, Rome, existing cities—as well as the city in speech, and the Righteous City, the City of God. If it will not make such considerations, then, in all likelihood, it falls back on Lord Acton's "despotic theories," theories that do not know the "ways of freedom," nor the true being of man, but only the disappointment over the corruption of the intellectuals.

"Thought," Aristotle said, "moves nothing; what moves us is thought aimed at some goal and concerned with action" (1139a36–37). The difference of political philosophy is that it is genuinely concerned with the thought that "moves nothing" as well as with the thought that is concerned with those actions that lead to our end. Political philosophy is different because its own questions lead it to concern itself about the content of the end. This end is most enigmatically described as the "city of righteousness." It is not seen merely as either "the highest of the social sciences" or as "the handmaid of theology," but as the true understanding of *that which is*, however it be known to us, provided that we have asked the right questions and have heard answers to these questions as asked.

When the subject of "leisure" appears in Book Eight of *The Politics*, we are suddenly aware that the most important things take place not in constructing, refounding, or even running the polity. They arise rather in all that is done while living in it. What are the serious occupations of leisure? What things are to be done simply because they are true or beautiful—something to be understood in contrast with Pilate's cynical "what is truth?" (John, 18, 38)? Plato's answer to this question was "singing, dancing, and sacrificing" (803). Aristotle's answer is philosophy (1279b11–15) and, perhaps, music as itself ordered to philosophy. Political philosophy exists so that the politician, who can prevent these noble things, can also come to see that he best let them be what they are. The way of the politician and the way of the philosopher are not the same, but they do depend on each other if we are to be both open to the whole and aware that we cannot, by our own powers, fully attain it.

Notes

1. Eric Voegelin, "Political Science and the Intellectuals," Paper presented at the 48th Annual Meeting of the American Political Science Association, August 26–28, 1952, 1.

2. Lord Acton, "Review of Sir Erskine May's *Democracy in Europe*"(1878), in *Essays in the History of Liberty: Selected Essays of Lord Acton*, edited by Rufus Fears (Indianapolis: Liberty Classics, 1985), I, 63.

3. Just how dangerous they might be was the theme of Paul Johnson, *The Intellectuals* (New York: Harper, 1988), and Raymond Aron, *The Opium of the Intellectuals*, translated by T. Kilmartin (New York: Norton, 1957).

4. Eric Voegelin, *Order and History*, vol. 4 of *The Ecumenic Age* (Baton Rouge: Louisiana State University Press, 1972), 142–43.

5. Stanley Jaki, *Jesus, Islam, Science* (Pickney, Mich.: Real View Books, 2001), 1–31. See also Ralph Lerner and Mushin Mahdi, "Introduction," *Medieval Political Philosophy* (Ithaca, N.Y.: Cornell University Press, 1978), 1–20.

6. See Josef Pieper, *Scholasticism: Personalities and Problems of Medieval Philosophy*, translated by R. and C. Winston (New York: McGraw-Hill, 1960) 147–51; Heinrich Rommen, *The Natural Law: A Study in Legal and Social History and Philosophy*, translated by T. Hanley (Indianapolis: Liberty Fund, [1947] 1998), 51–55.

7. See below, chapter 8; also James V. Schall, *At the Limits of Political Philosophy* (Washington, D.C.: Catholic University of America Press, 1996), chapter 3, "Modernity," 49–70. The phrase "the modern project" is from Leo Strauss, *The City and Man* (Chicago: University of Chicago Press, 1964), 6.

8. Charles Schulz, *Here Comes Charlie Brown!* (New York: Fawcett, 1958).

9. Leo Strauss, "What Is Political Philosophy?" *What Is Political Philosophy? and Other Essays* (Glencoe, Ill.: The Free Press, 1959), 9. See Hans-Georg Gadamer, "Aristotle and the Ethic of Imperatives," in *Action and Contemplation: Studies in the Moral and Political Thought of Aristotle*, edited by R. Bartlett and S. Collins (Albany: State University of New York Press, 1999), 66.

10. Leo Strauss, "Jerusalem and Athens: Some Preliminary Reflections," in *Studies in Platonic Political Philosophy*, edited by Thomas Pangle (Chicago: University of Chicago Press, 1983), 147–73. See Susan Orr, *Jerusalem and Athens: Reason and Revelation in the Works of Leo Strauss* (Lanham, Md.: Rowman & Littlefield, 1995).

11. Leo Strauss, "On the Mutual Influence of Theology and Philosophy," *Independent Journal of Philosophy* 3 (1979): 111–18.

12. St. Augustine, "On the Trinity," in *Basic Writings of St. Augustine*, edited by W. J. Oates, vol. 2, 667–878 (New York: Random House, 1948).

13. See Etienne Gilson, *Reason and Revelation in the Middle Ages* (New York: Scribner's, 1938). See also James V. Schall, "Possessed Both of Reason and Revelation," in *A Thomistic Tapestry: Essays in Memory of Étienne Gilson*, edited by Peter Redpath (New York: Rodopi, 2003), 177–93.

14. Leo Strauss, *City and Man* (Chicago: University of Chicago Press, 1964), 1.

15. See Roger Scruton, *The West and the Rest* (Wilmington, Del.: ISI Books, 2002), viii.

16. See Rousseau, *Social Contract*, I, 7, and II, 7.

17. See Joseph Owens, *Human Destiny: Some Problems for Catholic Philosophy* (Washington, D.C.: Catholic University of America Press, 1985).

CHAPTER TWO

~

On the Paradoxical Place of Political Philosophy in the Structure of Reality

Every human being and every society is what it is by virtue of the highest to which it looks up. The city, if it is healthy, looks up, not to the laws which it can unmake as it made them, but to the unwritten laws, the divine law, the gods of the city. The city must transcend itself.

—Leo Strauss, *The City and Man*[1]

I will argue that genuine subjectivity is to be attained through the redemptive return of doxological dispossession, thus ensuring that the subject is neither autonomously self-present, nor passively controlled from without (the pendulum of 'choice' available to the citizen of our immanentist city).

—Catherine Pickstock,
After Writing: The Liturgical Consummation of Philosophy[2]

For these sophists desire that demonstrative arguments should be given for all things; for it is obvious that they wanted to take some starting point that would be for them a kind of rule whereby they could distinguish between those who are healthy and those who are ill, and between those who are awake and those who are asleep. . . . Still, they are not deceived in their own minds so that they believe the judgments of one who is asleep and the judgment of one who is awake to be equally true. And this is clear from their acts. . . .

—Thomas Aquinas, *Commentary on Aristotle's Metaphysics*,
Bk. IV, C. 15, #709

13

Summary: We do not normally ask about where political philosophy exists within reality because we conceive it as a human or practical consideration, which it is. Yet, a political philosophy that mis-understands itself easily can claim itself to determine what reality is. Thus, placing political philosophy in the right place is part of placing reality itself in the right theoretical place. Each is to be seen after the manner in which it is.

I

Philosophic discussions sometimes lend themselves to nonphilosophic beginnings. It seems proper to start with a tract that ended in the last days of the twentieth century with the death of its author. The scene at the theater is the "Tenth Annual Tiny Tots' Concert." Present are Marcie, Peppermint Patty, Charlie Brown's little sister Sally, and a diminutive girl with long hair, wearing a head-band. Peppermint Patty tells us right off that she "hates" such "Tiny Tot Concerts." Sally in turn complains, "Every time we come to one of these concerts, they play 'Peter and the Wolf.'" In the next scene she continues, "They must think we don't understand anything else." The little girl with the head-band, sitting to Sally's left, asks her, "Don't you like 'Peter and the Wolf'"? Sally replies, "I don't know . . . I've never understood it."[3] We find this account amusing because we understand, without need of further explanation, what it means to say that we do not understand, while at the same time we have just claimed that we do understand.

That is to say, as the passage from St. Thomas that I cited in the beginning affirms, we possess the first principle of being and knowledge without our having formally to elaborate it, namely, a thing cannot be and not be at the same time. We cannot deny the principle without implicitly affirming it. Our acts often make our thoughts clear when we do not admit their clarity especially to ourselves. Even when we would be skeptics, we reveal something that is not skeptical. Our very rational power is given to us. As Samuel Johnson put it in a letter to James Boswell, on February 9, 1776, "Providence gives the power, of which reason teaches the use."[4] Without the implicit truth of the principle of contradiction, we could not know that we reason badly. Without this principle, we could not be taught reason's use.

In a conversation at the University of Leyden in Holland, on May 20, 1975, the French philosopher Emmanuel Levinas was asked by Professor H. Phillipse: "Is philosophy a diversion for you, as it was for Pascal?" To this question, Levinas enigmatically responded, in a phrase to which I shall return later, "if the undivertable can be a diversion, and if a diversion can be undivertable." Phillipse next inquired, "Is the philosophical attitude—which is in essence a skeptical attitude—not in contradiction with the attitude of faith?" Levinas distinguished the meaning of "skeptical," a point with which I began these considerations on political philosophy. "'Skeptical' only means the fact of examining things," Levinas affirmed,

> the fact of posing questions. I do not at all think that a question—or, at least, the original questioning—is only a deficiency of answers. Functional and even scientific questions—and many philosophic ones—await only answers. Questioning *qua* original attitude is a relation to that to which no response can contain, to the "uncontainable"; it becomes responsibility. Every response contains a "beside the point" and appeals to an un-said (*dé-dit*).[5]

The fact is, there are questions to which there are answers, even when we realize that every answer arises out of a reality that is "uncontainable" by our own minds, themselves open to *what is*. This questioning is not skepticism but a manifestation of what Socrates called intellectual *eros*, an awareness and pursuit of the revelatory nature of being.

II

"Examining things" is what we do when we philosophize. We would not bother to do this examining if we thought a priori that we could know nothing of what we examine. The burden of knowing what political philosophy might be involves the effort to distinguish and identify what it is not. This may be a skeptical enterprise, if you will, but it has the prime purpose of knowing about things as such. It seeks to identify where and how political things fit into the order of reality. "Philosophy is the intellectual activity that works with distinctions," Robert Sokolowski has written.

> Philosophy explains by distinguishing. This does not mean that philosophy just asserts distinctions and lets it go at that; rather, it works with distinctions, it brings them out and dwells on them, dwells with them, showing how and why the things it has distinguished *must* be distinguished from one another. . . . The activity of making distinctions always has something contemplative about it. Whenever we make a distinction, we become somewhat disconnected from whatever practical or rhetorical activity we may be engaged in.[6]

That is to say, the effort to distinguish things at one level simply means that we want to know what they are independently of our wanting to know what to do with them or make of them. In this sense, there is an unavoidable philosophical aspect to our reflecting on political things, even though politics is what Aristotle called a "practical" science, one directly ordered to doing, to acting, not making or contemplating.

The "place" of any philosophy is, properly speaking, within the human mind while it actively thinks about *what is*, about what is not the human mind itself or anything in it. Our "consciousness" depends initially on the fact that we have a mind that comes to be in act, that is, that comes to know something. Thus, consciousness also depends on what is other than mind. What is not mind is not itself necessarily conscious even though it has some intelligibility to it, something not of its own making. The human mind, that power that is *capax omnium* ("capable of all things") only knows itself indirectly, in knowing what is not itself. In this sense, it is not a divine mind that knows all in knowing itself. It remains a limited, finite mind, yet, still mind, still open to all things, to *what is*. Therefore, it is capable of receiving what it is not.

This capacity of knowing all things is why finite beings can be content not to be gods themselves. To talk of philosophy, moreover, is to talk of the knowledge of the whole, to seek this whole. To talk of precisely "political" philosophy, on the other hand, is to talk of certain conditions that allow us to continue this enterprise of thinking, of seeking to know, to love the whole. Political philosophy addresses first the politician to convince him to let philosophy itself be. Political philosophy in this sense always remains under the shadow of Socrates and Christ, both nonwriters of books, both killed by the best existing states of their time.[7] But it also wants to know the status and intelligibility of precisely political things, the things we call political.

Among the *things that are*, we find human cities. Indeed, it is worthy of note in the beginning that the description of the whole, as in Plato, the Stoics, and Augustine, is after the manner of a "city"—"The Republic," the "Cosmopolis," the "City of God." Human cities as such are not, properly speaking, "things," though there are things, primarily human things, within them.[8] Existing human beings are the substantial realities that ground the ontological basis of cities. As we see in ruins everywhere, minus human beings, minus cities. Human cities, while not totally or metaphysically "unreal," do not fall into the category of substance, however un-Hegelian but downright Aristotelian this observation might sound. Human cities do not exist without human beings, without human beings acting for some purpose, some end. Cities fall in the category of *ad aliud*, of "relation." They indicate the order of actions existing among rational beings acting practically to achieve their chosen ends, ends themselves revealed again and again by their chosen goals, as Aristotle described it so well in the first book of his *Ethics*.

And human beings themselves do not exist of their own making. Political science does not make man to be man but taking him from nature as already man, causes him to be good man—to summarize the words of Aristotle (1100a30–32; 1102a8–10; 1258a21–23). *What it is to be man* is not itself an idea concocted from nothing or originally formulated by man. Rather, it is something learned or discerned by reflecting on some already present order of being and action within him, already within a world, a *cosmos*, that exists. We find ourselves *to be*, and to be human beings, not turtles or trees or torrents of rain. Human beings want to know the truth of things, including the truth of what their cities are, together with the truth about their own status in substantial reality.

"The experiences of reason and spirit agree on the point that man experiences himself as a being who does not exist from himself," Eric Voegelin wrote in his second German lecture on "The Development of Diagnostic Tools."

> He exists in an already given world. The world itself exists by reason of a mystery, and the name for the mystery, for the cause of this being of the world, of which man is a component, is referred to as "God." So dependence of existence (*Dasein*) on the divine causation of existence (*Existenz*) has remained the basic question of philosophy up until today. This was formulated by Leibniz in the classic proposition that metaphysics has to deal with two questions: Why is there something, why not nothing? And one second question, Why is this something as it is? These why questions place at the beginning of all reflections on man, what we can call, with classical philosophical expression, the etiological problem of the existence of man and the world.[9]

Voegelin insists that at our own beginning, we cannot but know that what we are is not caused by any efficacious action or thought of our own. We can, perhaps, deny that we have this wonderment about ourselves in our fragile being, but this denial again puts us back at the skeptical question. We affirm something in our very denying of it. Moreover, Voegelin's second question, "Why is this something as it is?"—the question of form—also involves in the case of man the Aristotelian affirmation that man is by nature a political animal, a city-living being, again not something of his own making.

III

Years ago in Spokane, I heard a lecture by the great historian of philosophy, Etienne Gilson. His lecture concerned itself with the starting point of philosophizing. This starting point, I recall him vigorously affirming, was the certainty of the evident propositions that 1) "there are things," and 2) "I know them." To doubt these starting points makes it impossible ever to begin. He reminded us that there is nothing clearer than this experience and affirmation. Even the denial of things or knowing them involves things and knowing. Even if we be Descartes himself, we cannot find something clearer from which we might "prove" that there are things or that we know them. Starting points are not known by prior "proofs," as Aristotle reminded us in Book Six of his *Ethics*. The habit of first principles means that some things are known of themselves, *per se nota*, self-evident truths, as they came to be called. They are known in the first act of knowing anything else, hence, their firstness. The attempt to prove all proof is an infinite regression that results in knowing nothing.[10]

Gilson at a certain point in his lecture took a glass of water that was on the podium. He held it in front of us. We wondered what he was about. He placed the glass of water in his hand and showed it to us. "If I said that what I have in my hand was a block of wood," he provocatively told us, "you would all sit up and pay attention. You would be curious. But if I said that it is a glass of water, you would say, 'so what?'" Gilson let this account sink in a bit. No one protested that the glass of water was really a block of wood. The dream world and the real world were assumed to be different. Then he added, with some rhetorical force, "but the truth is that it *is* a glass of water and *not* a block of wood. True things may be very common things that we know all along. It is falsity that often strikes us, makes us pay attention." I have never quite forgotten that glass of water that was not a block of wood, that "there are things and I know them."[11]

A friend of mine, to continue this theme, Professor Thomas Martin, was asked to give the eulogy in Arizona for his friend and mentor, the late professor Richard Arlen Wood, who had been for many years a famous professor of philosophy at Northern Arizona University. Wood had a great influence on Martin and generations of students at Northern Arizona. Martin, in his eulogy, recalled the first time he encountered Wood in a class at Flagstaff. Martin, through his recollection of Wood, makes Gilson's point in another way.

"I stood there remembering the first time I had met Dick Wood at NAU in 1973 when he walked into 'Philosophy 353: Man and Reality. . . .' Twenty-five of us were seated in the classroom when in walked this man with his hair slicked back, wearing brown jeans, a western shirt, and cowboy boots," Martin recalled.

> He stopped and stood eyeing the class while twitching the corner of his mouth, straightening out his mustache with his forefinger and thumb. He frowned and looked about as though he were searching for something to say. He took a puff on his half-smoked cigar and began to read the roll.

After reading a few names, he suddenly stopped and asked a student sitting in the front row, "Do you have a mind?" "Yes," the student brightly responded. "Well, you will like this course and reading Descartes' *Meditations* because he also had a mind about which he is going to tell us. Do you have anything in your mind?"

"I have a lots of things in my mind," the student replied. "That's nice, but could you give me an example of one thing you have in your mind?" Wood asked. "Well, currently I have you, Professor Wood, in my mind." "I am in your mind?" Wood wondered. "Well, it's not really you that is in my mind, but an image of you which has come through my eyes to my mind," the student explained.

"An image of me has come through your eyes and is in your mind?" "Exactly," the student affirmed. "So do you see me or do you see an image of me?" "I see an image of you," the student acknowledged. "Have you ever seen me?" Wood wanted to know. "No, I have only seen an image of you," the student replied. "Then how do you know that this is me if you have only seen an image of me?" "I don't," the student admitted. "Then to whom are you speaking?" Wood asked. No response.[12]

This amusing classroom scene, of course, illustrates what we mean by the crisis of modernity, the inability to get outside of ourselves to a reality that we did not create or know before we encountered something *that is*. This something is the cause of our knowledge because *it is*.

Modern political philosophy is, at bottom, the product of this inability to get outside of ourselves so that, as a result, what we really know is only ourselves with no possible check on ourselves by what is not ourselves. When Machiavelli, in his famous chapter 15 of *The Prince*, made it impossible, as he thought, for men to pass from what they "do" do to what they "ought" to do, or vice versa, he left the will of the Prince and the wills in the Republic free to create any form of man they wished. By destroying Plato, nothing stood in the way. The Prince became an artist, not a politician, or better he became an artist whose subject matter, whose raw materials, were human beings themselves devoid of any intrinsic form.[13] No check on the Prince's actions was to come from the "form" of *what man is*, the form by which he knows that he himself did not make himself. What ought to be is what already exists, as Hegel is later to postulate the logical conclusion of this position for us.

IV

In a famous essay, to recall, Leo Strauss asked the question, "What Is Political Philosophy?"[14] Clearly, intellectual clarity asks us to distinguish political science and political philosophy. Likewise, we need to be aware of the distinction of reason and revelation, of philosophy and science. Hence, if we ask about the "paradoxical" place of political philosophy in precisely the "structure" of reality, we imply that there are both political things, including the question of the best regime, and human practical reason out of which political things initially flow. We also affirm that reality is not a "chaos" but a "structure," that is, an "order." We can make sense of political things.

I use the word "paradoxical" about the place of political philosophy in the structure of reality because the subject matter of political reflection, namely, human actions insofar as they are blameworthy or praiseworthy, do not reach reality apart from human thinking and choosing (1110b1–2). In other words, the fact that man is "by nature" a political animal, one whose full being is not available to him without the city, means that, unlike other beings in their flourishing, human beings must actually "act" for political things to exist and thus for themselves fully to exist. Likewise, man must actually "think" if he is going to understand where these actions are to be located in the order of things.

The intellectual virtue of the moral virtues is precisely "prudence," the virtue that supplies the form or content to the will so that we can know what the act we put in existence really is (1140a25–28; 1143a25–36). The wide variety of ethical and political things, of which Aristotle speaks, is due to the fact that their subject matter is variable among both good alternatives and evil ones. The potential variability of human choice and understanding in each individual prudential act means that it could have been "otherwise." This "otherwiseness," as it were, must be included within the meaning of the act or else it cannot have its note of praise or blame. This latter note is what indicates what it is in the order of things. This is why the so-called social sciences cannot "know" their subject matter after the manner of those sciences whose subject matter is by nature invariable. Modern social sciences often lack this inner sense of altereity. Hence their method is "reductionist," that is, it presupposes that reality must be as its method demands. Classical political science does not assume this insistence that reality and a mathematical method of knowing it correspond because political science cannot expect more certitude than its subject matter allows (1094b12–16).

Aristotle often uses the analogy of the doctor and the politician to shed light on political things (1144a2–6). This distinction goes back to the difference between art and prudence. Political things are *recta ratio agibilium*, ("right reason in acting") whereas artistic things are *recta ratio factibilium* ("right reason in making"). What is the point of this distinction for our purposes here? The doctor knows that human health is a normal reality that occurs if nothing goes wrong. What it is to be humanly healthy is not something the doctor "makes." He presupposes this given healthfulness as his first principle of action. His task is not to ask, what is essentially the philosopher's practical question, "what do I do when I am healthy?" but rather "how do I become healthy when I am sick?" The doctor, as Plato warned us, is a dangerous man to us if he is our enemy, since he knows best how to inflict damage on us (332d). He can use his knowledge *qua* man for good or ill, but not *qua* doctor where he can use it only for our good, the end of the art. Once we are healthy, the doctor's task is finished. He does not tell us how to live well. Good doctors can be unhappy men; indeed, they can be evil men.

Aristotle tells us to examine the typical "motion" of all things—the movement of the stars, of the plants, of the animals. He also tells us to examine our own "motions." The ethics, economics, politics, poetics, and rhetoric are designed to clarify one or another aspect of human "motion." Certain things are in the universe because human beings are in the universe. Political philosophy exists because of this peculiar human "motion" by which human beings interact to achieve a common good in which the human being can flourish. Political science is called an "architectonic" science, that is, it is a directive knowledge with a focus on action (1094a11–17). We can step back from this active knowledge to analyze in general what men do or do not do in their personal, familial, or political actions. The organization of this knowledge into intelligible form results in *The Ethics* and *The Politics*.

Political philosophy appears when it is necessary to justify, before the politician, the nonpolitical being of man, both what is private and what is transcendent. The same man is politician and metaphysician. Essentially, political philosophy exists to explain that there are things that transcend man, that the highest things, not merely political things, are worth spending time on. In this sense, political philosophy points to metaphysics and revelation, to the things that are brought up by, but not answered by, political life. Without this more contemplative thought, man cannot be *what he is*. This is the meaning of that famous passage in the sixth book of *The Ethics* of Aristotle where he writes:

> Wisdom must be intuitive reason combined with scientific knowledge—scientific knowledge of the highest objects which has received as it were its proper completion. Of the highest objects, we say, for it would be strange to think that the art of politics, or practical wisdom, is the best knowledge, since man is not the highest being in the world. . . . It is evident also that philosophic wisdom and the art of politics cannot be the same; for if the state of mind concerned with a man's own interests is to be called philosophic wisdom, there will be many philosophical wisdoms . . . (1141a18–30).

This less than highest status of politics too is the reason why Aristotle tells us not to listen to those who tell us only to look to and work for "human" things even though we be humans (1177b30–78a4). The very condition of our humanness points to what is not "human" but which is "mind." Mind is related to mind. Man remains a rational being for whom all his non-rational powers and capacities are related to his highest faculty, itself ordered to *what is*.

V

The passage in classical philosophy that is most central to political philosophy as such is found in Plato's *Gorgias*, the famous passage in which Callicles, the intelligent, smooth, handsome politician, the man whose god is the *demos* itself, ceases to answer Socrates' questions (505c). It is at this point, shades of *The Apology* itself, that we know that Socrates is dead. As a philosopher, his hold on life is only guaranteed by his ability to speak with the politician who always retains the power to kill him. Political philosophy is not merely the philosophical consideration of political things but the effort to convince the politician to allow the philosopher to continue in the city with his (the philosopher's) own task. The philosopher's task in turn is to lead the politician at least to an awareness of what is not simply politics, itself deprived of any criterion but itself.

Leo Stauss put the issue well in his essay "On Classical Political Philosophy." The precarious status of philosophy in the city is contingent on rendering the politician, who ordinarily has no time or inclination for such things, benevolent to the higher things.

> The adjective "political" in the expression "political philosophy" designates not so much a subject matter as a manner of treatment; from this point of view, I say, "political philosophy" means primarily not the philosophic treatment of politics, but the political, or popular, treatment of philosophy, or the political introduction to philosophy—the attempt to lead the qualified citizens, or rather their qualified sons, from the political life to the philosophic life.[15]

In both Plato and Aristotle, the bridge that allows the politician to open himself to things he does not fully understand is largely provided by music and poetry, both of which, as we know from the same sources, can equally corrupt the soul if they themselves are disordered. Plato recognized that the only way he could "defeat" Homer and the corrupting nature of poetry would be for himself to provide philosophy with its own poetic attraction and enchantment. This Platonic poetic counterpart to Homer, designed to counteract his charm with an even greater charm, is called, precisely, *The Republic*.[16]

"There is aesthetic creation because there is *creation*," George Steiner wrote in his *Real Presences*, a title with obvious philosophical and theological overtones.

> There is formal construction because we have been made form. Today, mathematical models proclaim access to the origins of the present universe. Molecular biology may have in reach an unraveling of the thread whose beginning is that of life. Nothing in these prodigious conjectures disarms, let alone elucidates, the fact that the world *is* when it might not have been, the fact that we are in it when we might, when we could not have been. The core of our human identity is nothing more or less than the fitful apprehension of the radically inexplicable presence, facticity and perceptible substantiality of the created. It is; we are. This is the rudimentary grammar of the unfathomable.[17]

Steiner's observations follow from Voegelin's two questions, "Why is there something and not nothing?" "Why is this thing as it is?"[18] Political philosophy is located at the conjunction of everyday politics and the wonderment about the highest things. Reality would not be complete without it if by reality we mean not merely *what is* but the accurate understanding of *what is*. Both of these, the reality and the understanding, seem necessary in a world that includes intelligence as well as being, which includes the intelligence of being.

Leo Strauss states bluntly that "'scientific political science' is in fact incompatible with political philosophy."[19] Strauss implies here that the students of "scientific political science" do not engage in the classic enterprise of political philosophy so that there is an unacknowledged lacuna in the proper understanding of human things. In attending to the fact that the subject matter of politics is human actions insofar as they are good or bad, praiseworthy or blameworthy, political philosophy can avoid that "scientific" neutrality that methodologically leaves out the essential nature of these acts.[20] To be "value-free" means literally not to understand what is to be investigated, what is to be known. Modern social science in this sense means that reality continues but it has no proper intelligence to illuminate it. This is why Strauss suspects that the political philosophy that does look to this reality as known by practical science and action is incompatible with modern social science.

"The social scientist is a student of human societies, of societies of humans. If he wishes to be loyal to his task, he must never forget that he is dealing with human things, with human beings," Strauss explains in his essay, "Social Science and Humanism."

He must reflect on the human as human. And he must pay due attention to the fact that he himself is a human being and that social science is always a kind of self-knowledge. Social science, being the pursuit of human knowledge of human things, includes as its foundation the human knowledge of what constitutes humanity, or rather, of what makes man complete or whole, so that he is truly human. Aristotle calls his equivalent of what now would be called social science the liberal inquiry regarding the human things, and his *Ethics* is the first, the fundamental, and the directive part of that inquiry.[21]

"The liberal inquiry regarding human things" recognizes that the "social sciences," in the Aristotelian sense, are a kind of "self-knowledge." That is, they realize that their subject matter has passed through and reflects on "the human as human." This understanding also implies that the mind knows that there are things that are not "human" both below and above man. It is aware of the beasts and the gods as well as men. The place of political philosophy in the structure of reality is at the point where the subhuman, the human, and the transcendent meet. Yet, they meet not as hostile combatants but as members of an ordered whole, a whole that includes beings who can freely reject what they are.

VI

In the beginning of these considerations on the place of political philosophy in the structure of reality, I cited, in addition to the passage from Aquinas on skepticism, a passage from Leo Strauss in which he pointed out that of its very nature, the city looks not to laws that it can unmake but to those it cannot, because man did not make himself to be man. The city must transcend itself, or perhaps better, the substantial beings among whom the city is a relation have ends that go through and beyond the political. In a further passage, I cited Catherine Pickstock, in a remarkable book pointing to, as she puts it in her sub-title, the "liturgical consummation of philosophy" (see below, chapter 10). Pickstock intimates that human consciousness cannot be guaranteed by ideological constructs or by "autonomous self-presence," the only alternatives available in an "immanentist" world, as she puts it. It can be grounded only by a "redemptive" return of "doxological dispossession," caused by a proper human response to the transcendent, a response that implies that man does not "make" his own salvation.

Earlier, I had cited the response of Levinas to the question of whether the absolute could be a "diversion," of whether, following Pascal, and indeed Plato and Aristotle, the relation of man to transcendence was one of "serious play," as Plato put it in *The Laws* (803a–04b). "Doxological dispossession" means that human completion is not a response to itself or to what it has itself made—to recall Voegelin's questions about our awareness that we do not create ourselves to be or to be what we are. Doxology, praise, causes us to let go of the illusion that we are the end of our own actions in any absolute sense. All our actions, including our political ones, while remaining what they are, point beyond themselves. If we do not allow for this pointing, we do not understand what we are or the nature of that "good," as Plato called it, that lies at the origin of things.

Political philosophy takes us back to the proper being of cities in relation to man and to his own personal destiny. Cities are not things that will be saved. Any empire, be it Roman, Holy Roman, British, Soviet, or whatever, "declines and falls," to use a famous and still haunting expression. Important as they might be, cities and empires are passing things, even though they be also human things intended to surpass the length of the lives of their individual citizens. The Greek classics, when they explained politics, explained them as an order of human actions by which citizens were praiseworthy or blameworthy, and this not just in some ephemeral sense. It was in and through the city that the citizen transcended the city. As Strauss put it at the end of his explication of Aristotle's *Politics*, man transcended the city only by what is highest in him, only by pursuing "true" happiness.[22] Modern political philosophy, with its "immanentist" background, as Pickstock intimated, has presented an alternate to the limited state either in terms of a this-worldly, universal ideology in which all good is seen to be a product of the state or in which the individual stands by himself as the maker of all value and the definer of all things, including himself.

"Doxological dispossession" suggests that what is worthy of man's highest praise is not the state. It is not even man himself. Since the state is a good, however, it can itself be setup as apparently worthy of total human commitment. No one, perhaps, has put the alternative better than C. S. Lewis's famous Screwtape in his advice to his colleagues about how to distract the human being from his major purpose. It seems fitting to close this chapter on the place of political philosophy in the structure of reality by citing—who else?—the devil!

Screwtape advises his fellow devils that human beings must be fostered in a certain delusion—not "diversion"—to recall Levinas. Ordinary human beings have a real presence in the world but also they have a real awareness that they did not cause their own being. Human beings then must be deluded into believing that the fate of nations is *in itself* more important than that of individual souls. The overthrow of free peoples and the multiplication of slave states are for us [devils] a means (besides, of course, being fun); but the real end is the destruction of the individuals. For only individuals can be saved or damned, can become sons of the Enemy or food for us. The ultimate value, for us, of any revolution, war, or famine lies in the individual anguish, treachery, hatred, rage, and despair which it may produce.[23]

Political philosophy is itself an effort to place the nations in a proper perspective in regard to their being. The fate of nations, however exciting and capable of being made to seem more important than it is, is not the central focus of political philosophy which points through the city to what transcends it. It points to the beings capable of being saved or damned, to beings capable of praise, of responding to the glory that man did not make.

Human beings are precisely, in Steiner's phrase, "real presences." We do not see their image in our eyes, but we see them. We know to whom we are talking; we know that we did not cause ourselves to be or to be what we are. Do not listen to those, as Aristotle told us, who, being human, tell us to concern ourselves only with human things, with the fate of the nations. Human things, as Plato remarks, do have a certain importance, but compared to the "divine seriousness," they are diversions. But man remains the political animal even in the highest things. We do have the power to distinguish between being awake and being asleep, as Aquinas put it.

In the end, "doxological dispossession" is the highest form of being awake. It is this awakeness to which the city points. It is the paradoxical place of political philosophy in the structure of being that the being of the city finds itself in its rightful rank, in its rightful category of relation, amid the things that are. The highest life, as Aristotle said, is not the political life, but the contemplative life, the life which, compared to political live, is "divine." But to the degree that the philosopher does not convince the Callicleses of this world to make a place for these higher considerations, to that very degree will political philosophy fail in its mission both to the city and to that which transcends the city. Political philosophy must be thought into existence in order that *what is* might be complete in knowing its own word.

Notes

1. Leo Strauss, *The City and Man* (Chicago: University of Chicago Press, 1964), 152.

2. Catherine Pickstock, *After Writing: The Liturgical Consummation of Philosophy* (Oxford: Blackwell Publishers, 1998), 170.

3. Charles M. Schulz, *Dogs Don't Eat Dessert* (New York: Topper Books, 1987).

4. James Boswell, *Boswell's Life of Johnson* (London: Oxford, 1931), I, 638.

5. Emmanuel Levinas, "Questions and Answers," in *Of God Who Comes to Mind*, translated by Bettina Bergo (Stanford, Calif.: Stanford University Press, 1986), 86.

6. Robert Sokolowski, "The Method of Philosophy: The Making of Distinctions," *Review of Metaphysics* 51 (March, 1998): 516, 524.

7. See James V. Schall, "The Death of Socrates and the Death of Christ," in *At the Limits of Political Philosophy* (Washington, D.C.: Catholic University of America Press, 1996), 123–44.

8. See James V. Schall, "The Reality of Society according to St. Thomas," in *The Politics of Heaven and Hell: Christian Themes from Classical, Medieval, and Modern Political Philosophy* (Lanham, Md.: University Press of America, 1984), 235–52.

9. Eric Voegelin, *Hitler and the Germans* (Columbia: University of Missouri Press, 1999), in *The Collected Works of Eric Voegelin*, vol. 5 31, 86.

10. See Ralph McInerny, "Are There Moral Truths That Everybody Knows?" in *Common Truths: New Perspectives on Natural Law*, edited by Edward McLean (Wilmington, Del.: ISI Books, 2000), 1–18; C. S. Lewis, *Mere Christianity* (New York: Macmillan, 1952), 17–42.

11. Gilson's great book has recently been republished, Etienne Gilson, *The Unity of Philosophical Experience* (San Francisco: Ignatius Press, 1999).

12. Professor Thomas S. Martin, "Eulogy for Richard Arlan Wood," Epiphany Episcopal Church, Flagstaff, Arizona, June 19, 1999.

13. See Charles N. R. McCoy, *The Structure of Political Thought* (New York: McGraw-Hill, 1963), 159–66.

14. Leo Strauss, "What Is Political Philosophy?" in *What Is Political Philosophy and Other Studies* (Glencoe, Ill.: The Free Press, 1959), 9–55.

15. Strauss, *What Is Political Philosophy?* 93–94.

16. See Gene Fendt and David Rozema, *Plato's Errors: Plato, a Kind of Poet* (Westport, Conn.: Greenwood, 1998).

17. George Steiner, *Real Presences* (Chicago: University of Chicago Press, 1989), 201.

18. "Why should there be art, why poetic creation? The question is an exact analogue to that posed by Leibniz: why should there be being and substance, why should there not be nothing?" ibid., 200. Similar questions are found in *Conversations with Eric Voegelin*, edited by R. Eric O'Connor (Montreal: Thomas More Institute Papers/76, 1980), 2; Vatican II, *Gaudium et Spes*, no. 10.

19. Strauss, *What Is Political Philosophy?* 14.

20. See E. B. F. Midgley, *The Ideology of Max Weber* (Aldershot, Hants.: Gower, 1983).

21. Leo Strauss, "Social Science and Humanism," in *The Rebirth of Classical Political Rationalism: An Introduction to the Thought of Leo Strauss*, edited by Thomas L. Pangle (Chicago: University of Chicago Press, 1989), 6.

22. Strauss, *The City and Man*, 49.

23. C. S. Lewis, *The Screwtape Letters* (New York: Macmillan, 1977), 170.

~

CHAPTER THREE

The Philosopher's Study
of Political Things

And of course Sir Ambrose (Plessington) himself remains as great a mystery to me as ever. I have often wondered, since, why he should have betrayed his allies. . . . But he was an idealist; he believed in the Reformation and the spread of knowledge, in a community of scholars like that described by the Rosicrucians in their manifestos or by Francis Bacon in *The New Atlantis*, which tells how the natural sciences will return the world to its Golden Age, to that perfect state before the Fall of Man in Eden. On his return to England (1600's) Sir Ambrose must have been sorely disillusioned. What he discovered among the denizens of the War Party were not enlightened scholars like those in Plato's Academy or Aristotle's Lyceum, but rather thieves and murderers as ignorant and evil as any found in Rome or Madrid.

—Ross King, *Ex Libris*[1]

In all later epochs, *the philosopher's study of political things* was mediated by a tradition of political philosophy which acted like a screen between the philosopher and political things, regardless of whether the individual philosopher cherished or rejected that tradition. From this it follows that the classical philosophers see the political things with a freshness and directness which have never been equalled. They look at political things in the perspective of the enlightened citizen or statesman. They see things clearly which the enlightened citizens or statesmen do not see clearly, or do not see at all. . . . They do not look at political things from the outside, as spectators of political life. . . . (Classical political philosophy) is free from fanaticism because it knows that evil cannot be eradicated and therefore that one's expectations from politics must be moderate.

—Leo Strauss, "What Is Political Philosophy?"[2]

Summary: Presupposed to any clarification of the relation of reason and revelation lies the question of the relation of the philosopher to the politician. Until this relationship is examined, the question of revelation cannot be properly addressed. Classical political philosophy sought to find a place for the philosopher within the city such that the politician would be rendered benevolent, not hostile to the philosopher. The politician in turn had to realize the dangers to the city both of a false or distorted philosophy and of a philosophy, true as far as it went, but one that did not account for all that is.

I

In Ross King's novel *Ex Libris*, we read the account of an "idealist" who does everything he can to preserve books and knowledge in the midst of the wars of the Reformation. The Catholics were considered to be the enemies of knowledge, yet knowledge, especially the "new" knowledge of science, would, presumably, save us. We could, by this very science, so it was contended, reverse the myth of the Fall and, by our own powers, return man to the Garden wherein perfect harmony existed between man and nature. The relation man-to-God—the so-called theological-political problem—was held to have little effect on either politics or humanity. Politics was a "gnostic" problem rather than a metaphysical or theological one. That is, man had within himself all the intelligence and resources needed to solve his own problems. Man was precisely "autonomous"; he provided his own law to himself presupposed to nothing but himself. Neither his thoughts nor his deeds transcended the city.

Yet, it turns out, underneath it all, men remain pretty much the same in all times and all places. Neither politics nor the new science seems to get at the bottom of things. No new regime remains "new" for long, even with new religions. The very term "modern" had to be replaced by "post-modern," but there is no stopping there either. We can already anticipate a "post-post-modernity," though whether any of it is anything more than carrying out in reality certain principles already implicit in philosophy remains to be seen.

Those, in any case, who had been thought to be "reformed" in London turned out, in the end, to be cheats and murderers, just like the Catholics in Madrid or Rome. Neither Machiavelli nor Hobbes really disagreed with such "realist" observations, though both were "modern" founders because they too thought that their worldly or scientific politics could in fact "improve" things, but not by virtue or persuasion, as the classical writers thought. The moderns thought that some "best" regime could be "designed" that would lessen or completely remove the recurrent and perhaps perennial disorders found in all historically existing polities. This "design" did not need to take into consideration the self-modification of the interior soul of man, as the classical writers had thought.

The scholarly members of Plato's Academy or Aristotle's Lyceum in Athens were not reduplicated in modernity, not in London or Paris, much less in Rome or Madrid. This turn of events, which seemed to be contrary to the expectations of modern political science, surprised the moderns, though it probably would not have surprised Plato or Aristotle. The "turn" of philosophy to practice and technique, which Bacon had recommended with such enthusiasm, actually implied a rejection of any independent or permanent order of things, especially of a standard of human things that could not be "otherwise," as Aristotle put it. In their searchings for perfection, the moderns abjured both the classical tradition and the intervening revelational corpus, a corpus that neither Plato nor Aristotle knew, though not a few thought that Plato especially must have had some inkling of it, so insightful was he.

Even the classical politicians, however, understood the importance of learning. Pericles, for all of Plato's dislike of him, praised learning and culture as the basis of Athenian political glory. We read earlier in King's novel that "a library is like an arsenal, a locus of power. After all, had not Alexander the Great planned a library at Nineveh that he claimed would be as much an instrument of his rule as his Macedonian armies?"[3] But of course, when libraries are designed as instruments of power, they are not really libraries. Libraries are rather designed to help us both to know and to preserve our knowing. They are not, by themselves, "knowledge," which is always in the active mind of a knower. Libraries were as valuable to the weak as to the strong, perhaps more so. Knowledge stands before power and beyond it as well as with it.

Indeed, as the classical authors knew, the end of politics is not politics, but the leisure to behold what is beautiful and to know *what is*, to know that which not even politics can change. Politics was one of those things, like virtue, to which it was directed, that, by being itself, pointed to what was not itself. The nobility of politics, while real, was also in that to which it pointed. Like philosophy, it too was an *ancilla*, a handmaiden in the service of higher things. A politics closed in on itself is a politics that did not understand the *what is* of political things.

The classical philosophers, though they knew civic life from the inside and spoke its language, as Strauss intimated, did not engage much in actual politics, not because they did not think it was interesting—Aristotle writes a book on the topic—but because they understood that something else was more interesting. Socrates, indeed, remained a "private" citizen lest he be killed sooner in his city (32e). The amusing stories of Thales, the philosopher, with his winepress monopoly or the laughter of the Thracian maidens over the philosopher so self-absorbed that he fell into a hole, were designed to demonstrate the paradox that philosophers could be rich or practical if they thought it worthwhile. But they had found something so interesting that they preferred to be poor, preferred to fall into holes in the road, to the laughter of the maidens, rather than give up discourse about the highest things.[4]

We have come to understand in the modern world that certain philosophers who become politicians—I think of Lenin—are very much more dangerous and more difficult to eliminate than tyrannical politicians who are motivated mostly by greed or pleasure. Aristotle is praised for writing two books, one on politics and the other on metaphysics, as if to remind us that the two are not the same. Plato is sometimes accused, especially in modern times, of causing tyranny because he writes his metaphysics in books entitled *The Republic* and *The Laws*. Clearly, the proper relation of politics to philosophy is fundamental for both philosophers. The politician can kill any philosopher if he so wills.

The deviant philosopher, the sophist, however, can corrupt the morals or order of any polity. The relation of politics to philosophy or of philosophy to politics is not a one way street on either side. We must recall the trials of Socrates and Christ here, for it was these trials and their gruesome results that solidified forever the question of whether the philosopher could live safely in existing cities, even decent ones like Athens, Jerusalem, or Rome. And if he could not, the question necessarily arose, out of actual experience, of whether there were a city in which he would be at home? Even more immediately, the practical or constitutional question became, is there a way of rendering the politician open to philosophy or revelation at least to the point that he does not kill the philosopher or prophet?

II

In Leo Strauss's essay, "What Is Political Philosophy?" we recall that the classical thinkers approached political things directly, not through modern scientific method according to which method alone they see or do not see all that they see. Moderns see what the method allows them to see, but the actual political things they do not see. The classical political language, however, was common language. Man, including philosophic man, was already involved in politics before he had any "theory" of politics. The philosopher possessed a sober and coherent understanding of what men were likely to do, of what we could expect of political things. But the politician also possessed such knowledge, often more clearly than the philosopher did.

The greatest danger to politics was not so much from philosophy, the contemplation of the highest things, but rather from a theoretical "fanaticism," to use Strauss's word, that allowed no moderation, no realization of the origin of evil in the human will. By knowing that not all evil could be eradicated, especially by politics, then, at least something prudential, something feasible might be put in place to modify existing evils. Degrees of both good and evil existed.[5] For the Greeks, the first of these moderating possibilities was virtue. Later, with the revelational tradition, a second alternative was grace. Neither virtue nor grace necessarily "determined" anything. Nor were either under the direct control of the political, though it could indirectly witness their effects and thus legitimately use them for its own purposes.

The members of Aristotle's Lyceum certainly understood this caution about the abiding presence of evil among us. Aristotle could perceptively describe "good" regimes and "bad" regimes. He followed the paths by which one regime passed from one order to the other. Good regimes could become less good. Bad regimes could become worse. Sometimes it was possible, often with the help of the philosopher, to turn the soul even of a tyrant toward the good. This interior "turning" was often thought to be the quickest way out of the dire consequences of the worst regimes. Aristotle had a criterion by which regimes were distinguished one from another. But he was very cautious in recommending political change. He thought that experience mattered even though it was not an excuse for stagnation. He was aware of the variety found in particular things, especially in human things. No two human acts were ever exactly alike, hence the primacy of the virtue of prudence.

Again, Aristotle thought that things could become better, but also worse. He did not understand "progress" to mean that things always improved. He understood prudence to mean that sometimes they did not. One could never assume that virtue would pass from teacher to pupil, or from one generation to the next, or even that it would remain in the same soul over a period of a lifetime. This was a "realism," unlike certain later "political realisms," that did not defend what was objectively wrong. But it was completely aware of the difficulty involved when it came to changing political things. It acknowledged that sometimes things improved. Contemporary idealists too often, as it turned out, created more terrible tyrannies than the classical tyrants ever thought of, even though many of the means employed by modern tyrants, or "totalitarians," as we are wont to call them, were also rather accurately described by Aristotle—the keeping the populace busy and exhausted, the not allowing friendships, the control of all conversations, the nothing private (1314a13–29).

III

St. Thomas himself, in his *Treatise on Law*, had emphasized that law was made for men, "the majority of whom were not perfect" (I–II, 96, 2). This latter affirmation was a statement of everyday observation that needed theoretic explication but no academic "proof." Its truth was pretty obvious to most men. If the politician expected too much of law, itself an "external" principle of order and action in one's soul, as Aquinas put it, he found that most men would be unable to practice what was in fact good (I–II, 90, Introduction). This incapacity would cause an inner discouragement and external disrespect for the law on the part of most citizens. It would make things worse by making attainment of law's purpose seem hopeless. Not everything could be expected of everyone.

In spite of this prudential caution, however, political society still needed the best things at least somewhere within it. But these "best things" did not arise from politics even though man was a political animal and political things were not in principle bad. The "highest things" appeared freely, almost unexpectedly, almost as if there were something "beyond politics," to use a phrase of Christopher Dawson, at work in every existing polity.[6] The relation of politics to the "highest things" was not, in principle, one of antagonism, however much it turned out to be in practice because of the questions of will and vice.

St. Thomas, likewise, was a reader of Aristotle, but one who had at his disposal the order of revelation with which to examine the abiding "wickedness" in men of which Aristotle spoke (1267a42). In a sense, we can say that the effect of revelation on Aristotle's politics, as Aquinas saw it, was to reinforce and to elevate both the contemplative and practical sides of human living and thinking. Also it explains, in more detail, under the title of Original Sin, the true nature of this tendency to "wickedness" that Aristotle had noticed.

But St. Thomas also understood that the practical life could not be helped unless the contemplative order also was left free to confront certain unsettled issues in the classical philosophers, particularly those relating to friendship.[7]

The practical life, the political life, was not itself safe unless there were at least some individuals within its sphere who were devoted to the contemplative life.[8] At least some philosophers needed to direct themselves to the whole, to the order of all things, not just to political things. In the revelational tradition, these contemplatives did not have to be philosophers in the technical sense, just as workers did not have to be slaves.

Yet, why could we not expect, by our own wits and science, to remove the effects of the Fall and produce among us a New Eden? A central answer to this question from the revelational tradition was that we had here "no lasting city," even if the city we did have were just. This realization was but another version of establishing the proper location of the best city, Augustine's heritage from Plato. We had a "best regime," but it was not an actual political regime. To be sure, much of the great drama of life, often that which determined one's final status, did take place in actual cities. The "lasting-city," the city in speech, was, nonetheless, a city that could be described fairly accurately by Aristotle or Plato.

The "moderation" of actual politics was the result of understanding this delicate distinction between two "real" cities, the confusion of which has been the cause of much of the idealism and, indeed, of much of the terror of modern political reality. It was the genius of Augustine to take Plato seriously, to "ground," as it were, the city in speech in such a manner that it saved both philosophy and actual cities. At the same time, Augustine addressed himself to issues that properly concerned both cities but to which neither, by themselves, could or did adequately respond. All existing cities, all cities in speech had about them an aura of incompleteness even when they were at their best, as in Athens or Rome, as in *The Republic* of Plato and *The Republic* of Cicero. The best existing cities and the best cities in speech had the effect not of completely satisfying us but of causing us to wonder what yet needed to be added. Both cities brought us to the "limits" of political philosophy, something that is precisely the service political philosophy provides both to metaphysics and to revelation.

IV

In the Myth of Er, the memorable account of the ultimate results of human action in the last book of *The Republic* of Plato, we come across a passage that has always puzzled readers who were political philosophers. When read carefully, the passage actually seemed to undermine any enthusiasm political philosophers might have for their discipline. *The Republic* is the book that, more than almost any other, is the charter of our freedom as well as of our learning because it admonishes us, indeed teaches us, how to have, in our own souls, a city in speech, lest we be overly committed to actual cities and their ultimate dangers. In this passage, Socrates shows the importance not of the next life, though he does not mitigate that importance, but of this life, of what goes on in this world.

Socrates makes his point by telling the tale of a final judgment in which all those who die, including those with heinous crimes on their souls, are given a second chance to choose a better life, better than the one they chose the first time around. We implicitly assume that, though we need not, we would obviously choose better a second time. The question remains, however: are these souls likely to choose better, even if given a second chance? It is a sobering passage, especially for anyone who might think that virtue can be achieved in any other way but by our choosing it, by our first knowing *what is*.

Each soul is to go before the Judge who is to render the final decision in session before the life of the one judged passes into the hands of the goddesses of past, present, and future so to live out his choice. As it turns out, each one is very much influenced by the kind of life that he lived on earth the first time around, in the actual life that he knew. Often terrible choices would be made from motives of bitterness and envy, or hatred and vengeance. Thus, the second choice was frequently as bad as or worse than the first choice. This unexpected eventuality is understandable because the purpose of the whole myth is to teach us the importance of our present choices, to let us see their transcendent meaning. But there is no escape in a second or third or fourth life which is the ultimate argument against any theory of reincarnation, of any effort to improve a failed life by having it "live again." One life is sufficient. If we choose wrongly in this life, we will not choose any better in another. The whole effect of the account is to teach us the radical importance of this life. The myth has, in a certain sense, the same effect as the doctrine of hell in revelation, namely, that our acts have, or can have, ultimate consequences from which we cannot escape without our restoring order.[9]

But what interests me here about this account of Er is the curious case of the man who appears to be a good politician. He is, in the beginning, no Callicles, no stubborn, though attractive tyrant. The Judge has assured those coming before his seat that a reasonable life will be open for anyone, first or last, "who chooses it rationally and lives it seriously." The first choosers are not to be rash; the last are not to be discouraged. No reason seems to exist why someone who led a less good or terrible life the first time would not choose a better one.

After setting down these conditions, the man who comes up first before the Judge actually "chose the greatest tyranny" the second time around. What is very surprising, and why I am interested in this passage here in the context of philosophy and political philosophy, is just who was this tyrant? As I said, he was not Cleon nor Alcibiades, at least not originally. Perhaps he was, like the frightening, competent, handsome Callicles, a man who loved philosophy in his youth, but who subsequently rejected it in ruling the city (*Gorgias*, 485a).

This same man depicted in the Myth of Er, however, ended up doing terrible things. How so? We can understand perhaps Cleon or Alcibiades doing dire things, but not this man. Yet,

> in his folly and greed he chose it (tyranny) without adequate examination and didn't notice that, among other evils, he was fated to eat his own children as a part of it. When he examined at leisure the life he had chosen, however, he beat his breast and bemoaned his choice. And, ignoring the warning of the Speaker (Judge), he blamed chance, daemons, or guardian spirits, and everything else for these evils but himself (619c)

This scene puts the problem right at the doorstep of the man himself. The relationship of our destiny to our choice was never put more clearly by a philosopher.

But what is interesting for my purposes here is the sort of man this tyrant was in this present life. At first sight, we might think that he had also lived a dissolute or tyrannical life here in some actual city. Not so. "He was one of those who had come down from heaven, having lived his previous life *under an orderly constitution, where he had participated in virtue through habit and without philosophy.*"[10] One could hardly overestimate the importance of this explanation, or be more astonished by it. We normally would not have expected that someone, who had good habits and who lived in an orderly constitution or regime, would have chosen to become a tyrant. At the same time, we cannot help but thinking that we should strive to live in virtue in an orderly regime, even if we have no depth in philosophy. Cities, after all, are not made up only of philosophers. In fact, we could not have a city with only philosophers in it.

Socrates' point here is a momentous one. Nothing guarantees virtue but philosophy, the philosophy of *what is*. It is quite possible, to find an example of the sort of situation Socrates anticipates, to have, say, senators, who are even Catholic, who go to church, but who still vote, with all sorts of rationalizations, pro-abortion, that is, implicitly vote to eat their own children. Socrates' point suggests that we are not safe until and unless we see and acknowledge the point of what is right. Habit, constitution, religion will not by themselves save us from ourselves, from responsibility of what we choose. The tyrant, in the Myth of Er, had all sorts of excuses for his actions, but none were allowed. Socrates allows no escape from our own choices. No real safety is found in virtue and good political regimes. We are always in danger, even as virtuous men in a reasonably good regime, of eating our own children unless we actually understand why we should not, unless, in other words, we are philosophers.

What this passage from the Myth of Er brings up, then, is the relation of philosophy to good regimes, in which politicians have habits of virtue. But these same politicians are not philosophers. They do not see the point of virtue, to what it is directed, even when they practice it. When the crisis comes and they are asked to face up to the real good as it presents itself, they choose against it. They are distracted. They have all sorts of reasons. They do not examine things carefully. They claim to square circles. They are busy with "important things." Or as Chesterton put it in *What's Wrong with the World*, "our modern politics are full of noisy forgetfulness; forgetfulness that the production of this happy and conscious life is after all the aim of all complexities and compromises."[11] There is a place for "perplexities and compromises" but not at the expense of the good or the right, of *what is*. Socrates' main point remains. We can choose against reason, against the good, even in good regimes, even with habitually virtuous men. This is why the worst things can happen in the best of regimes, and, a pari, the best things in worst regimes.

V

The story is told of the nineteenth-century English politician and philosopher John Morley. Once, while campaigning for office, he closed his address at a political rally by asking the listeners to vote for him. Suddenly, an angry gentleman jumped up and shouted, "I'd rather vote for the devil." To which outburst, Morley calmly responded, "Quite so, my good man, but in case your good friend declines to run for this office, may I count on your support?"

If the tyrant in the Myth of Er was but one step away from philosophy in his practice of virtue in a good constitution, John Morley was content to be but one step away from the devil to secure his seat in Parliament. All along, we have been granting that most people are not perfect, nor are most people tyrants. Yet, somehow, there seems to be a struggle at the highest level of intelligence and will of such proportions that all of heaven and hell depend on its outcome. This is certainly the teaching of Socrates, as it is the teaching of Christ.

Aristotle again enters the discussion at this point because we are reluctant to see how virtue and good regimes are dangerous. In Book Ten of his *Ethics*, Aristotle tells us that there are two kinds of happiness, one political and one contemplative. They are not the same, but they are not unrelated. The effort to make the city of man look as much as possible like the City of God is not, as such, an unworthy ambition. In principle, nothing is wrong with imitating, however imperfectly, the best. Indeed, this may well be why there is a creature who is not God in the universe.

Carens Lord, in his *Education and Culture in the Political Thought of Aristotle*, writes to this point:

> If a life of activity and rule is the best life simply, the perfection of that life will appear to be the exercise of "sovereignty over all" (1324a31–41). In fact, however, most men are somehow aware that political activity by itself cannot be the end of the best life. Political activity is indeed productive of happiness, but not intrinsically so: most men engage in politics not for its own sake but because of the rewards that accompany it. . . . In Aristotle's view, true happiness consists in the leisured enjoyment of the mind in the pursuit of speculations and thoughts which have no end beyond themselves, in other words, in the activity of philosophy.[12]

Two questions might arise out of this analysis: 1) if "most men" are in politics because of rewards, does this mean that there is, contrary to Aristotle, no real role of the state even in the promotion of virtue?[13] Christ had said that the purpose of rule or authority was not to lord it over the subjects but to serve them (Matthew 20, 24–28). And 2) granted the contemplative life as a proper good, a proper way of life, does the philosopher as a man have any relation to those who are poor or suppressed or in need? That is, is there a way to orient contemplation to action when necessary because of the very disorder of politics or economics? In the revelational tradition, the emperor bears the sword to punish wrongdoers (Romans 13, 3), while no one, neither king nor philosopher, is exempt from the love of one's fellows, granted that philosophers and politicians are both needed. Not everyone can do everything, which is the meaning of a "common" good, of specialization, of the multiplicity of actually good things to be done.[14]

In line with these questions, we find a remarkable passage in the Book Ten of Aristotle's *Ethics* that reads as follows: "Still, even though no one can be blessedly happy without external goods, we must not think that to be happy we will need any large goods. For self-sufficiency and action do not depend on excess, and we can do fine actions if we do not rule earth and sea; for even from moderate resources we can do the actions expressing virtue"

(1179a2–5). This passage is surely the charter of the common man not only in politics but also in philosophy. Recalling Socrates' tyrant who possessed virtue in a reasonably good regime, here we find Aristotle himself suggesting that normal people can practice virtue. They do not have to be emperors or kings. They do not have to be rich. Granted that we need some worldly goods, we do not need any excess of them.

Earlier on, Aristotle had made the same point in a different way: "For virtue and understanding, the sources of excellent activities, do not depend on holding supreme power. Further, these powerful people have had no taste of pure and civilized pleasure, and so they resort to bodily pleasures" (1176b18–21). This passage, in fact, is very close to the point of *The Republic*, namely, that politicians who lack an inner life, who have "no taste of pure and civilized pleasure," will be found pursuing "bodily pleasures." This was Carens Lord's point also.

This leaves us with the following problems: 1) what is to save us from bad philosophers? and 2) what is the relation between the good politician and the good philosopher? Perhaps, more basically, are politics and philosophy, granted their respective and relative autonomy, themselves adequate to confront the problems that inevitably occur both in politics and philosophy? On empirical grounds, the revelational tradition has suspected they are not in both cases. Something more seems necessary even for virtue, and something more than philosophy seems to be needed even for philosophy to be philosophy. *Credo ut intelligam* ("I believe in order to understand"), as Augustine put it.

VI

One final passage in Aristotle's *Politics* seems pertinent to our considerations here. In Book Two, Aristotle is speaking of Phaleas of Calcedon, who "asserts that the possessions of the citizens should be equal" (1266a39). Aristotle doubts this will work. Aristotle can be amusing. He tells us here that "no one becomes a tyrant in order to get in out of the cold" (1267a13). Aristotle thinks that if people commit crimes because they are hungry, the solution is pretty simple. See that they have some property on which to grow their own food. What about those who commit crimes because of some excess of enjoyment? Here, to recall Strauss's phrase, what they need is "moderation" (1267a9).

The really difficult question follows. People do not commit injustices only for "necessary things." Why do they do them, then? Some people commit excesses because they "want enjoyment through themselves alone." They are the "autonomous" men we have spoken of in modernity. Is there a remedy for these latter, by far the most dangerous, types? There is, thinks Aristotle. They should seek a remedy "in philosophy" (1267a12). What a remarkable answer! Aristotle does not just say in philosophy, but that they should find a remedy in the "pleasures" of philosophy, in the delight in knowing *what is*.

What about the politician in all of this? The fact is, he does not have time to be a philosopher. He is absorbed in many things, worthy things for the most part, that need attending. But should he also be attuned to higher things? How can this come about? Aristotle seems to turn to this question in Book Eight of *The Politics* where he speaks of education, particularly in music, a word covering all the arts. Even though the politician is not a philosopher, he ought not to be, like Callicles in power, contemptuous of philosophy. The politician ought to have tastes and habits that enable him to tend to, to recognize the philosophic good from the right ordering of his passions through his music.

As Plato saw, such a man is still vulnerable because he does not see the light. On the other hand, his political task is a needed one. He is a danger to the philosopher because he has the power to kill him. The philosopher must render him benevolent to the highest things even when the politician does not himself "delight" in them. The philosopher's study of political things is the other side of the politician's less vivid awareness of philosophical things. It is a dangerous relationship whose tension should not be underestimated. We know that Christ and Socrates were killed in ostensibly legitimate trials by the best existing states of their time. Though he is aware of the corrupting influence of the sophist, Plato is more directly concerned with the politicians who kill philosophers. Yet, even though he has the power to kill the philosopher if he chooses, we are hard pressed not to think that, in the end, a philosopher may be the more dangerous character. Aristotle for his part was concerned with both the politician and the philosopher and their living together. This is the import of a book on politics and a book on metaphysics, not to mention a book on poetry. It is true, as Strauss said, that "fanaticism" is a danger arising to the polis from the philosopher. Increasingly today, any claim of truth is considered "fanatical."

Yet, it may well be that existing cities are under pressure both from bad and from good philosophy. The city in speech and the City of God are not intended to be cities of this world. But they are intended to express the limits of any city of this world. And these limits are at the point in which cities do or do not realize that the true home of man is not a political one in this world. This latter realization is not, as we might be tempted to think, a sign of discouragement, but a liberty that guarantees a space beyond politics. At the same time it does not deny that things in this world can be better. The revelational tradition addresses itself to both of these points and, in fact, secures them.

It is possible to live virtuously in an orderly regime and still not grasp the outlines of what Strauss called "the City of Righteousness, the Faithful City."[15] This is indeed the origin of tyranny, as Socrates suspected. But the philosopher's understanding of political things ought to be perceptive enough to make him realize that man's end is not a political one, however much he is also a political animal. It ought to make him perceptive enough also to realize the man's end is not found in philosophy alone, though he must be philosophic enough to see that without philosophy he could never see why this limitation is so. Philosophy implies an opening to *all that is*. The philosophy that leads to "fanaticism" closes itself from this opening. The most dangerous "fanatics" are not those who hold absolutes, but those who do not. The politics that kills the philosopher, in its turn, lacks the moderation and the virtue that would limit itself to its own competency.

Athens, Jerusalem, Rome, Madrid, London, Paris—these are the cities of our heritage—classical, medieval, modern. It is in them that the city in speech and the City of God have previously and still come to our attention. Alexander of Macedon, Aristotle's pupil, intended to build a library at Nineveh. He did build a library at Alexandria, the city that bears his name. He was a man of power but also a philosopher who died young. Socrates told us that tyrants could arise from men who studied philosophy in college or even from men with the habit of virtue who lived in orderly constitutions but who lacked philosophy. Scripture tells us that we have here "no lasting city." We read *The Republic* of Plato to build a city of speech in our souls. The Psalmist (87) says, "Glorious things are said of thee, O City of God"—such are the undying themes of political philosophy.

Notes

1. Ross King, *Ex Libris, a Novel* (New York: Penguin, 1998), 391–92.

2. Leo Strauss, "What Is Political Philosophy?" in *What Is Political Philosophy and Other Studies* (Glencoe, Ill.: The Free Press, 1959), 27–28. Italics added.

3. King, *Ex Libris* 350.

4. See James V. Schall, "The Death of Plato," *The American Scholar* 65 (summer 1996): 401–15.

5. See James V. Schall, "A Meditation on Evil," *The Aquinas Review* 7 (#1, 2000), 25–42; "Evil and Political Realism," in *At the Limits of Political Philosophy* (Washington, D.C.: Catholic University of America Press, 1996), 71–88; "The Natural Restoration of Fallen Angels in the Depths of Evil," in *Faith, Scholarship, and the Culture in the 21st*

Century, edited by Alice Ramos and Marie George (Washington, D.C.: Catholic University of America Press/American Maritain Society, 2002), 251–68.

6. Christopher Dawson, *Beyond Politics* (London: Sheed & Ward, 1939).

7. See James V. Schall, "Aristotle on Friendship," *The Classical Bulletin* 65, 3/4 (1989): 83–88.

8. See Josef Pieper "The Purpose of Politics," in *Josef Pieper—an Anthology* (San Francisco: Ignatius Press, 1989), 121–23.

9. See James V. Schall, "Regarding the Inattentiveness to Hell in Political Philosophy," in *At the Limits of Political Philosophy: From 'Brilliant Errors' to Things of Uncommon Importance* (Washington, D.C.: Catholic University of America Press, 1996), 89–102.

10. Hackett edition of *Complete Works*. Italics added. Bloom's translation of this passage reads as follows: "He was one of those who had come from heaven, having lived in an orderly regime in his former life, participating in virtue by habit, without philosophy."

11. G. K. Chesterton, *What's Wrong with the World* (San Francisco: Ignatius Press, 1994), 5.

12. Carens Lord, *Education and Culture in the Political Thought of Aristotle* (Ithaca, N.Y.: Cornell University Press, 1982), 197.

13. The best discussion of this point is still that of Yves Simon, *A General Theory of Authority* (Notre Dame, Ind.: University of Notre Dame Press, 1980).

14. See discussions on the "common good" in *Josef Pieper—an Anthology* (San Francisco: Ignatius Press, 1989), 64–67, and Yves Simon, *A General Theory of Authority* (Notre Dame, Ind.: University of Notre Dame Press, 1980), 26–29. *The Aquinas Review*, vol. 4, no. 1 (1997) republished the famous texts and controversy on the common good by Charles De Koninck and I. Th. Eschmann. See also Clifford Kossel, "The Moral Views of Thomas Aquinas," in *Encyclopedia of Morals*, edited by V. Ferm (New York: Philosophical Library, n.d.), 11–22.

15. Leo Strauss, *The City and Man* (Chicago: University of Chicago Press, 1964), 1.

CHAPTER FOUR

~

The Role of
Christian Philosophy in Politics

Man's conquest of himself means simply the rule of the Conditioners over the conditioned human material, the world of post-humanity which, some knowingly and some unknowingly, nearly all men in all nations are at present labouring to produce.

—C. S. Lewis, *The Abolition of Man*, 1947[1]

Summary: What the present chapter adds to the previous one is the fact that certain philosophic truths have arisen within philosophy itself as a result of the necessity to clarify the very possibility of accepting revelation. What is curious is the relevance of these philosophic positions to the practice of philosophy, especially in understanding what the human person, the basis of any civil order, really is in his highest meaning.

I

James Boswell tells us that, as he was not in London in the year 1770, he did not have much conversation with Samuel Johnson. However, instead of his own memory and notes, he was able for this same year, 1770, to include in his renowned biography some of the *Recollections* of Johnson by the Rev. Dr. Maxwell, of Falkland, in Ireland. These recollections of the Rev. Dr. Maxwell are the source from which the following famous and amusing observation comes: "A gentleman who had been very unhappy in marriage married immediately after his wife died: Johnson said, 'it was the triumph of hope over experience.'"[2]

45

More to the point of a link between Christian philosophy and politics, however, though this very Christian philosophy too has something to do with the complex relation of hope and experience, we might recall two other passages from the same *Recollections*. The first passage reads as follows:

> Speaking of Boethius, who was the favourite writer of the middle ages, he (Johnson) said it was very surprizing, that upon such a subject, and in such a situation (referring to his impending condemnation to death by the Emperor), he (Boethius) should be *magis philosophus quam Christianus* (more a philosopher than a Christian).[3]

Many thinkers before us, no doubt, have also been surprised by Boethius's unexpected source of "consolation," whereby on such an ominous occasion as his own condemnation to death, he preferred to meditate on Socrates rather than Christ; he preferred philosophy to revelation.

My own approach here, however, though happily lacking the same urgency, will be rather different from that of Boethius. Reversing Johnson's remark about philosophy and Christianity, I will maintain the contrary position, to wit, *eo magis Christianus, quo magis philosophus*. When the chips are down, of course, I do think it better to be a Christian than a philosopher, though I doubt that such chips are ever really down. But I would suggest that precisely by being a Christian, by carefully reflecting on the exact Christian doctrines to see how it is possible to grasp what they might mean, one is a better philosopher, as philosopher.

No doubt this position recalls St. Thomas. It is also a view that rather often results in some considerable academic unpopularity if not downright animosity. It often ends in a kind of cultural ostracism or academic death, in a situation that itself no doubt could wish for some sort of consolation, philosophic or Christian, or otherwise.

The second passage pertinent to this theme of Christian philosophy and politics reads: "To find a substitute for violated morality, he (Johnson) said, was the leading feature in all perversions of religion." If I might read this passage somewhat contrariwise, it suggests that an authentic, nonviolated morality would need to rely on a religion that was not perverted. The theoretical substitute for the violated morality, I take it, would be the intellectual effort to justify and put into existence as the form of the polity and individual life what was in fact contrary to classical morality.

This articulated substitute would initially take the form of a religion-like moral system, an ideology, if you will, that contained a kind of coherent consistency within the terms of the denial itself. This consistent ideology would systematically reject the essential points proposed by classical religion, meta-physics, and morality. Its final perfection would be its successful organization of an actual political, if not world, order. This is, in its own way, the carrying out of Aristotle's remark that if man were the highest being, politics would be the highest science. The principal role of revelation in politics, I think, is to reinforce Aristotle's understanding that man was not the highest being in the universe. Thus, man would be freed of the temptation to think that he was the highest being, a temptation that, when not theoretically counter-acted, results in the practical effort to establish an alternate Kingdom of God on earth, however it be called.

II

To speak of precisely "Christian philosophy" is rash enough, I suppose, let alone the almost unheard of implication that such philosophy might have a "role" in or even a relationship with politics. On the other hand, in these days of rapidly increasing and radical separation of church and state, the topic is intriguing, however much neglected in academic discourse.[4] The net effect of an exaggerated divergence between religion and politics is to elevate a certain kind of philosophic discourse, usually the discourse of tolerance or relativism, into the position of the sole arbiter of what subjects are allowed to be seriously spoken in the public forum. Christian philosophic speech in this context loses not so much its legitimacy as its voice or, perhaps better, it loses an intellectual framework in which its voice can be understood.

In the beginning of this chapter, I cited C. S. Lewis's perceptive remark about how the human raw material, in "the world of post-humanity," as he called it, in our world that now exists, would be looked upon as something malleable before the will of zealous political "conditioners." Politico-philosophic leaders, including democratic ones, in the name of their sub-stitute vision of reality, would employ the power of the state to achieve their theoretic purposes. They would seek to put into being what is con-trary to the natural structure of human worth and dignity and, likewise, contrary to the explicit statements of Catholicism about itself and its un-derstanding of the worth and meaning of the human person.

Let me now cite, in the context of these remarks about philosophy, Chris-tianity, and politics, from a speech originally given September 25, 1992. I cite it mostly, I think, because it illustrates better than anything else the thesis of the "culture wars," namely, that we are now, within this and other polities, entered into such radical divergences of opinion about what human life means that no real compromise, the essence of practical politics, is likely or even possible.

"The argument against abortion is based not only on the data of faith but also on reasons of the natural order, including the true concepts of human rights and social justice," the passage reads.

> The right to life does not depend on a particular religious conviction. It is a primary, natural, inalienable right that springs from the very dignity of every human being. The defense of life from the moment of conception until natural death is the defense of the human person in the dignity that is his or hers from the sole fact of existence, independently of whether that existence is planned or welcomed by the persons who give rise to it. Every reflection on this serious matter must begin from the clear premise that procured abortion is the taking of the life of an already existing human being. . . . There can be no "right" to kill an already existing though yet unborn human being.[5]

These words were spoken to the Irish bishops by John Paul II—words that have been often repeated.[6]

What is to be noted about these remarks in particular, however, is that they claim to be spoken not merely in the name of religion but rather by religion *in the name of reason*. Indeed, they are made by a religion that insists that reason is not contradictory or alien to its doctrines and practices, one that insists that it must give valid reasons to show this consistent relationship. Today, in fact, the real cultural conflict is not between reason and science—what the Holy Father said is, from a scientific point of view, absolutely accurate. Rather, the conflict is between such political ideology with its substitute countermorality and science.

III

I would initially suggest, then, that the role of Christianity in politics is a philosophic one. It is to maintain the accurate statement of the truth of things, of *what is*, even the truth of science when science will not stand up for itself. It is to perform this clarification even when the words we use, like "choice," do not accurately describe the fact to which they refer. We destroy millions of already begun human lives with no scruple and little compunction. We do this drastic act in the name of a theory, in the noble name of "rights," in fact. This justification leads us to suspect that we must be much more careful than we have been in using the concept of rights.[7]

We are now also legally permitted to use, with decreasing limits, the remains of aborted fetuses for human experimentation, another policy change we have been bequeathed by the new conditioners. And we use these human remains precisely because they are human and therefore most apt for human purposes—scientific, cosmetic, or replacement of organs. The contradiction is patent. We kill the incipient life because we say that it is only "potentially" human; then, we use the fetal products in the noble name of the common good, because it is actually human. The justifying principle stated in 1992 in the U. S. Supreme Court's *Planned Parenthood vs. Casey*—"At the heart of liberty is the right to define one's own concept of existence, of meaning, of the universe, and of the mystery of human life"—makes it quite impossible, as an intellectual principle, to distinguish between a Hitler and a Mother Teresa, between a monster and a wise man. Ralph McInerny had it right, "We live in a time, philosophically speaking, when a lot of people have just given up on the pursuit of truth."[8]

In thinking about this topic of Christian philosophy and politics—abortion is my least favorite topic and I hate even to allude to it—I had originally intended to suggest something perhaps outlandish. In truth, I wanted to argue that political philosophy occupies a kind of privileged place between philosophy itself and revelation, while the contact between revelation and everyday practical life is almost immediate. Eternal decisions are made in the course of our regular days, whether we be philosophers, senators, doctors, or janitors, whatever be our polity, the best or the worst. There is, as it were, a Thomistic reason for the latter point and a Platonic reason for the former.

Political philosophy has to explain or justify the existence of the polity so that it does not kill its philosophers or saints (or babies) when the polity realizes that something clearly disordered exists within it. The truth of things, the whole of things, is properly the object of both philosophy and revelation. Though there is such a thing as truth known by intuition, even in politics, the truth of politics largely depends on the truth of articulated philosophy.[9] Man does not make man to be man, Aristotle told us, but taking him from nature as already man, makes him to be good man. Nor does man live by bread alone, as Scripture taught. But both those who are to live the truth of things, and for Christianity this includes in principle everyone, and those who teach this truth must be allowed to live and to speak. Their very existence cannot be hostile to a polity, even when either they or the polity itself is disordered. In principle, indeed, their existence is the polity's purpose for existing, that is, to allow the highest things to exist within the context of the ordinary things. And among the highest things is the proper understanding of man, without which understanding there is no limit to politics.

But the spiritual life of the philosopher or saint, at its highest, in what transcends politics, consists, in part, in seeking to resolve the different claims of truth in such a manner that reason and faith are allowed to operate and to conclude issues in conflict. This is the Platonic point. The recurrent hostility of politics to truth—the best existing city killed Socrates, the best Empire killed Christ—is not good politics; the hostility of philosophers to truth is not good philosophy.

The Thomistic point is that the civil law is made for the generality of citizens, the majority of whom are neither perfect nor are they philosophers (I–II, 96, 2). This practical wisdom is not intended to suggest that therefore what the citizens "do" do—the Machiavellian issue—is quite the best norm for civil polity. Rather it is that most people need something more than their own experience and reason to know and do what is right. This something more is the purpose or "reason" for revelation. This is why it was "necessary," to use St. Thomas's term (I–II, 91, 4).

The things that are done that are wrong, however, remain wrong both in themselves and in their consequences, even when they are tolerated or proposed as good. It is probably not worth the effort to try to prohibit all wrongs or make a law about all right. The moral life is a thing that we ought, for the most part, to choose and reason to by ourselves. But for most people, it will be religion that will incite them to anything approaching the good life that is needed for the survival of any polity, let alone that is needed to save their souls. When Augustine finally came to address the topic of why the Romans declined, he found the answer in a moral context, in the way the Romans lived as judged by standards that even the Romans themselves understood. A careful reading of many of the things we confront every day makes it seem that the sober Romans, at their worst, would have been surprised at what we do to ourselves.

IV

Over a decade ago, Irving Kristol caught some of this issue about religion and political decline. The rise and fall of liberalism is directly related to the rise and fall of secularism in American life, he remarked. "Secular humanism" is already showing signs of sterility and collapse. There is nothing on the left to replace this secular humanist position. But there is another kind of alternative. "Today, it is the religious who have a sense that the tide has turned and that the wave of the future is moving in their direction . . . ," Kristol continued.

> Religion is . . . most important because it is the only power that, in the longer term, can shape people's character and regulate their motivation. . . . The reason is simple: It is not possible to motivate people to do the right thing and avoid the wrong thing, unless people are told, from childhood on, what the right things and the wrong things are.[10]

The link between an accurate description of what we do and what we ought to do, whether the link be made by reason, as John Paul II indicated, or by religion, as Irving Kristol maintained, needs to be the continuing raw material of political philosophy, of what it is that it reflects on. What gives this question added complexity in more recent years is the general concern about the internal integrity of religion itself—the terrorists coming out of Islam, the scandals caused by disorders in the Catholic episcopate and priesthood.

The things that are done that are wrong, to repeat, remain wrong both in themselves and in their consequences, even when they are politically tolerated. In one sense, we might observe that religion as such is not under attack when its members do wrong things because they are wrong things.[11] The problem arises when what is wrong is specifically defined as what is right. That individual Christians are capable of, even at times likely to do wrong things is part of the Christian faith itself, the doctrine of the Fall. This is why there is an intimate link between the doctrine of forgiveness and the right order of polity even when many wrong or evil things occur.[12] The doctrine of forgiveness was never intended to be a justification of wrongdoing, but rather an acknowledgment of it.

Religion is only under attack when the wrong things themselves come to be intellectually considered to be right, or, in political terms, to be "rights," that is, when the affirmation of wrongs becomes itself enshrined in the laws and coercive power of the state as what is to be done. Thus, as St. Thomas argued, it is probably not worth the effort to try to prohibit all wrongs or make a law about commanding all virtues (I–II, 96, 2, 3). The moral life is a thing that we ought for the most part to choose and reason to by ourselves. This is the profound meaning of the adage that we should hate sin but love the sinner. We do not love the sinner when our political theory of tolerance becomes an intellectual definition of right and wrong, the content of which depends on nothing other than whatever one's definition is. Religion has premises in reason, not just in will.

In this sense, if I understand him rightly, St. Thomas would suggest that polities that do not right themselves with the prod of revelation will end up by being more and more unreasonable. They will continue to lower their sights and call the results "reality." Chesterton suggested that a people that sets out to be "natural" somehow ends up by becoming "unnatural." This unreasonableness or unnaturalness will manifest itself in conduct. This disorder will henceforth be defined as custom or good. This is Johnson's "violated morality" that results in a perverse substitute for religion. Activities and institutions contrary to reason and to the understanding of reason in which it is embodied in a given human nature, that, as such, has no specific origin in any human making, replace the activities and institutions said to manifest and support classical morality and religion.

V

What is the role of Christianity in politics? Linus has been diligently preparing for the school Christmas play in which he is to recite the passage that begins, "And the Angel said unto them, fear not: for behold, I bring you good tidings of great joy which shall be to all the people." Lucy is listening to this recitation. She even compliments him, since he had embarrassed them all by forgetting his lines in the Christmas play of the previous year. Linus puts his coat on and prepares to go to the play. He is in a good mood. "I TOLD you I knew it," he boasts to Lucy. "I have a memory like the proverbial elephant." As he walks outside in the evening darkness, he happily and accurately repeats these lines again and again. However, in the next scene he suddenly reappears at Lucy's door. "What in the world? I thought you just left?" she exclaims. Thoroughly dejected, Linus replies, "I did, but I came back." Finally, to Lucy with eyes shut in disbelief, he explains, "I forgot where the Church is."[13]

Now, of course, this is the point I want to underscore in this matter of philosophy and politics. In thinking of these issues, we too do not want to forget where the Church is. In the first place, the New Testament is not a revelation about polity. Politics is not revelation's object. We will look in vain in the Gospels for a description of how to organize the state or how to promote policy. The role of philosophy for Christians is to elucidate what the state is when revelation does not give any particular guidance on the subject. Indeed, the role of revelation is to incite more accurate, more philosophical thinking about what the state is itself to be.

The Scripture is, no doubt, brash enough to tell us that there are things of Caesar (Matthew, 22:22). No other religion ever said that Caesar has his own justifications, that he has things to do that are perfectly proper to him. But this same Caesar in practice can be a tyrant. Under his authority, neither Christ nor Paul nor Peter survived. The obedience to the emperor that Paul advised to the Romans seemed paradoxical when this same obedience meant the elimination of Paul himself (Romans, 13:1–7). Surely the effect of revelation was not, as Nietzsche suspected, intended to promote tyranny by default.

But emperors who were not also philosophers of sorts were not the real threat. Brutality and individual corruption were normally passing things in history. Their evil was easily recognized and admitted. The really dangerous political leaders, as we have indicated, were those who had some grounding in philosophy, something about which Aristotle had already warned. Furthermore, Aristotle thought that the only cure of philosophical disorder was more philosophy, that is, correct philosophy. Paul himself, to be sure, looked upon the philosophers with a most skeptical eye (1 Corinthians, 1:17–25). The wisdom of this world seemed closer to foolishness to him.

But if we put these strands of thought together, in the context of the role of Christian philosophy in politics, we can see that the fact that there are things that "belong to God" implies that there are things that do not belong to Caesar. The great drama of political philosophy is to protect the legitimacy of a place wherein truth can be spoken and lived. It does this best, if we re-call Aristotle, through music and poetry, through virtuous habits, that enable the actual politician to sense the truth without ever himself having had the time fully to know it. Some very intelligent actual politicians, to recall Callicles, loved to talk philosophy in their youth. But on reaching political power, they chose to put it aside. They refused to talk about the relation of their ideas to truth, at which point they became, in Plato's dialogue, the most dangerous of men. Callicles, as the model of such rulers, remains, I think, a very contemporary politician.

VI

"Have I forgotten where the Church is?" someone might ask at this point. Here, I cannot help but recall Charles N. R. McCoy, who remains the most insightful of Catholic thinkers who have devoted themselves to the under-standing of political philosophy. He was concerned with the nature and di-rection of the modern mind as it has intellectually argued itself into inde-pendence from any norms of nature or revelation, into a kind of autonomous freedom that sees human nature as a kind of raw material open to its own re-fashioning. During the time that McCoy (1930s to 1970s) wrote, the most dangerous refashioners or conditioners seemed mainly to be Marxists. Yet, in reflecting on him, he was amazingly aware, not unlike the Holy Father him-self in *Centesimus Annus*, of a kind of incipient democratic tyranny that would, if anything, be more dangerous than marxism.

What I would propose here, then, is that McCoy came the closest to de-scribing in accurate philosophic terms what has gone wrong and why in the modern era. I do not mean that he is some kind of uncanny seer, but I do mean that the hard intellectual work required to understand the situation in which we find ourselves is depicted in his writings. Though he may, like Strauss, have been too harsh on Burke, and, unlike Strauss, too hard on Plato, McCoy understood why many contemporary liberal and conservative minds were not so much in opposition to each other but rather represented two sides of the same coin. McCoy admired Marx for seeing that both were lacking critical intelligence about the need for intelligence at the center of things. For Marx this was the human intelligence, for McCoy it was the Prime Intellect to which human intelligence was in some sense open.[14]

Furthermore, McCoy saw that religious thinkers themselves were more and more imitating in their theology philosophical principles and attitudes from modernity that could only transform religious thinking into pious versions of what was going wrong in the secular world. McCoy, I sometimes think, is more important for theology than he is for political philosophy. He understood why it is, in a sense, that we have so few "Catholic" universities wherein intellectually the validity of the defined positions of the Church is presented and argued as relevant to philosophy and especially to politics.

But in order to make the point I want to make in this chapter, let me cite a remark of Charles Taylor. Taylor sought to explain the origins of the notion of authenticity as it has come to be understood in modern philosophy. What interests me here is the understanding of authenticity as the antithesis to and almost parody of the magnanimous man of Aristotle or the saint of Christianity. We aspire more and more to be led by such apparently autonomous and authentic men, those whose warrant is self-realization and whose freedom consists in putting their own ideas into reality, with no check from *what is*.

"Being true to myself means being true to my own originality, and that is something only I can articulate and discover," Taylor remarked.

> In articulating it, I am also defining myself. I am realizing a potentiality that is properly my own. This is the background understanding to the modern ideal of authenticity, and to the goals of self-fulfillment or self-realization in which it is usually couched. This is the background that gives moral force to the culture of authenticity, including its most degraded, absurd, or trivialized forms.[15]

It is easy to see that some form of authenticity is a Christian virtue, that we need to know what we do. We need to take into consideration our own unique lives, yet not be hypocritical. But a Christian authenticity would begin, it seems, with Voegelin's remark, based in a true humility, that "we all experience our own existence as not existing out of itself but as coming from somewhere even if we don't know from where."[16]

VII

Why I want to refer to McCoy in this context, however, is not because of his doubts about the project of Strauss to revive classical political philosophy. McCoy himself subscribed to the need for some radical revival of political philosophy as such. But he doubted the success of such an endeavor without a Christian component to this revival. St. Thomas was more than a welcome preserver of Aristotle. St. Thomas deepened philosophy, however, precisely because of revelation. His philosophical conclusions as such did not take a form that a non-Christian could not understand or accept even though they were stimulated by the need to clarify revelational things.

Charles N. R. McCoy explained how such modern authenticity came to conceive that it gave law to itself, how it came to hold that there was no place for a natural law and a revelation addressed through it. McCoy had a great appreciation for Rousseau and Marx and considered them philosophers of great insight in understanding the meaning and direction of modern political philosophy. With the presumed death of marxism, we might wonder about the validity of McCoy's thesis. McCoy's thought was based on the awareness of an abiding prudence or practical wisdom that existed in certain strands of the political tradition, strands articulated best in Aristotle and St. Thomas.

Claes Ryn has justly remarked, in the context of both Strauss and McCoy, that "choosing between modern and pre-modern thought is not a real possibility."[17] Ryn argued against a kind of abstract intellectualism that did not really embody principles in reality. The Thomist notion of prudence and the Christian doctrine of Incarnation are, of course, very much along these lines that point to the importance of the body in philosophy. Indeed, even Marx, as McCoy thought, was concerned with a kind of species-man whereby everything of the universe came to exist in each person, though it seems that Aristotle's notion of friendship might be a better solution to the same problem.

The question asked today is whether the intellectual critique of modernity as something intrinsically opposed to human life in the Aristotelian or Thomist sense remains viable. Paul Johnson has asked, in this regard, whether totalitarianism was "dead"? Or does it reappear in new ideologies and movements, perhaps even more dangerous because more democratic?[18] Do these newer movements not have the same intellectual roots as marxism only, on its fall, to follow a different, more subtle path?

It is on this point of the troubling nature of philosophic modernity that McCoy was most perceptive. In his essay, "The Dilemma of Liberalism," he wrote:

Liberalism's primal act of imagination whereby it establishes its essence and existence in the enhanced sense of freedom consequent on the Humean principle that the aberrations in nature are ever so conformable to reality as its apparent intentions issued in autonomy and other-direction. This condition is

overcome by the profounder insight that . . . by the law that reduces the material and mental spheres to a common denominator the aberrations in nature become the exemplar for freedom in the world of culture and civilization. The way
to autonomy then must lie, as Marx most clearly perceived, in destroying all the
"intentions" in nature. . . .[19]

Autonomy and authenticity are to be manifested in culture and civilization.
Their sign of societal existence is their replacing the intentions of nature
that see man as already a formed being whose end or good is given to his intellect to know. His truth consists in the degree to which he conforms his free
life to nature and nature's God's purpose in causing him to be in the first
place. This purpose, which is first to know *what is*, is, likewise, his own good,
a good that is given to him by the cause of his being. Religion, family, limited state, science, morals, and law all take their being and meaning from
these intentions in nature.

These human realities—family, limited state, religion, morals, law, and
science—"are the indefectible principles and natural associations," McCoy
continued,

and they are not among the facts in accord with which we must live—in a people's democracy. But they are precisely the things upon which, in the classical
tradition of the West, all free governments have depended. And the reason for
this is that all of these things are nothing but participations of that intellect
that is "separable indeed but [does] not exist apart from matter" in the life of
that Prime Intellect upon whose perfect freedom, indeed—as Aristotle well
understood—"depend the heavens and the world of nature."[20]

The intellect that is "separable from matter but does not exist apart from it"
is of course the human intellect. Its freedom is not original with itself, but it
is an essential property of its *what is*, its being.

The human good is, as it were, given to it and given to it as something it
could not imagine in its highest reaches. Aristotle said that man does not
make man to be man but taking him from nature as already man makes him
to be good man. The freedom of man has to do with his goodness, not with
his being. That is, a freedom of man to be something other than man is neither a liberty nor a glory more exalted than what he is. The claim of modern
political theories is that the institutions in which this good is fostered are
themselves not presupposed to the real good of man. They must be changed
or eliminated because their existence interferes with the ambition of authentic and autonomous man to refashion man free of any divine or traditional claim. This position, thus, must be based on positions that refuse the

freedom that comes from the truth of man's being. McCoy saw here that free government depends on the Western tradition that saw the first purpose of philosophy to be that of knowing the given being of man as a limit on its own activities. It is in this sense that Western civilization, the civilization with the universal purpose, as Strauss rightly called it, must directly come under attack if an alternate structure of man, rooted in the denial of any claim to a right order of human things, is to exist.[21]

VIII

In a short essay entitled, "The Purpose of Politics," Josef Pieper has commented on the dangers of the exclusively political, on the view that politics is, contrary to Aristotle, the "highest science." A politics that is based on an unlimited freedom rather than on the truth that makes us free leaves us, Pieper thought, subject to "the deadly emptiness and the endless ennui which bounds the realm of the exclusively practical." This result, Pieper went on to explain, is the result of the destruction of the *vita contemplativa*, of the capacity to account for the "intentions" in nature. In this situation, it is possible to

> see new and forceful validity in the old principle: "It is requisite for the good of the human community that there should be persons who devote themselves to the life of contemplation." For it is contemplation which preserves in the midst of human society the truth which is at one and the same time useless and the yardstick of every possible use; so it is also contemplation which keeps the true end in sight, gives meaning to every practical act of life.[22]

Thus both the democratic polity that allows the philosopher to exist, even though it thinks him a fool, and the best practical polity that knows its own limits and knows that there are things that are not Caesar's have within their structures the intellectual means for their own preservation.

But, as Thucydides, Plato, and Aristotle imply, it is out of the democratic polity that the philosophical tyrants arise. The philosophic tyrants are not content merely with their own good but require that the whole of reality be ordained to their own project, a project that is conceived to be the proper understanding of things, particularly human things. When we have come to this point, in conclusion, we realize that C. S. Lewis's word was very perceptive, the "conditioners." We do live among those who presume to deal with only "conditioned human material." Lewis called this simply "post-humanity."

The role of Christian philosophy in politics is, at its briefest, to prevent such a post-human order of things from coming about by demonstrating, in contrast, the truth of right order. The first step is to understand how this post-humanity is coming about. And that understanding, practically speaking, will not happen without revelation, without a clear understanding of the responses that revelation gives to the unanswered philosophic questions, together with a clear understanding of disorder in the human soul. The alternate answers are in place. Samuel Johnson already had it correct in 1770— "To find a substitute for violated morality was the leading feature in all perversions of religion." The substitutes take over the public world. This is why, even as philosophers, we cannot forget where the Church is. *Eo magis Christianus, quo magis philosophus.*

Notes

1. C. S. Lewis, *The Abolition of Man* (New York: Macmillan, 1978), 86.

2. James Boswell, *Boswell's Life of Johnson* (London: Oxford, 1931), I, 420.

3. Ibid. See also on Boethius, Josef Pieper, *Scholasticism: Personalities and Problems of Medieval Philosophy* (New York: McGraw-Hill, 1960), 25–42.

4. See Étienne Gilson, "What Is Christian Philosophy?" in *A Gilson Reader*, edited by A. Pegis (Garden City, N.Y.: Doubleday Image, 1957), 171–91.

5. John Paul II, "Catechetics and the Defense of Life," *The Pope Speaks*, 36 (January/February 1993), 55. See also Robert George, *In Defense of Natural Law* (Oxford: Oxford University Press, 1999), chapters 8 and 11; Hadley Arkes, *First Things: An Inquiry int the First Principles of Morals and Justice* (Princeton, N.J.: Princeton University Press, 1986), chapters 16 and 17.

Sometimes it is suggested that the Church has changed its position about the moment of conception as the beginning of life because St. Thomas, following Aristotelian biology, thought life began later. The question of when life begins is one of scientific fact. St. Thomas based himself on the best thought he knew. The principle he used and that used by John Paul II about the beginning of life are the same. Today we know more of the experimental side of this inception.

6. See John Paul II's Encyclical, *Evangelium Vitae* (1995), in *The Pope Speaks* 40, no. 4 (1995): 199–281.

7. See Mary Ann Glendon, *Rights Talk: The Impoverishment of Political Discourse* (New York: The Free Press, 1991); Henry Veatch, *Human Rights: Fact or Fancy?* (Baton Rouge: Louisiana State University Press, 1985); Robert P. Kraynak, *Christian Faith and Modern Democracy: God and Politics in the Fallen World* (Notre Dame, Ind.: University of Notre Dame Press, 2001); Ernest Fortin, *Collected Essays*, edited by J. Brian Benestad (Lanham, Md.: Rowman & Littlefield, 1996), 3 vols.; James V. Schall, "Human Rights as an Ideological Project," *American Journal of Jurisprudence* 32 (1987), 47–61.

8. Ralph McInerny, "Interview," *National Catholic Register*, January 24, 1993.

9. See Jacques Maritain, "On Knowledge through Connaturality," in *Natural Law: Reflections on Theory and Practice*, edited by W. Sweet (South Bend, Ind.: St. Augustine's Press, 2001),13–24.

10. Irving Kristol, "The Coming Conservative Century," *Wall Street Journal*, February 1, 1993.

11. See George Weigel, *The Courage to Be Catholic* (New York: Basic Books, 2002).

12. See Hannah Arendt, "Irreversibility and the Power to Forgive," in *The Human Condition* (Garden City, N.Y.: Doubleday Anchor, 1959), 212–19; James V. Schall, "On Forgiveness," *Crisis* 17 (January 1999): 59.

13. Charles Schulz, *And the Beagles and the Bunnies Shall Lie Down Together* (New York: Holt, 1984).

14. Charles N. R. McCoy, *The Structure of Political Thought* (New York: McGraw-Hill, 1963); *On the Intelligibility of Political Philosophy: Essays of Charles N. R. McCoy* (Washington, D.C.: Catholic University of America Press, 1990).

15. Charles Taylor, "The Sources of Authenticity," *Canadian Forum* (January/February 1992): 5.

16. *Conversations with Eric Voegelin*, edited by R. Eric O'Connor (Montreal: Thomas More Institute Papers/76, 1980), 9.

17. Claes G. Ryn, "Universality and History: The Concrete as Normative," *Humanitas*, 6 (fall, 1992/winter, 1993): 19.

18. Paul Johnson, "Is Totalitarianism Dead?" *Crisis* 7 (February 1989): 9–17; see *The End of Democracy: The Judicial Usurpation of Politics*, edited by M. Muncy (Dallas: Spence, 1997); James V. Schall, "A Reflection on the Classical Tractate on Tyranny: The Problem of Democratic Tyranny," *American Journal of Jurisprudence* 41 (1996): 1–20.

19. McCoy, *Intelligibility*, ibid., 84. See also James V. Schall, "Transcendent Man in the Limited City: The Political Philosophy of Charles N. R. McCoy," *The Thomist* 57 (January 1993): 63–95; "'Man for Himself': On the Ironic Unities of Political Philosophy (McCoy)," *Political Science Reviewer*, 15 (fall 1985): 67–108.

20. McCoy, "Dilemma," ibid, 85.

21. Leo Strauss, *The City and Man* (Chicago: University of Chicago Press, 1964), 3.

22. Josef Pieper, *Josef Pieper—an Anthology* (San Francisco: Ignatius, 1989), 123.

CHAPTER FIVE

~

On How Revelation Addresses Itself to Politics

The economic problem is a . . . problem which has been solved already: we know how to provide enough and do not require any violent, inhuman, aggressive technologies to do so. There is no economic problem and, in a sense, there never has been. But there is a moral problem, and moral problems . . . are not capable of being solved so that future generations can live without effort.

—E. F. Schumacher, A Guide for the Perplexed, 1977[1]

It will be observed, that Johnson at all times made the just distinction between doctrines contrary to reason, and doctrines *above* reason.

—Boswell's Life of Johnson, 1784[2]

Summary: Aristotle had remarked that virtues are acquired by performing acts of virtue. Aquinas added that the law cannot command our interior movements of the soul. Moreover, since there are "things of Caesar," these exist in their own right. Thus revelation must direct itself to politics indirectly, through the souls of those who are active in cities.

I

The New Testament contains a number of perplexing statements that apparently have to do with economics. St. Paul said, for example, that a workman is worthy of his hire, from which we conclude that a workman who does sloppy or dishonest work is morally wrong. Likewise, an employer who does not pay a fair wage is unjust. But we are not told how the market or the company or the government or the worker, for that matter, decides what in truth is a fair price or wage or how to achieve either. Nor are we told how the consumer is related to the worker and to the employer both of whom, along with the government, can conspire against the consumer if they are in selfish collaboration. If revelation does not deal specifically with these latter things, we might wonder, what good is it? What might be the significance of revelation in apparently not deciding all these unsettling questions of mankind?

In one famous parable, on the socially inadmissible grounds that the owner can do with his money as he pleases, we see the master of the vineyard paying those who worked only the last hour of the day the same wages as those who labored all day (Matthew, 20:1–16). This parable evidently suggests some powerful difference between justice and charity, for it is the workers, not the master, who are chastised. Justice binds us but mercy frees us. Evidently we need both and they are not the same. Demands for justice can corrupt the inspirations to mercy. I have often called justice the most terrible of the virtues because it deals only with relationships, not, as in friendship, with the persons who have the relationships. The owner's wealth in the parable did not come unjustly. Many workers could not find jobs all day. The master of the vineyard took pity on them and gave them something to do, even for a short time. In justice, he could have left the excess laborers at the hiring hall. The hired workers who were paid the same amount for an hour as those who worked ten surely had to wonder about this. No union would stand for such an arrangement.

However, such is human nature, those who were paid a just wage for a full day's work from morning subsequently complained about those who were given the same amount of wages without putting in the same amount of work. Since we are not saved in justice, we can be saved at any time in mercy. The last will be first. Doesn't God seem to be treating the world unfairly when He saves some at the last hour who have done everything wrong but who finally repented? In the order of salvation, how much we do is not the most salient factor. Some do much more, some considerably less, yet all receive the same reward, though the Father's house has many mansions. Some angels differ from others in glory. The problems of the world evidently are not adequately or fully met with what we know about justice and order. Saint Thomas in a famous passage remarked that the world is created in mercy, not justice (I, 21, 4).[3] To the pure humanist, perhaps no more scandalous passage exists in the Angelic Doctor's remarkable works.

And on either side of Christ, we find two thieves, one of whom remarked that both were being punished justly, but Christ, what evil had he done?

Christ turned only to one of the thieves to tell him that he would be with Him in paradise. Ought Christ better to have saved both or none? Why this discrimination since both were guilty? Was His mercy unequal and did it violate justice and equality, those contemporary virtues that seem to have absorbed and judged all the others? Why is justice such a harsh virtue, something that even the ancient writers understood with their doctrine that modified it with equity (*epichia*)? Why is the modern slogan "faith and justice" and not "faith, liberty, and justice" or even more, "faith, hope, and charity"? Does it not seem odd that Pope John Paul II in *Centesimus Annus* (#5) would say that we cannot even solve our social problems without the Gospel, as if to imply that somehow even the natural virtues are related to the prior purpose of revelation?

The older brother of the prodigal son, to recall another related parable, labored all his days for his father but was never given so much as a kid with which to party with his friends. The other son blew all his inheritance on riotous living but was still greeted with celebration by his father. Did not the older brother have a legitimate gripe? Was the father being unfair, that favorite word of those who think the world is made only in justice? Was the older brother wrong or foolish in working hard for his father all his days? Should he not have joined his brother and wasted his substance so that his father would welcome him too? Evidently not. But there were ways to repair our faults and sins that did not appear to follow the laws of justice. Indeed, it is doubtful that justice by itself can repair the violations of justice. The point was not, then, that the brothers, to win their father's love, should have both gone off to a far country carousing and wasting their inheritances. But, along with the older brother, we can be tempted to think or do wrong even when we are doing right, especially when we think that only justice rules our relationships within our families or polities or with God (Luke, 15:11–32).[4]

II

St. Paul also said that he who does not work, neither let him eat, clearly a hard saying in these days of universal compassion and welfare economics (2 Thessalonians, 3:10). St. Paul at one point, I believe, made tents to support himself (Acts, 18:1–3). St. Paul was like Smith-Barney; he believed in making money the old-fashioned way, by earning it. Generosity is not supposed to substitute for personal effort and can even destroy it by undermining incentive. Something is wrong with the pure free-loader, wrong with his outlook on the world, his view that something is his simply because he thinks he needs it. The world is not better off if everybody is given everything with no creative input or responsibility on the part of each one. This seemingly ideal situation was, after all, the original condition of man in the Garden of Eden and we know what happened there. More than one flourishing economic sector has been destroyed by unconditional gifts from private, national, or international sources. Even when grace builds on nature, it is designed to complete the intrinsic purpose of nature, not to eradicate it. The poor generally want and are expected to have some title for their incomes that comes from their own dignity, from themselves. This system of mutual contribution is what Catholic social thought has called, since Pius XI's Encyclical *Quadragesimo Anno*, "subsidiarity."[5]

The poor, we are told, will be always with us (Matthew, 26:11–12). As St. Paul said in Galatians, all Peter, John, and James asked Paul and Barnabas to do at their famous conference in Jerusalem was "that they should keep the poor in mind," something they were most disposed to do (Galatians, 2:1–10). But what exactly does it mean to "keep the poor in mind"? Can we help the poor if we have erroneous or silly ideas about wealth production and distribution, about work and government? St. James said that we were not supposed to go about telling the poor to be blessed and good without actually doing something for them (2:18). Is just anything we do, however, all right or enough? Does keeping "the poor in mind" also have something to do with the ideas, intentions, virtues, and methods whereby wealth is produced? The "poor" in fact have been in modern thought the primary justification for the expansion of the absolute state and for totalitarian theories. Their "cause," if I might put it that way, has become one of the primary substitutes for God in the modern world, this in a world wherein we are told by revelation to be "mindful of the poor."

Mary was praised for breaking an expensive alabaster vase to pour oil on Christ's feet, something that seemed to Judas, but not to Christ, to be a waste (Luke, 10:38–42). The world would not be better off if there were no market for fine perfumes. If we produced only necessities, we would probably not even produce necessities, a theme that recalls the Second Book of Plato's *Republic*. Perhaps wealth and poverty were not in absolute opposition to one another. Perhaps the only way we could help the poor was to produce wealth that was distributed inequitably but still in a world where all received more. Moreover, if the poor will always be with us, this truth must mean that the complete elimination of poverty, at least in some comparative sense, is not possible and therefore the claim to do so is quite dangerous. On the other hand, in the beginning, all were poor, so that one of the greatest of human resources is the knowledge of how not to be poor. How to produce wealth, without which knowledge all will simply remain poor, is not something directly taught in revelation but was left for us to discover by ourselves.[6]

Envy is a vice of both the rich and the poor. No greater contempt of the poor can be shown than to presume that they do not sin against each other or to believe that all their sins are occasioned by their material wants. Many a poor family and many a poor nation do not think that they must steal or lie or kill just because they are poor. This is one of the great slanders of our time, without denying Aristotle's observation that we need a certain among of material goods to be virtuous (1332a1). No doubt envy is a much more serious moral disorder than greed, which is itself a serious disorder.

Aristotle indeed had already located the primary causes of civil disorders in excesses of greed and envy, that is, in spiritual not material things. The fact that envy is rarely preached about or examined as a moral and theological problem, one related to the reasons for the failure of economic well-being, is a telling indictment on the shallowness of our popular religious and moral social theories. This view about the poor being always with us seems to suggest that utopias are in fact dangerous if they propose precisely to eliminate poverty completely by their schema, by their reform formulae. Looking back from the twenty-first century, we can still agree with Paul Johnson in *Modern Times*. The real scourges of this era are rooted precisely in those philosopher-politicians, who, motivated by their failure to discover any truly transcendent good, have sought to eliminate poverty by reforming society before reforming man after the manner of philosophical or revelational guidance.[7] The real problem of contemporary democratic theory is whether it has not itself accepted these dubious theories as operative principles in the public order.

III

We live today in a world in which ironically the poorest of the rich societies are infinitely richer than the richest in other societies, both ancient and modern. And the grand projects to make every poor man rich ought not to end up by making every man, rich and poor, to be poorer. There is no greater imaginary moral disorder than a theory of what I call "gapism" or distributionism that conceives the world as a finite pie. In such an image, the reason the rich are rich is because the poor are poor; the rich are therefore unjust by definition because the only place they could have acquired their wealth was to take it unjustly from someone else. Nothing causes more useless and dangerous envy than this theory uncritically lodged in the minds of otherwise good men, very often religious men, who have never really thought about the conditions of wealth production and distribution. No one denies, of course, that a certain amount of injustice does go on in this world, but the primary sign of this injustice is not the fact that some have more and others less.

Only monks, it seems, are equally poor and this by rule. This is why they are vowed to live unlike other men, not because wealth is evil but because they themselves witness to what is not bought by riches. Yet these same monks built abbeys and libraries and magnificent churches. Some later economists saw in this unexpected phenomenon of the vow of poverty producing great wealth the paradox that wealth comes initially from saving, from accumulating and not spending everything we garner. Moreover, a large portion of the tourist industry of the modern world derives from how these accumulated savings were ultimately spent on building beautiful buildings and artifacts. What wealth made, at its best, was worth seeing. If you can imagine Rome, for instance, without its beautiful and impressive buildings, churches, paintings, music, roads, arches, and, yes, spaghetti, all in the name of austerity, you can imagine a place to which few people would go to visit.

Wealthy nations somehow seem to be those countries that have learned to save but only if they also invent and experiment and know about the world market. It is almost impossible to keep unproductive wealth except by the methods of the absolute state. "He who loses his life will save it" has also turned out to be a good principle of economic productivity. Without risk, without trying what has never been tried before, without improving what we have, what we have soon disappears. Needless to say, we need to decide not merely what we can have, but what we want. As E. F. Schumacher said in the passage I cited in the beginning, we know how to solve the problem of poverty, what we do not know so easily is how to solve the problem of virtue. That is to say, lack of virtue and of generosity is related to a lack of wealth or to a failure to use it properly.

Interestingly, the word for the old Hebrew or Attic coin, the talent, has come to mean not so much money as the brains with which to produce wealth or the ability to learn about how to make things. John Paul II makes this very clear in *Centesimus Annus* that the source of wealth is not material but spiritual, a notion that has been common in economic circles for some time. Countries with enormous physical resources are often very poor, while those with hardly anything can be very rich if they have both talent and certain virtues. The failure to understand the significance of this truth is what lies behind almost all of the failures of modern religious and social thought to understand the real problems of the poor in the modern world. The ultimate source of wealth is not goods or property or things, but the human mind.

But the human mind, subject as it is to the human will, is also the primary arena of order and disorder. Talents not only can be buried, but they also can be used for positively harmful purposes. The most dangerous criminal, the most dangerous politician is the intelligent one motivated by zeal and directed by wrong ideas, not simply the ones seeking solely their own ends or interests. The brains of the policeman, the criminal, the lawyer, and the professor, for that matter, can be measured with the same IQ. The talent buried in the ground is much less harmful than the ten talents employed to gain power or prestige for immoral or unjust purposes.

A Christian forgets at his peril that the origin of evil, to recall the account in Genesis of the Garden, does not arise from man's lack of material goods. The Fall occurred to first parents who, in the Garden, had, as it were, everything. Thus, it is not correct or possible to locate the ultimate origin of evil in something lacking, even though evil, when it occurs, is what is lacking in a good being or action. Genesis, it strikes me, is most perceptive. The Fall occurred when men sought to be like gods in a world in which everything was given to them, given to them evidently not in justice but in generosity and kindness.

The Fallen Angel was, by all accounts, among the most intelligent of the angels. This is why St. Paul told us soberly that our struggles are not against flesh and blood but against principalities and powers, to warn us that the cause of human disorder is not in things but in the spirit (Ephesians, 6:10–18). We cannot study social history without studying moral history. We cannot study moral history without studying intellectual history, including particularly salvation history. The effort fully to understand ourselves apart from the understanding of ourselves found in revelation is itself futile. The "whole truth about man," as the Holy Father calls it, is not known only by human knowledge, especially by a human knowledge, however good in itself, that systematically excludes from the consideration of itself what has been taught in revelation.[8]

IV

The servant, preferring to keep his coins unproductively rather than putting them in a much more profitable entrepreneurship, buried his talent rather than risk the disfavor of a just Lord. This precisely "unprofitable" servant who was admonished at least to gain some interest from the bankers, was condemned, not praised. Even a low rate of commercial interest was better than collecting nothing. This parable, to recall, was recounted in a world that thought usury in the strict sense was a sin. The point of this parable of the unprofitable servant, to be sure, was not primarily a dissertation on economics. Rather it was a discussion of the way that God dealt with us. What is characteristic of Christianity, something inherited from the account in *Genesis* of the relation of man to nature, is that we are not "creators" of wealth ex nihilo, from nothing, but we are able to do things with what has been given to us for the purposes for which we are created.

Why the physical world does not achieve its own purpose without man has much directly to do with why man does not define his own end, which is not simply a contract with the world for its improvement nor even something due directly to his nature. Schumacher cites the marvelous medieval Latin aphorism, *Homo non proprie humanus sed superhumanus est* ("Man is not properly speaking human but superhuman").[9] This does not mean that man will become something other than man, a Nietzschean superman, for instance, but that he himself, not by his own but by a divine design, is slated to be himself in a more complete manner than his own reality would anticipate or even imagine. Man will not demonstrate his worthiness to be related to the inner life of God by first himself, by his own powers alone, organizing the world apart from God. Rather he will first order himself to God after the outlines suggested or commanded to him by God Himself. In following these new laws, he will be able to understand how it is that the world can achieve its end and how his own end is higher in each single instance of a human life than the whole material world itself. Much of human intellectual life, however, consists in refusing to accept this priority. Ultimately, I think, this unwillingness to accept the scriptural priority of purpose, end, and means is the primary source of the opposition to the Church today insofar as that Church explains itself after its own nature, as it does, say, in John Paul II's *General Catechism*.

To mix up the priorities is not merely a technical mistake but a moral and theological one. The proper use of our talents is not apart from the primary mission we have to know and serve God, and this in the order of His guidance and not of our own preferences or whims. The perplexities and directives of revelation about how and why to observe the commandments, not forgetting to include the new commandment which Christ has given us, are, when worked out, some of the main reasons why we can understand the real nature of the world and of ourselves.[10] They incite us to discover the reasons why we can and should know about nature and its development. In order for us to deal scientifically with the world, we must first believe that the world can be known in some sense, that it is not an illusion, that it has a relatively stable order that did not come directly from man's own mind. These are theological propositions derived from the Old and New Testaments, without which nothing much would be done in the world.

The disorders in the physical world or in the economic world are most often the results, not the causes, of man's own personal relationships to God and neighbor. If we notice carefully the implications of John Paul II's insistent teaching on what is called "social sin," it is remarkable how the Holy Father consistently locates any social sin in prior personal sins, a doctrine wholly in line with Aristotle and St. Thomas and largely in opposition to modern relativist ethical and political theory. Disordered regimes, as both Plato and Aristotle rightly taught us, are the results of disordered souls. This is a very ancient doctrine, confirmed again and again in revelation, but it is also a very necessary doctrine, hardly heard in the schools for a quarter century.

Moreover, although we are judged by whether we give a cup of water to someone who needs it, nowhere do we read in the New Testament about how to develop a water purifying system or aqueducts like the Romans did, things that are said to have saved more people's health than almost anything else in medical history. Water was changed to wine at Cana. Water was used by John to baptize Christ. The Jewish law forbad pork in part it seems because of its dangers to health. But these sacred prohibitions and uses are not direct contributions to the problem of pure water throughout the world, a problem that still exists but whose solution we surely know in great detail. We are, to be sure, to pay particular attention to the poor and needy. But we find in Scripture no discussion about whether generous welfare programs run by the state help or destroy poor families and individuals or reduce solvent ones to penury, as the evidence of experience seems to indicate that they often do.

Thus, the very incompleteness of the New Testament in, particularly, social and political matters, let alone economic ones, is, I think, to be looked upon as God's compliment to the goodness of human nature insofar as it was uncorrupted by The Fall—itself incidently one of the most fundamental doctrines having to do with the public order. There is no more socially devastating teaching than that which says that man is intrinsically good, that there is nothing disordered in his soul, that therefore evil lies outside of his personal life whether he be rich or poor or in-between, that he can be made good by certain structural changes in economics and politics.

V

The New Testament also has important things to say about the state, but not many. The New Testament is not a book of economic or political theory, or if it is, it is a very poor one. Revelation evidently was initially intended to instruct men on what they could not know by themselves, not what they could. Samuel Johnson's above-cited remark about knowing things against reason and things above reason is to the point. The principle of contradiction as an intellectual tool ought to enable us by ourselves to know the things against reason. But our reason needs to be instructed by a higher reason for those things we want to know above our reason, about the inner life of God and whether God, made man, has dwelt among us.

The fact that we can derive certain quite wise and valuable insights in both politics and economics from the Old or New Testament serves as a kind of confirmatory hint that what they contain is not against but within the proper order of things, of the whole, of what is not against reason and of what is above it. Revelation and good sense are somehow related, even when revelation takes the most unexpected turns or recommends the most improbable things, like loving our enemies and doing good to those who hate us, without at the same time naively releasing all the most hardened criminals from prisons to prey upon an unsuspecting populace.

Though St. Paul wrote a short letter to a slaveholder (Philemon), revelation was not directly concerned about freeing the slaves in some political sense or about inventing aid programs for the poor or describing the proper structures to regimes. He wrote about the one thing necessary. We were to seek first the Kingdom of God, but not to try to establish it by our own efforts. Christ refused the temptation to turn stones into bread either as a sign of His power or as a sign of His ability to help the hungry (Matthew, 4, 1–10). The Kingdom of God was not some sort of model political order in this life. We can never read enough of St. Augustine on this score.

Indeed, a long series of philosophers, such as Hobbes and Rousseau, have accused Christianity in particular of a kind of incivism for its concentration on things said to be more important than economics or politics, an accusation, when sorted out, that implies that politics are more important than eternal life. The two may not be in conflict with each other, but then again they can be. Both Aristotle and Plato understood something of this priority of the things of God, which is no doubt why we can trust them in many things of this world in ways that we cannot trust more modern thinkers who confuse God with the world, or confuse the race of men in the world with God.

The moral and religious efforts devoted to virtue, to sacrament, to worship were said to deflect men from giving their full attention to certain worthy political and economic enterprises. St. Augustine, on being confronted with this charge, simply pointed out that Christians, because of their beliefs and practices, made better soldiers and citizens than others. The vow of poverty seemed to deny the goodness of the efforts to produce things, but in practice it seemed to have been at the origins of modern accumulations of wealth and capital. Christ implied that man did not live by bread alone, that we should consequently seek first the Kingdom of God, which was not a political regime, and all these other things would be given to us.

This priority seems to imply, as I have said, that disorder of soul will lead to disorder of economics and polity, so that if we do not get the first relationship to God correct, we will never get the latter in proper order. Christ's admonitions also seem to suggest that the important things of life can be achieved even if we do not live in well-appointed political or economic conditions. Apparently, the greatest of saints can live in terrible regimes, even in terrible prisons and labor camps all their lives and reach the highest sanctity. Often it seems persecution or suffering is the way that the new law is best and most forcefully made known throughout the world. Likewise, those who live in the most affluent and developed society from some technical point of view can in fact choose lives of the worst moral and physical degradation.

The two most famous passages in the New Testament about politics are those from St. Matthew (22:22) about rendering to God the things that are God's and to Caesar the things that are Caesar's and from St. Paul where he tells us to obey the emperor who bears the sword to correct our wrongdoings (Romans 13:1–7). When they are forbidden to preach the Good News by the Jewish authorities, in a third pertinent passage, John and Paul ask in Acts (4:5–22) whether they should obey God or man? They leave no doubt which is to be more important in case of conflict. Thus, there were limits to what the state might command even when it was rendering to Caesar. The New Testament, a revelational document, states clearly that the state is normal, natural, to be expected. It says in its own way what Aristotle said when he emphasized that man is by nature a political and social animal.

Christ at His trial even tells Pilate, who would be the equivalent of some governor of a small state, that he would have no authority over Christ were it not given to him by His Father (John, 19:1–11). The fact that the state could and did kill Christ did not mean either that it acted justly or that what Christ taught was not true. If Pilate has some authority, obviously he did not get it from the Old or New Testament. Nor did he concoct it from his own imagination. Cicero had already provided a pretty decent explication of the legitimacy of the state to the Roman mind. Caesar is already in operation by the time Christ is born. In fact, He is born where He is born because of an edict of Caesar Augustus. He is born when Rome has already conquered Palestine. Yet, Christ never discusses, as Cicero did, whether a republic or an empire were a better form of regime. Even less does Christ tell Pilate that he is a usurper, but He acknowledges that he has some limited authority over Him.

Christ does not give Pilate a lecture on the evils of capital punishment or on civil revolution, though He does seem to accept an organization with authority to deal with certain difficult and conflicting civil problems over the ages. Many have subsequently faulted Christ for this failure suddenly to correct slavery or other civil and economic woes of the world, as if this is what He should have been occupying Himself with. If He had a perfect economic and political program, such people imply, they would surely believe. But subsequent experience has been long enough to make us doubt this proposition. Both good men and evil men can draw good or evil out of good. This is one of the main political lessons of Christ's Crucifixion at the hands of what was perhaps the best state in the ancient world. This-worldly institutions were not what Christ was about, even though doing what He advised redounded to the good of the civil and economic orders.

One of the apostles, Matthew, was a tax collector. Christ was asked about the power to tax, itself a sign, if anything is, of the power and legitimacy of the state. To answer the question He does not denounce the taxing powers of the state, nor does He suggest a flat tax instead of an income tax. The Romans never did in fact figure out a good way to collect taxes, one of their few organizational weaknesses. Rather, Christ asked for a coin and inquired of a hostile audience, "whose head was found on it"? The answer was Caesar's. So Christ said to his questioners, not that Caesar had no authority nor that Caesar was an illegitimate occupant of Palestine nor that He preferred a sales tax, but that Caesar did have authority. That is to say, the New Testament recognizes that political authority is itself legitimate.

The New Testament thus presupposes that there is a legitimate argument for political authority that is not derived from revelation. Might we say that it presupposes Aristotle and Cicero, the philosophers? Revelation is not contrary to reason but insists we know what we can find out from our own sources before we will recognize the validity of what it presents above reason. However, just because Caesar has legitimate taxing power does not itself determine the rate or type of taxation that is best. Presumably, there can be and often are unjust taxes in any civil order. Just because the state has some power does not mean that it has absolute power.

Again we are left with the impression that Christ was not particularly concerned with whether Roman taxing policies were within due proportion or were always used for legitimate purposes. Christ seemed to like members of the Roman legion that occupied Palestine, something no doubt supported by taxes. We know from ancient taxing policies, however, that there was much wrong with the ways taxes were collected. We know too from the famous "bread and circuses," that the use of the monies collected often by force and corruption from the empire were used to support in leisure a corrupt populace, for base and immoral purposes, even for persecuting Christians.

A Christian about to be tossed to the lions in the Roman Colosseum, presumably, was not primarily worried about whether Roman taxing powers were being legitimately used or collected in the business of importing lions to Italy. Paul and Peter, moreover, were evidently martyred under the Emperor Nero, a none too pious man, to whom this same St. Paul told the Romans to be obedient (Romans, 13:1–7). We do not reasonably conclude from that admonition that everything Nero did was commendable. We do not conclude that St. Paul, contrary to Plato and Aristotle, was eulogizing tyranny as the best form of rule. But if he was not, it must follow that we have some other source of knowledge about political and economic things than what we find in revelation, again without denying that what we find in revelation has implications even for political rule and economic order.

VI

The commandments that the New Testament reaffirms from the Mosaic Law are stated generally in a negative fashion. We are told not to do certain things, ever. "Thou shalt not." John Paul II has made a brilliant statement of the meaning and reason for this approach in his *Veritatis Splendor*, almost the only modern public document, along with *Fides et Ratio*, that speaks directly of truth, particularly of moral truth, and this as it relates to freedom. Many critics over the centuries maintain that this classical statement found in the Commandments is too negative. On the other hand, the New Testament does tell us to love one another, to do good to those who hate us. Both negative and positive commands are put before us. Why so? If we examine carefully the things we are commanded not to do, both in the order of acts and in the order of thought and willing—we are not to do or covet doing—we find a list of things that are so basic to human well-being that their violation, even once, bears an intrinsic relationship to human worth and dignity.

Thus, killing, stealing, lying, coveting, or committing adultery strike at the very heart not only of society but of the inner life of the human person who commits the sin and of those who suffer it. Chesterton as usual put it best:

> The silliest sort of progressive complains of negative morality, and compares it unfavourably with positive morality. The silliest sort of conservative complains of destructive reform and compares it unfavourably with constructive reform. Both the progressive and the conservative entirely neglect to consider the very meaning of the words "yes" and "no." To give the answer "yes" to one question is to imply the answer "no" to another question; and to desire the construction of something is to desire the destruction of whatever prevents its construction. This is particularly plain in the fuss about "negative morality," or what may be described as the campaign against the Ten Commandments. The truth is, of

course, that the curtness of the Commandments is an evidence, not of the gloom and narrowness of a religion, but . . . of its liberality and humanity. It is shorter to state the things forbidden than the things permitted; precisely because most things are permitted and only a few things are forbidden. . . . It is better to tell a man not to steal than to try to tell him the thousand things that he can enjoy without stealing; especially as he can generally be pretty well trusted to enjoy them.[11]

It is precisely because we do not do these forbidden things that, generally, we will be able to do the hundreds of positive things.

The human race is told in Genesis to increase and multiply, to have "dominion" over the earth, to found cities and countries, and to learn of and to name *what is*. That is, it is told of the myriads of things that are there for it to accomplish in every life, but at the same time revelation contains a warning about those things that are most likely, in any given instant, to overturn inner and external integrity, to set man at odds with woman, to set mother against mother-in-law, and brother against brother. The positive things there to be done are not listed, only the negative ones that would undermine the possibility of doing rightly anything proceeding from our natural faculties responding to grace.

Indeed, as St. Thomas pointed out, those things that Christ added in the New Testament, on examination, enable us better to do those things that needed most to be done. "Even recognizing the relative autonomy in the secular order, chapter 25 (31–46) of the Gospel of Matthew makes it plain that the human community needs the 'theological virtues,'" Romano Cessario has written.

Indeed, our eternal happiness depends on it. In other words, the human project finds its true bearings in the Church. "I was hungry": agriculture, food and drug administrations, lunch programs and relief to the indigent, food processing, and so forth. "I was thirsty": ecological provisions for safe natural resources, alcoholic beverage bureaus, wine merchants and oenologists. "I was a stranger": immigration and naturalization departments, social welfare for displaced persons, refugees and resident aliens, the hotel industry. "Naked and you clothed me": social welfare agencies, manufacturers and clothiers, the garment industry, with its preference for low cost labor. "I was ill": hospitals and clinics, drug manufacturers and pharmacists, doctors and nurses, the medical education establishments. "In prison and you came to visit me": criminal justice systems, lawyers and police forces, prison guards and rehabilitation workers. . . . How much do people need to know in order to fulfill these offices successfully? It would provide an interesting exercise to ponder how much each of these endeavors requires a direction that only the Church can provide.[12]

Ironically, in this approach, it is only by adding to what we know from reason or the Old Testament that the real earthly goals of mankind might, but need not, be accomplished.

It is true that human beings have something to do on this earth during the time they live here. But it is also true that God does not command in detail the definite projects and systems that lie before the human race. Man is to reach his end in part through his own activity, though even here not as a Pelagian effort that implies his own complete autonomy. The admonition to "seek" something else first before all these things are added to us remains at the paradoxical heart of any successful effort even to accomplish what is possible in this world.

How is it that we go about helping others, as we are told to do and as we generally want to do? We immediately notice that we can have good intentions but that what we do to help does not always work. We have all met people who know well how to work or help others but who choose not to do so. There is somehow a difference between desire and performance. We even sometimes need to be protected from the good intentions of others.

Charlie Brown is on the mound winding up. Evidently the batter hits a pop fly near the pitcher's mound. Charlie yells, "I got it! It's all mine!" But Charlie is a rational animal. As he circles looking up in the air for the fly, we hear him arguing with himself: "If I catch this ball, we'll win our first game of the season." This rare event of winning evidently is desirable.

But then Charlie shows some doubt about his own abilities, so he prays to God, "Please let me catch it! Please let me be the hero! Please let me catch it! Please!" Charlie wants to be a hero, but doubts his own capacity so he calls on divine aid which usually aids Charlie in ways he does not desire. So he reasons further, knowing about the Fall and undeserved merit, "On the other hand," he says to himself still getting under the pop fly, "do I think I deserve to be the hero?" He would not want to be an undeserving hero to whom God has given the power to catch the ball.

Next, Charlie shows some concern for his neighbor: "The kid who hit it doesn't want to be the goat." Charlie's heroism is some batter's humiliation. But since baseball of its very nature requires some heros and some goats, he reasons further, "Is a baseball game really this important? Lots of kids all over the world never even heard of baseball." Charlie echoes the mothers who used to tell their children to eat their suppers because kids in China are starving. He brings in the poverty and deprivation problem: "Lots of kids don't get to play at all, or have a place to sleep, or. . . ." At this crucial point, of course, the ball hits his glove and bounces to the ground before an astounded Charlie. The catcher rushes up to ask, "Charlie Brown how could you miss such an easy pop fly?" To which query Charlie replies, "I prayed myself out of it."[13]

Why, in conclusion, do I cite Charlie Brown in this context of revelation, politics, and economics? It is to remind us that, like baseball, our performance in life is itself related to our ideas and our motives, to what we hold valuable, to how we understand the world and our place in it. Charlie's conflicting desires, his indecision over personal glory, the worth of the game, and the concern for the other batter make it impossible for him to perform even the most simple of pitching tasks, namely, to catch a pop fly.

Revelation addresses itself to reason, to politics by clarifying what it is that we exist for, what the world is about, what is our end and our happiness. We will not get the world right if we get ourselves wrong. Revelation, as I have suggested, does not directly teach us about tax policy, about the form of regimes, or about how to produce pure water and abundant food. But it does indicate the immense importance of each human being, of the power and scope of human intellect and enterprise, of the meaning of the world and its relation to our own destinies. We can be free to do the myriads of delightfully positive things because we are, by observing the commandments, liberated from those acts that destroy any real possibility of our doing what ought to be done.

As Chesterton said, "it is better to tell a man not to steal than to tell him of the thousands of things he can do without stealing." In short, the poor are not poor because the rich are rich. The only way anyone can reach that abundance in which human life best flourishes is that everyone learn, probably at different rates, how to become richer. In short, we must know what things are against reason and what are above it; we must know that the economic problems are solved but that the moral problems of choosing to live rightly and virtually reappear in each life and in each era and constitute the real drama of mankind. These are the things that we can do that we will be judged upon in our search for that Kingdom to which we are destined, not of this world, but still addressed to those of us in this world about what we in fact do in this world.

Homo non proprie humanus sed superhumanus est. No doubt this attention to supernatural truth is, at first sight, the least likely way in which we should expect revelation effectively to address itself to politics or economics. Ironically, in the end, since other ways, often imaginatively tried throughout history, have not in fact worked, it might just be the most fruitful way we can proceed even in solving our own problems, even though revelation, as such, as we shall see (chapter 10), is primarily directed to things beyond politics.

Notes

1. E. F. Schumacher, *A Guide for the Perplexed* (New York: Harper Colophon, 1977), 140.

2. James Boswell, *Boswell's Life of Johnson* (London: Oxford, 1931), II, 576.

3. See James V. Schall, "On the Disappearance of Mercy from Political Theory," *The Politics of Heaven and Hell: Some Christian Themes from Classical, Medieval, and Modern Political Philosophy* (Lanham, Md.: University Press of America, 1984), 253–78,

4. See Allan Bloom's discussion of this point in analysis of "On Christian and Jew: 'The Merchant of Venice,'" *Shakespeare's Politics* (Chicago: University of Chicago Press, 1964), 13–64.

5. Yves Simon prefers the word "autonomy" but with the same connotations as subsidiarity, *A General Theory of Authority* (Notre Dame, Ind.: University of Notre Dame Press, 1980), 137–39.

6. See James V. Schall, *Religion, Wealth, and Poverty* (Vancouver: Fraser Institute, 1990).

7. Paul Johnson, *Modern Times* (New York: HarperCollins, 1985).

8. See *The Whole Truth about Man: John Paul II to University Faculties and Students* (Boston: St. Paul Editions, 1981).

9. Schumacher, ibid., 38. The sentence is from Saint Thomas, *de Caritate* 1.

10. See James V. Schall, "Foreword: The Very Graciousness of Being," in John P. Hittinger, *Liberty, Wisdom, and Grace: Thomism and Democratic Political Theory* (Lanham, Md.: Lexington Books, 2002), ix–xx.

11. G. K. Chesterton, "Negative and Positive Morality," *The Illustrated London News*, January 3, 1920, in *Collected Works* (San Francisco: Ignatius Press, 1989), vol. 32, 17–18.

12. Romano Cessario, "The Sacramental Mediation of Divine Friendship and Communion," *Faith & Reason* 27 (spring 2002): 9.

13. Charles M. Schulz, *Dogs Don't Eat Dessert* (New York: Topper Books, 1987).

CHAPTER SIX

~

The Relation of Political Philosophy to Metaphysics and Theology

Si aliqua potestas est summum bonum, oportet illam esse perfectissimam. Potestas autem humana est imperfectissima; radicatur enim in hominum voluntatibus et opinionibus, in quibus est maxima inconstantia. Et quanto major reputatur potestas, tanto a pluribus dependet; quod etiam ad eius debilitatem pertinet; cum quod a multis dependet, destrui multipliciter possit. Non est igitur in potestate mundana summum hominis bonum.[1]

—Thomas Aquinas, *"Quod Felicitas Non Consistit in Potentia Mundana,"*
Summa Contra Gentiles, III, 31

Summary: Metaphysics is considered the highest of the philosophical sciences by Aristotle, while the medievals considered theology to be the "queen" of all the theoretical and practical disciplines because of revelation's origin in the Divine Intellect. Politics was considered to be a "practical science," indeed the highest of the practical sciences. Political philosophy looked on political things not primarily about its own well-being but about its relation to other sciences. It defended the legitimacy of political things. Whenever political philosophy or politics itself became the "highest science, it necessarily sought by its own methods to replace metaphysics or theology or both as the explanation of what is.

I

In *The City and Man*, Leo Strauss made this oft-repeated observation: "In our age it is much less urgent to show that political philosophy is the indispensable handmaid of theology than to show that political philosophy is the rightful queen of the social sciences, the sciences of man and human affairs."[2] Clearly here are related theology, political philosophy, philosophy itself, and the social sciences. No particular present "urgency," in Strauss's view, demanded that the relation of theology and philosophy be taken up. Without specifically dealing with the relation between theology and philosophy, that would acknowledge that there is a fundamental issue about their relationship, Strauss chose to select for the more important issue, at least for his time (1964), the relation of political philosophy to the social sciences.

These social sciences Strauss called "the sciences of man and human affairs." Political philosophy he designated cryptically as precisely the "queen," not the "king," of these sciences. Politics was indeed that discipline that dealt with man qua mortal, insofar as he came into being, lived, and died in this world. Philosophy was the preparation for death, not for living.[3] In Plato, the discussions of philosophy arose at the death of the philosopher. The philosopher sought to call the potential philosopher to the kind of "living well" that would preserve moral equanimity even when the best existing state killed, in a civic trial, the best man.

Just what did Strauss have in mind by this use of a word like "handmaid," particularly when it is replaced by the word "queen"?[4] "Handmaid" indicates an apparently subordinate or inferior role. At first sight, Strauss seemed to be exalting the position of the "queen" of the social sciences at the expense of philosophy and theology. But did he intend this conclusion? Did he not restrict this exalted position of the "queen" of the social sciences to an issue of current concern, to the status and stature of marxism and modern social philosophy?

"In our age," then, in the context of Strauss's analysis at the time he wrote it, must refer to the relation of the Marxist world in its intellectual roots to the philosophic nature of the universal civilization, to the West. The West is the only place where the question of philosophy, the universal consideration as such, arose.[5] Philosophy itself was the consideration of the whole, a whole that included the classics and even needed to consider the civilizations that do not claim to belong to the universal civilization. In retrospect, now that this particular "urgency" that caused the "queen" to be more important "in our age" than the "handmaid," certain other considerations come to the fore. With the apparent demise of socialism—a new form seems always to return— could it be hinted that the other relationships, between political philosophy and philosophy, and both to theology, together with theology's own relation to reason, have suddenly become more central?

Perhaps Strauss meant no more by this "handmaid" and "queen" usage than that it is better to be first in Gaul than second in Rome. Political science is the highest of the practical sciences in classical thought. Strauss did not find the "mutual relation" of theology and philosophy to be more than a kind of agreement not to step on each other's turf or, perhaps better, a doubt about whether differing turfs actually exist.[6] In a sense, he did not wrestle with the reason and revelation question in a more positive manner because, as he remarked in *Natural Right and History*, he did not hold the same faith, the same "biblical revelation," in which this question most immediately arose.[7] This position is itself one of philosophical import as it implies that a philosophy prodded by a faith is not "philosophy" even though it deepens philosophy as such.[8] Philosophy's very essence of a search for the whole is self-limiting, not wanting to know the whole except on its own terms.

On the other hand, Strauss's famous caution may have implied that an intellectual disorder in the practical sciences, especially in political philosophy, makes it more difficult to speak properly of the highest things, a discourse toward which political life itself points. Strauss remained Socratic enough to realize the dangers of speaking of forbidden things in democracies and in their academies. There were other kinds of "death" besides hemlock—obscurity, indifference, exclusion from discourse, the refusal to question about which Voegelin referred.[9] Strauss hinted indirectly that the other social sciences were disordered because they did not know their proper relationship to political philosophy, which was itself disordered in modernity by an option to ground itself in autonomous will and not in *what is*.

II

Scholastic philosophy, of course, was concerned to understand political philosophy as the "handmaid" of theology—not merely political philosophy, but philosophy as such.[10] Theology was the "rightful queen" of the intellectual disciplines in this tradition. Both philosophy and theology claimed to be knowledges of the whole. The question was whether this claim was mutually irreconcilable? But this scholastic understanding of philosophy was not intended to make philosophy or political philosophy other than what it was in itself.[11] The principle that "grace built on nature" was indeed a valid one and implied nothing less than that if nature were meaningless, so was grace. Strauss himself noted the radicalness of this position in his discussion of the relation of philosophy to Islam, Judaism, and Christianity.[12]

The New Testament was not designed as a substitute for Aristotle's *Politics* or *Metaphysics*. The "things of Caesar" remained properly Caesar's (Matthew, 22:22). To hold this rightfulness of place for politics was not "against" this revelation, but what the revelation itself maintained. Indeed, from the viewpoint of political philosophy, this latter congruity between faith and reason is perhaps the more remarkable aspect of revelation. Revelation persisted in speaking in terms intelligible to philosophy, or better, in terms not contradictory to it. It spoke in terms, when spelled out, that are addressed to those limits of politics already found in the classical writers.[13]

But the "things of God" did entail confronting the question of the relative status of politics in the order of things. Was politics, as Aristotle held (1141a20–23), the highest of the practical sciences, but not the highest science as such? If politics were the highest "science," would it not be itself a metaphysics, a science of *all that is*? But if politics were "limited" because not all questions and methods fell under its scope, did this limitation not mean that its own content and order were to be related to those sciences higher than itself? The limits of politics were thus designed to open to members of any polity questions that politics itself could legitimately pose but which it could not adequately or fully answer. Politics in its self-understanding had something "moderate" about it.

Josef Pieper, as we have seen in "The Purpose of Politics," emphasized that ethical and political activity, while being good, points to something beyond itself, to something that is not practical or aimed at some deed or making. Once we have achieved our practical purpose, what sort of reality takes over for us? The contemplative life completes the active life, though the active life, as Aristotle pointed out in the *Ethics*, has its own kind of happiness (1178b33–79a33), particularly in acts of solid prudence. Yet, the final purpose of the active life, without denying itself, is to make the contemplative life possible.[14] Implicitly reflecting Book Ten of Aristotle's *Ethics* in which we find two kinds of happiness, practical and contemplative, both legitimate, both related to one another, Pieper has touched on the essential aspect of political philosophy. This aspect is its concern with the purpose or end of the active life itself, with the fact that the active life, the political life, is not itself the highest activity, however good it is in itself.

One might wonder, however, whether the urgency of which Strauss spoke in showing political philosophy as the "rightful queen of the social sciences" is demanded by social science itself? Or is the relation of theology and political philosophy already intellectually established so that lesser urgencies might come to the forefront? Surely, if this resolution between revelation and reason is already in place, however much neglected or misunderstood, the figure that most comes to mind is Thomas Aquinas.

Did Strauss mean, then, that before we could properly confront the question of the relation of revelation and politics we must first accurately establish the nature of modern social science, almost as if social science might in modernity be conceived as itself a substitute for metaphysics or revelation?[15] Was not this after all the problem with that famous lack of "moderation" and the embrace of "enthusiasm" that is so dangerous in modern political movements? And was it political philosophy that was most needed, even in religion, to prevent the utopianism so rampant in the social sciences from infecting theology? Perhaps the crises in theology have their origins in this theoretical problem with the social sciences, a problem that theology itself has so often not understood.

III

After the collapse of marxism, then, surely itself a considerable problem for the integrity of modern social science, since no social science "predicted" such a collapse, we can ask whether the priority of political philosophy to other social sciences does not become rather more pressing? Indeed, it has been noted that it was a pope, John Paul II, rather than social science, who came closest to "predicting" the fall of marxism."[16] Is there not, as Strauss often suggested, something disordered in the modern social sciences themselves, in how they conceive themselves and their purposes? Strauss seems justified in worrying about the intrinsic disorder in the social sciences themselves.

Marxism, to be sure, when it flourished, presented itself as a "scientific" view of the world. But it was itself the product or result of movements and ideas that were not original to it. It was related to Epicurus, about whom Marx wrote his dissertation, and to Machiavelli's "founding" of modernity, and to Hegel's effort to explain all things in one system. In one sense, marxism was an effort to answer the question of the highest good within a philosophical system that excluded any transcendence at the origin of what is.[17] Marxism was an effort to substitute human collective intelligence for divine intelligence as the explanation of order in human affairs and, through them, of order in nature.

The effort to "recover" classical or medieval political philosophy, an effort we primarily associate with Strauss, Eric Voegelin, Maritain, and Hannah Arendt in particular, makes this endeavor, at first sight, appear as a kind of retrogressive enterprise, even when what is being recovered are the principles whose very rejection was the cause of much modern social and political disorder.[18] With the collapse of marxism, it is perfectly legitimate to inquire whether its practical chaos in the empirical order requires also a rejection of the philosophic grounds upon which it was originally based? Or does another version of this same modernity, liberal relativism, post-modernism, or deconstructionism, for instance, now prove in effect to be valid or at least feasible?

But if the problem lies with modernity itself, then, neither the Marxist nor the liberal approaches will stand the test of reason and in fact are not so standing this test.

Can a case be made for an analysis of the events of modernity that would argue that a reconsideration of St. Thomas is now not only valid but imperative? Interestingly, John Paul II, who by all accounts was instrumental in the de fact collapse of marxism, touched on this issue in his philosophical works.[19] His lecture, "The Perennial Philosophy of St. Thomas," given at the Angelicum University in Rome on November 17, 1979, addressed directly the "handmaid" question that Strauss had brought up.[20] Here, however, the "handmaid" status of philosophy is restored to its original meaning where philosophy becomes the word used to discuss the open relation of reason and revelation.

In terms of political philosophy, this position would mean that even though political philosophy is the "queen" of the social sciences, the social sciences themselves, including political philosophy, are insufficient. By being what they are, they remain open to the whole that they do not comprehend within their own methodologies and competencies. Science, metaphysics, and theology are needed to complete our understanding of political philosophy.[21] This further consideration, however, was not due to any intrinsic defect in political philosophy—"man is by nature a political animal"—but to the very structure of *what is*.

IV

In order to make this case for a reconsideration of St. Thomas in the light of the historic present, therefore, it is necessary to recognize the limits of politics and to ascertain what it is that limits politics to be itself. In a well-known eulogy for Leo Strauss, Harry Jaffa argued that the grounds for respecting St. Thomas's work were that St. Thomas saved and explained Aristotle, the Philosopher.[22] This conclusion, of course, implicitly ignores the broader work of St. Thomas about Aristotle himself and about the place political philosophy held within the corpus of his works. While not denying the value of St. Thomas in "saving" Aristotle, still we might wonder whether St. Thomas's philosophical completion of Aristotle's own arguments was, in the order of philosophy itself, not in fact the greater significance to philosophy.[23]

Josef Pieper has noted that when St. Thomas cited Aristotle, he did not cite him because he was in need of an "authority" to back up his position. St. Thomas cited Aristotle because he thought what Aristotle argued was true on the grounds of Aristotle's own premises.[24] When St. Thomas disagreed with Aristotle, he did so directly and clearly on philosophical grounds. In other words, St. Thomas was able to understand the truth in Aristotle because he also understood the validity of the argument that established it, almost as if it did not make any difference who set down the argument in the first place.[25] The city of Aristotle was not the City of God, but Aristotle's work served in its own order to point to the latter.

Implicitly, of course, this position about Aristotle means that truth is not simply relative to time or place. A discourse with Aristotle is possible because *what is* is, because of the stability of human nature over time and because of the spiritual nature of the soul that makes thought as such possible. Both of these latter positions, the stability of human nature and the spiritual nature of the soul, were themselves positions argued and established philosophically by both Aristotle and St. Thomas. They are not "assumptions" based on some desire that they might be true in order to support revelation or metaphysics.

"The most authoritative text of the Christian Church, the New Testament, provides no code of conduct for the faithful in their day-to-day lives beyond the Ten Commandments and love of neighbor," an introduction to Thomas Aquinas rightly began.

> Moreover, the New Testament provides no systematic guidelines for the organization of human society. How are human beings to act in this or that situation? What is just in this or that situation? How should Christians form their conscience? What are the purposes of human society? How should human society be organized? What is the role of law in human society? To help answer these questions, the Christian Church of necessity turned to philosophers, to those who systematically reason about morals, politics, and law.[26]

This analysis, of course, is in basic agreement with Strauss's remark about the need to address the order of social sciences to each other in the context of their limits or ends. The "queen" of the social sciences might herself remain, to be what she is, a "handmaid."

The most "philosophical" question asked by political philosophy is "what is the best regime"?[27] Such a question, of course, obviously has roots in Plato. It is not without interest that this question appears within St. Thomas's thought as an aspect of his discussion on the Old Law, the Law of Moses (I–II, 105).[28] Clearly, the question is also an Augustinian one and no one took St. Augustine more seriously than St. Thomas. St. Augustine himself did not reject the Platonist and Ciceronian question of the location of the best regime as an unworthy one. Indeed, again recalling the Old Testament's usage of "the City of God," St. Augustine recognized that the question of its nature and location are both proper and necessary for political philosophy.[29]

V

With this background, how can we situate Thomas Aquinas in political phi-losophy?[30] Need our interest in him be merely "antiquarian"? Though there are literally thousands of observations and insights in the *Opera Omnia* of St. Thomas that have meaning for political life and thought, it is striking by comparison how little politics played in his system. It would seem that Aquinas himself was not overly interested in "the queen of the social sci-ences." Yet, Aquinas's very thought implied a fresh interest in all aspects of being, not the least political being.

Plato had suggested in *The Laws* (803), and Aristotle reiterated (1177b31), that by comparison, the affairs of men are intrinsically less inter-esting and fascinating than philosophy. Here is the same point in *The Re-public*: "For, presumably, Adeimantus, a man who has his understanding truly turned toward the things that *are* has no leisure to look down toward the af-fairs of human beings and to be filled with envy and ill will as a result of fight-ing with them" (500 c-d). The work of St. Thomas, I would suggest, relates to politics by spelling out in considerable detail the fascination of *what is* that arises beyond politics. In this sense, Aquinas saved politics from thinking it-self an adequate explanation of reality. This latter kind of political analysis, thinking itself the cause of reality, is the most subtle temptation of politics, as Aristotle hinted in *The Metaphysics* (982b29).

In his discussion of the relation of justice and mercy, a key question in which he deals with the fact that the world is not created in justice but in something more than justice, St. Thomas remarked that justice required us to return what was "due" to another, say a borrowed hundred dollars, but if we chose to give the person two hundred dollars instead, our action was not unjust (I, 21, 3).[31]

Mindful of Plato's good as higher than justice, though including it, St. Thomas saw the world filled with deeds that are more than justice, with mercy, generosity, and sacrifice. Justice is the political virtue, the virtue that orients us to others, to our proper relation to them. It does not, however, re-late to particular persons and characters in their uniqueness. This aspect of justice indicates that political philosophy naturally and normally points to what it cannot deal with on its own terms. Political philosophy intrinsically opens us to what is not merely justice. The treatment of friendship in both Aristotle and St. Thomas already hint at this openness.[32] Charity in St. Thomas is treated precisely as an aspect of friendship (II–II, 23, 1).

To be sure, St. Thomas's commentaries on Aristotle's *Ethics* and part of *The Politics* are obviously important. The "Treatise on Law" in the *Summa*

Theologiae (I–II, 90–109) serves as the context of most discussions of Aquinas's political thought together with his short treatise *De Regimine Principum* and the discussions on justice, war, sedition, toleration, usury, property, and other such questions in the *Summa Theologiae* and other works. It is fascinating to study these texts with a class to see how quickly it is realized that to understand politics, it is not sufficient to study merely political things.[33]

The "Treatise on the Law," for example, begins innocently enough perhaps with its "law is an ordination of reason, for the common good, by the legitimate authority, and promulgated" (I–II, 90, 1).[34] Soon we realize that we must quickly understand the difference among eternal, natural, divine, human, and the law of disorder (q. 91). Already we are into the structure of the *Summa Theologiae*, of why do things belong where they appear in the structure of the whole? We discover that law is dealt with as an external norm of action. We must know the internal principles of action and the capacities and ends of a being that can act freely in the first place.

This reflection leads back to questions about what are the different kinds of beings in the universe and how are they related to each other. In short, the political philosophy of St. Thomas, if we wish to begin with it in our theoretical reflections, as we may do, does what all great philosophy should do, namely, lead us to a consideration of the whole, to what are the limits of politics, not as a denigration of its importance but as an accurate understanding of *what it is*.

VI

Perhaps the most important reason why St. Thomas is to be reconsidered in a fundamental manner in political philosophy has to do with the question of science, particularly that science that has been in part responsible for the material improvement of the human lot. It has long been argued that religion and science were at loggerheads and that science progressed only with the elimination of religion. However dubious this theory is in itself, a basic question remains: why did science begin where it did? Are there any theological aspects to its origins and possibility?

It seems that the origins of science do require a view of God and of the world, in the absence of which, science will not begin or prosper. If God is conceived as pure will, while the secondary causes in nature possess no stability because of the arbitrary power of the divinity, then it appears that there will be no science. Moreover, science requires a view of the world that maintains that matter exists and is good. Its laws need to be discovered, not merely projected from the human mind onto a chaotic world with no intrinsic order to it, even if that order cannot be located in the world itself as to its own existence.[35] Science does deal with objective reality. Its "laws" work.[36]

Political philosophy is particularly related to such questions because it finds itself necessarily involved in the condition of the nations—in poverty, freedom, war, exchange—with the worthy condition of mankind. Recent modern experience has proved that not every system works, not every system produces justice, freedom, and truth, let alone abundance and prosperity. The legitimate variety of human polities has limits, precisely those limits that St. Thomas found in his discussion of natural law and the law of nations. That is to say, if the social affairs of mankind have wide and legitimate variety—in St. Thomas's terms, if there were positive laws, customs, and institutions less than the state—these diversities had some kind of basic grounding. This grounding St. Thomas called the "natural" law, a law that did not explain itself as to its own existence but existed insofar as each human being stood outside of nothingness as a certain kind of being not made by man.[37]

The natural law of St. Thomas was not simply the "natural right" of Strauss's Aristotle, still less the natural law or "human rights" of modernity as in Hobbes or Rousseau.[38] The natural law of St. Thomas was ontological, that is, standing outside of either the human mind or the human power to make, both of which were ordered to this same world as the cause or arena of their activities.[39] To the question of why it was a "law" and not just a "right," the whole of the metaphysics of St. Thomas is presupposed. That is to say, following Aristotle's notion that the human mind is *capax omnium*, capable of knowing all things, St. Thomas argued that finite things did not and could not cause themselves to be. If they existed, which they did, they bespoke a cause of their existence, a cause that was discovered through the stable finite being that each thing was in itself. The limited truth and good in finite things were grounds for understanding that finite things exist because of will, but not any will found in things themselves, even less by a will that seemed arbitrary.

This very natural law created for St. Thomas both in the citizen and in the philosopher a curiosity about further "law," about further understanding about the good in which things existed.[40] This very curiosity hinted that the knowledge of the whole to which philosophy was ordained was incomplete. Put in terms of St. Augustine, it meant that the City of God could not be identified with any existing city, or, for that matter, any city founded in speech and argument. In terms of St. Thomas, it meant that the natural law was rooted in being, but did not explain itself.[41] Thereby, political philosophy by being itself remained open to *what is*.

VII

In a remarkable essay, "The Possible Future of Philosophy," that has many points that parallel Strauss, though coming to a rather different conclusion, Josef Pieper, following St. Thomas, presented another understanding of the relation of philosophy and revelation that has great significance for political philosophy. First of all Pieper noted the "natural desire (of philosophy) to create a clear, transparent and unified image of the world."[42] Pieper remarked that a Gnostic theory might easily find the Incarnation, a teaching of revelation, to be merely a kind of cyclic confirmation of its worldview that the human mind understood all things, including revelation, by man's own powers.

Not unlike the remark of Glaucon in *The Republic* about what would happen to the just man in any existing city (362a), Pieper observed:

> But the fact that, within the framework (of actual historical events), mankind hated and killed the God-made-man "without a cause" (John, 15:25) and that yet this same death effected the salvation of man, who had committed the murder: these theological truths explode any tidy formula which anyone might conceive about the world.[43]

The point is that the Thomist principle of faith and reason not being in contradiction also includes the impossibility of human reason by itself to be able to claim complete understanding of the whole of the world, including the inner life of its cause.[44] In this sense, moderate liberalism and St. Thomas are in agreement with Strauss about the diversity of reason and revelation.

In his own alternative to Strauss's position that philosophy and theology's are unable to enter into intercourse with each other, however, Pieper maintained that the

> essential thing in philosophy is neither the avoidance of knotty problems nor the bewitchment of the intellect with plausible or conclusive proofs. Instead the essential thing is that not one single element of reality be suppressed or concealed—not one element of that unfathomable reality the vision of which is synonymous with the concept of "truth."[45]

This passage comes as close to any, I think, in clarifying the meaning of St. Thomas's political philosophy. Political philosophy is, in a sense, necessary in order that we might have a polity that allows us to philosophize in the first place. We need a polity that recognizes its own incompleteness, a polity based on moderation. It follows that revelation will be discovered in the existing polities not merely because it is there in the sacred books, as it were, but also because it is there in the questions that arise in the leisure toward which politics is naturally ordained.[46]

If St. Thomas was most careful about civil law being addressed to "human beings who were for the greater part imperfect" (I–II 96, 2), this position was taken because this imperfection did not prevent the highest things from being confronted in all existing polities and by each particular person in his own life. In the end, this freedom to grapple with the highest things even in any existing polity is a freedom that originates in most societies with revelation. This openness seems to be the true purpose of natural law in all existing polities, in which, as Aristotle said, we do not listen to those who tell us that "being human we should only deal with human things" (1177b32).

For St. Thomas dealing with political things, with the law, with the regime, even with the best regime, is the first step to securing freedom for confronting the divine things—both those divine things we can discover with our intellect and those which our intellect encounters in the "unfathomable reality the vision of which is synonymous with the 'truth.'" Thus, St. Thomas can quite legitimately observe about political philosophy: "*Non est igitur in potestate mundana summum hominis bonum.*"

In this sense, to conclude that human power is not the highest human good is precisely what is needed intellectually to allow politics to be itself. The great political disorders of modernity have almost invariably arisen not from classical tyranny but from philosophical politicians seeking to order all things by their political theories. At this level of discourse, at the level of politics and the highest things, Thomas Aquinas remains fundamental to the discourse of political philosophy.

Notes

1. "If some power is the highest good, it follows that it should be a most perfect power. Human power, however, is most imperfect. For it is rooted in the wills and opinions of men, in which there is the maximum inconstancy. And so much the more is power esteemed, so much the more does it depend on the many. This dependency, however, also pertains to its weakness, since what depends on the many can be destroyed in a multiplicity of ways. Therefore, the highest good of men is not to be found in worldly power."

2. Leo Strauss, *The City and Man* (Chicago: University of Chicago Press, 1964),1.

3. See James V. Schall, "Dwellers in an Unfortified City: Death and Political Philosophy," *At the Limits of Political Philosophy* (Washington, D.C.: Catholic University of America Press, 1996), 103–22.

4. It might be noted that the Blessed Mother in her response to the Angel at the Annunciation designates herself as "handmaiden" (Luke, 1:38).

5. Strauss, *The City and Man*, ibid., 3.

6. See Leo Strauss, "The Mutual Influence of Theology and Philosophy," *The Independent Journal of Philosophy* 3 (1979): 111–18. See also James V. Schall, "A Latitude for Statesmanship? Strauss on St. Thomas," *The Review of Politics* 53 (winter 1991): 126–47; "Reason, Revelation, and Politics: Catholic Reflections on Strauss," *Gregorianum* 62, no. 2 (1981): 349–66; no. 3: 467–98.

7. Leo Strauss, *Natural Right and History* (Chicago: University of Chicago Press, 1953), 164.

8. See Etienne Gilson, "What Is Christian Philosophy?" in *A Gilson Reader*, edited by Anton C. Pegis (Garden City, N.Y.: Doubleday Image, 1957), 127–92; Josef Pieper, *A Guide to Thomas Aquinas*, translated by Richard and Clara Winston (San Francisco: Ignatius Press, 1991), 147–60. These essays should be read in conjunction with Leo Strauss's famous essay "What Is Political Philosophy?" in *What Is Political Philosophy? and Other Studies* (Glencoe, Ill.: The Free Press, 1959), 9–55. See also James V. Schall, "What Is Medieval Political Philosophy?" *Faith & Reason* 16 (spring 1990): 53–62.

9. Eric Voegelin, *Science, Politics, and Gnosticism* (Chicago: Gateway/Regnery, 1968), 21.

10. See Étienne Gilson, *Reason and Revelation in the Middle Ages* (New York: Scribner's, 1938); Josef Pieper, *Scholasticism: Personalities and Problems in Medieval Philosophy* (New York: McGraw-Hill, 1964); Maurice de Wulf, *Philosophy and Civilization in the Middle Ages* (New York: Dover, 1953); Christopher Dawson, *Religion and the Rise of Western Culture* (Garden City, N.Y.: Doubleday Image, 1991); Frederick D. Wilhelmsen, *Christianity and Political Philosophy* (Athens: University of Georgia Press, 1980); James V. Schall, *Reason, Revelation, and the Foundations of Political Philosophy* (Baton Rouge: Louisiana State University Press, 1987).

11. See Jacques Maritain, "Relation of Philosophy to Theology," in *Thomism and Modern Thought*, edited by Harry R. Klocker (New York: Appleton-Century-Crofts, 1962), 305–06. See also Ralph McInerny, *Thomism in an Age of Renewal* (Notre Dame, Ind.: University of Notre Dame Press, 1966); John F. Wippel, *Metaphysical Themes in Thomas Aquinas* (Washington, D.C.: Catholic University of America Press, 1984); Ernest L. Fortin, "St. Thomas Aquinas," in *History of Political Philosophy* edited by Leo Strauss and Joseph Cropsey, 3rd. ed. (Chicago: University of Chicago Press, 1987), 248–75; Victor B. Brezik, ed., *One Hundred Years of Thomism* (Houston: Center for Thomistic Studies, 1981).

12. Leo Strauss, *Persecution and the Art of Writing* (Westport, Conn.: Greenwood, 1973), 17.

13. See Ralph McInerny, "Faith and Theology," *St. Thomas Aquinas* (Notre Dame, Ind.: University of Notre Dame Press, 1982), 145–62; Frederick Wilhelmsen, "Faith and Reason," *The Modern Age* 13 (winter 1969): 25–32.

14. Josef Pieper, "The Purpose of Politics," *Josef Pieper—an Anthology* (San Francisco: Ignatius Press, 1989), 121.

15. See E. B. F. Midgley, "Concerning the Modernist Subversion of Political Philosophy," *New Scholasticism* 53 (spring 1979): 168–90; "On 'Substitute Intelligences,' in the Formation of Atheistic Ideology," *Laval théologique et philosophique* 36 (October 1980): 239–53.

16. See George Weigel, *The Final Revolution: The Resistance Church and the Collapse of Communism* (Washington, D.C.: Ethics and Public Policy Center, 1992).

17. See Charles N. R. McCoy, "The Marxist Revolutionary Idea: Philosophy Passes into Practice," *The Structure of Political Thought* (New York: McGraw-Hill, 1963), 291–310. See also Charles N. R. McCoy, "The Historical Position of Man Himself," in *On the Intelligibility of Political Philosophy: Essays of Charles N. R. McCoy,* edited by James V. Schall and John J. Schrems (Washington, D.C.: Catholic University of American Press, 1989), 86–99.

18. See also Charles N. R. McCoy, "On the Revival of Political Philosophy," *Intelligibility,* 131–49; Henry Veatch, *Aristotle: A Contemporary Appreciation* (Bloomington: Indiana University Press, 1974), 3–20.

19. See Andrew N. Woznicki, *Karol Wojtyla's Existential Personalism* (New Britain, Conn.: Mariel, 1980); Karol Wojtyla, *Toward a Philosophy of Praxis,* edited by Alfred Bloch and George T. Czuczka (New York: Crossroads, 1981).

20. John Paul II, "Perennial Philosophy of St. Thomas," in *The Whole Truth about Man: John Paul II to University Students and Faculties,* edited by James V. Schall (Boston: St. Paul Editions, 1981), 222.

21. See James V. Schall, "On the Relation between Political Philosophy and Science," *Gregorianum,* 69, no. 2 (1988): 205–23; "Truth and the Open Society," in *Order, Freedom, and the Polity: Critical Essays on the Open Society,* edited by George W. Carey (Lanham, Md.: University Press of America, 1986), 71–90.

22. Harry Jaffa, "Leo Strauss, 1889–1973." *The Conditions of Freedom: Essays in Political Philosophy* (Baltimore: The Johns Hopkins University Press, 1975), 6.

23. See Ralph McInerny, "Thomas Aquinas and Aristotle," *St. Thomas Aquinas,* 30–74; Josef Pieper, *A Guide to Thomas Aquinas* (San Francisco: Ignatius Press, 1991), 43–62; Etienne Gilson, "Greek Philosophy and Christianity," *A Gilson Reader* (Garden City, N.Y.: Doubleday Image, 1957), 170–77.

24. Pieper, *Guide,* 54.

25. Ibid., 54–58.

26. William P. Baumgarth and Richard J. Regan, S. J., "Introduction," *Saint Thomas Aquinas: On Law, Morality, and Politics* (Indianapolis: Hackett, 1988), 14. See also Ernest L. Fortin, *Political Idealism and Christianity in the Thought of St. Augustine* (Villanova, Penn.: Villanova University Press, 1972).

27. See James V. Schall, "The Best Form of Government," *The Review of Politics* 40 (January 1978): 97–123.

28. See James V. Schall, "The Right Order of Polity and Economy: Reflections on St. Thomas and the 'Old Law,'" *Cultural Dynamics* 7 (November 1995): 427–40.

29. See James V. Schall, "St. Augustine and Christian Political Theory," *The Politics of Heaven and Hell: Christian Themes from Classical, Medieval, and Modern Politi-*

cal Philosophy (Lanham, Md.: University Press of America, 1984), 39–66. See also
Charles N. R. McCoy, "St. Augustine," in History of Political Philosophy, edited by Leo
Strauss and Joseph Cropsey (Chicago: Rand-McNally, 1963), 151–59.

30. On St. Thomas, see James A. Weisheipl, Friar Thomas D'Aquino: His Life,
Thought, & Works (Washington, D.C.: Catholic University of America Press, 1983);
G. K. Chesterton, St. Thomas Aquinas (San Francisco: Ignatius Press, 1986), G. K.
Chesterton G. K. Chesterton: Collected Works, vol. 3; Josef Pieper, The Silence of St.
Thomas (Chicago: Gateway, 1957); Charles N. R. McCoy, "St. Thomas and Political
Science," Intelligibility, 24–38; Etienne Gilson, The Spirit of Thomism (New York:
Kennedy, 1964); John Finnis, Aquinas: Moral, Political, and Legal Theory (Oxford:
Oxford University Press, 1998); Brian Davies, The Thought of Thomas Aquinas (Ox-
ford: Clarendon, 1992).

31. See McCoy, "Aristotle's Political Science and the Real World," Structure,
29–61.

32. See James V. Schall, Redeeming the Time (New York: Sheed & Ward, 1968),
216–24; "Aristotle on Friendship," The Classical Bulletin, 65, nos. 3 and 4 (1989):
83–88.

33. See James V. Schall, "The Uniqueness of the Political Philosophy of Thomas
Aquinas," Perspectives in Political Science 26 (spring 1997): 85–91.

34. See James V. Schall, "Truth, Liberty, and Law,"At the Limits of Political Philosophy (Washington, D.C.: Catholic University of America Press, 1996), 202–17.

35. See Stanley L. Jaki, The Road to Science and the Ways of God (Chicago: University of Chicago Press, 1978); Chance or Reality (Lanham, Md.: University Press of
America, 1986).

36. See J. M. Bochenski, "Law," Philosophy—an Introduction (New York: Harper
Torchbooks, 1972), 9–19; P. H. Hodgson, "The Freedom of Scientific Research,"
ΕΛΛΗΝΙΚΗ ΑΝΘΡΩΠΙΣΤΙΚΗ ΕΤΑΙΠΕΙΑ (Athens, 1985): 283–98.

37. See McCoy, "Natural Law, Law of Nations, and Civil Law," Structure, 88–98;
Yves Simon, The Tradition of Natural Law: A Philosopher's Reflections, edited by Vukan
Kuic (New York: Fordham University Press, 1965); Heinrich Rommen, The Natural
Law (St. Louis: B. Herder, 1947).

38. See James V. Schall, "Human Rights as an Ideological Project," American Journal
of Jurisprudence 32 (1987): 47–61; see Russell Hittinger, The First Grace:
Rediscovering Natural Law in a Post-Christian World (Wilmington, Del.: ISI Books, 2002).

39. See Raymond Dennehy, "The Ontological Basis of Human Rights," The
Thomist 42 (July 1978): 434–63.

40. See James V. Schall, "The Reality of Society according to St. Thomas," The
Politics of Heaven and Hell, 235–52. See also, San Tommaso d'Aquino: Doctor Hu-
manitatis (Atti del IX Congresso Tomistico Internazionale) (Rome: Libreria Editrice
Vaticana, 1991).

41. A number of recent studies on natural law are surprisingly relevant and interesting in regard to St. Thomas, see especially Henry Veatch, Human Rights: Fact or
Fancy? (Baton Rouge: Louisiana State University Press, 1985); Russell Hittinger, A

Critique of New Natural Law Theory (Notre Dame, Ind.: University of Notre Dame Press, 1987); John Finnis, *Natural Law and Natural Right* (New York: Oxford, 1980); Hadley Arkes, *First Things: An Inquiry into the First Principles of Morality and Justice* (Princeton, N.J.: Princeton University Press, 1986); Jay Budziezewski, *Written on the Heart: The Case for Natural Law* (Downer's Grove, Ill.: Inter- Varsity, 1997); Robert George, *In Defense of Natural Law* (New York: Oxford, 1999); E. McLean, ed., *Common Truths: New Perspectives on Natural Law,* (Wilmington: ISI Books, 2000: James V. Schall, "Natural Law Bibliography," *American Journal of Jurisprudence* 40 (1995): 157–98.

42. Pieper, "The Possible Future of Philosophy," *Josef Pieper—an Anthology*, 178. See Josef Pieper, *In Defense of Philosophy* (San Francisco: Ignatius Press, 1992).

43. Ibid., 179.

44. See M. D. Chenu, *The Scope of the Sumna* (Washington, D.C.: The Thomist Press, 1958).

45. Ibid., 179.

46. See Josef Pieper, *Leisure: The Basis of Culture* (New York: Mentor, 1952); Josef Pieper *In Tune with the World: A Theory of Festivity* (Chicago: Franciscan Herald, 1973); James V. Schall, *Far Too Easily Pleased: A Theology of Play, Contemplation, and Festivity* (Los Angeles: Benziger-Macmillan, 1976). See also John Finnis, *Natural Law and Natural Right* (Oxford: Oxford University Press, 1980), 371–410; Dennis Quinn, *Iris Exiled: A Synoptic History of Wonder* (Lanham, Md.: University Press of America, 2002).

~

CHAPTER SEVEN

From Curiosity to Pride: On the Experience of Our Own Existence

The metaphysical proofs of God are so remote from the reasoning of men, and so complicated, that they make little impression; and if they should be of service to some, it would be only during the moment that they see such demonstration; but an hour afterwards they fear they have been mistaken. *Quod curiositate cognoverunt superbia amiserunt.* This is the result of the knowledge of God obtained without Jesus Christ; it is communion without a mediator with the God whom they have known without a mediator. Whereas those who have known God by a mediator know their own wretchedness.

—Pascal, *Pensées*, #542[1]

The ground of existence is an experienced reality of a transcendent nature towards which one lives in tension. . . . There is that openness of the soul in existence which is an orienting-center in the life of man. . . . We all experience our own existence as not existing out of itself but as coming from somewhere even if we don't know from where.

—*Conversations with Eric Voegelin*, 1980[2]

Summary: If political philosophy, at its best, leaves us with an opening to the transcendent, at its worst, it leaves us with ourselves, with an autonomous world with origins only in ourselves. The Augustinian tradition has always understood this temptation to place man at the center of things not merely as a created being but as the cause of all being. Pascal's "curiosity" is likewise a warning against closing our

*personal and political selves off from our awareness that we are not, as Voegelin put
it, the cause of our own existence.*

I

In a famous passage at the beginning of his *Metaphysics*, Aristotle observed
that "all men by nature desire to know. An indication of this is the delight
we take in our senses; for even apart from their usefulness they are loved for
themselves" (980a23–24). This rather laconic passage in one of the greatest
of all books is, nonetheless, on examination, charged with surprise. It is not
just that we know but that we "desire" to know. We know that we know. We
know that we desire to know. We know that desiring to know is not itself
knowing. And the proof of this "desire" is nothing less than the "delight" we
take in our very knowing. The correspondence between knowing something
and the delight in knowing something intimates an unanticipated relationship, something that perhaps need not exist but, when it does exist, indicates
some kind of plan or order that is already present in us without our causing
it. We simply notice that it is there.

Furthermore, we do not just want to "know," but to know something. In
the beginning our mind is the famous *tabula rasa*, that alive power with nothing in it, a blackboard with nothing written on it. Our mind seeks to be in-
formed, to be written on, as it were. Our very act of knowing itself depends
on our first knowing something. It is not itself an empty "knowing" but a
knowing something out there, something capable of being known. Aristotle
already distinguishes here between what is useful for us and what is somehow
beyond use, something that is delightful by its own experience, something we
would do even if it were not also useful. We would still want to see, he tells
us elsewhere, even if we did not delight in seeing (1096b15–20; 1174a4–9).
Furthermore, he notices that what is for its own sake is more important than
what is useful for something else. The things that are for their own sakes are
more worthwhile, more elevated. When we know something, affirm it, we
are, on reflection, surprised that things in us are working, that in their working they delight us.

Aristotle is not giving us here a "theory" of knowledge. Rather he is guiding
our attention to what it is we regularly do if we would only pay attention, only
reflect on our own reality and its constituent activities. From the first, our own
reality, which is most immediate to us, is a reality that knows and delights in
knowing. Moreover, we do not begin our knowing primarily out of need, or
fear, or physical desire, as we might at first suspect. These things too can eventually be things or experiences that incite us to know, but our knowing them is

not itself a fear or a desire or a need. Knowing what fear is, for instance, is not the same as being frightened at something. The former is a knowledge and we delight in knowing it. Knowing what fear or need or desire is involves knowing the fullness of what we already are. We find that we can, on reflection, examine ourselves while knowing. Aristotle compares the light of seeing with the light of knowing. What is not us enlightens us, yet the light is also in us.

There is more. "*Nulla est homini causa philosophandi, nisi ut beatus sit,*" as Augustine put it in *The City of God* ("For man there is no cause to philosophize except in order to be happy." Bk. 19, 1). The very reason we philosophize, why we seek to know *what is*, to know the order of the whole in which we ourselves exist, is in order that we might be happy. Otherwise, we would not take the trouble to know. To be happy means that we are experiencing and directing our given faculties to operate on their proper objects, neither of which have we ourselves made. Aristotle had told us in his *Ethics* that the reason why we do all we do is precisely in order that we might be happy so that our lives are nothing less than an unavoidable examination of the things that might fulfill this search. "A man who is puzzled and wonders thinks himself ignorant," Aristotle realistically added. (982b37). This recalls Socrates' paradoxical wisdom, the knowing what he did not know.

To be puzzled and to wonder about things, evidently, indicate our condition, what we are to be about. On first being ourselves, we begin by not knowing, but we want to know. Our ignorance discontents us but we are pleased that it does. "For it is owing to their wonder that men both now begin and at first began to philosophize" (982b12). The study of the science that has no other purpose but to know is the free science. It is the first science, the one that exists for its own sake. It only seeks to know, and to delight in this knowing what it can know. Aristotle, in a marvelous insight, notes that it is this same wonder that caused men first to philosophize that now causes us to philosophize, to come alive, to become luminous to ourselves by knowing what is not ourselves.

The mind is a faculty of a certain kind of being. There are beings that know and know even when they also sense and feel. These beings are ourselves. "God, having made the heavens and the earth, which do not feel the happiness of their being," Pascal wrote, "He has willed to make beings who should know it, and who should compose a body of thinking members" (#482). We are capable of knowing *all that is*; we are *capax omnium*. We are designed so that what is not ourselves can, in the order of our knowing, become ourselves. We are not deprived of all things just because we are limited and finite things in our own makeup. To know is to be and to be ourselves in a fuller manner (*De Veritate*, 2, 2).[3]

Yet, when we know, we do not change what is known. What is known remains *what it is*, unless we, with the help of our knowing, act upon it to change it. But we are capable of knowing all things, including reflectively something of ourselves, of knowing that we too exist, that we too are not nothing. Nevertheless we know that we do not cause ourselves to stand outside of nothingness or cause ourselves to be what we are. That we are and what we are, both are given to us. They are the starting points of our mind's searching for *what is*; they are not the ending points of our own making. We know what we make; but we find ourselves already made, intricately made and ordered. This too puzzles us. What we are seems to bear imprints from beyond what we are, almost as if we were also somehow "words," somehow intelligible in our own uniqueness.

II

In English, at least, the phrases to be "curious" and to "wonder" can have the same meaning, but often, the former word, curiosity, has a slightly pejorative tinge. It means to be overly meddlesome or prying into things beyond proper bounds. Socrates was accused of this very vice. Perhaps, like Prometheus, who stole fire from the gods to aid man, there is a kind of defiance or challenge to the gods contained within much of our curiosity. The latter phrase, to "wonder," has a more innocent connotation to it. It is more accepting of what we are, even in our initial not knowing. Wonder indicates an honesty, an admission that we do not know something other than the fact that it is there, without our putting it there. Wonder also suggests that the desire to find out the reasons for things is essential to what we are. Rather, it simply is what we are in our fullness or completion. In knowing, we remain substantially ourselves. We do not want to be some other sort of being, even when we know about other sorts of beings within ourselves.

We delight in knowing what is not ourselves as if somehow this knowing of something not ourselves is designed to constitute our perfection, our happiness even. We notice, furthermore, that we do not know even ourselves directly. Nothing is more sobering, or more fascinating, than this realization that we only know ourselves indirectly. We know ourselves, as it were, reflexively in the very process of knowing something else. We are luminous to ourselves only when we are actually knowing what is not ourselves. We are, so to speak, given ourselves because we are given what is not ourselves. This is the grounding of both our dignity and our humility.

Things not ourselves, in our knowing, make us aware of ourselves, make us aware that it is an "I" that is knowing. My very self knows that I am a self, that I have a soul, that I look out on the world. And what most fascinates us in our own knowing, even of ourselves, is when it is another "I" that is being known. The whole drama of love and friendship, yes of hatred and enmity, begins here. Thus, we seem to disclose an order in our parts that leads everything we encounter back to our knowing faculty, to a power we have, which power, in turn, contains for us all that is not ourselves. Truth, as Plato says in *The Republic*, is to say of *what is* that it is, and of what is not, that it is not (477b; 478a). When we say of *what is* that it is, it is we who say it. That is, the *what is*, while remaining itself, also becomes luminous in our own *to be*, in our own reality. We wonder if somehow everything does not belong to us in some way. We wonder about this paradox wherein our seeming paucity of being is related to all actual beings.

Yet, the difficulty in knowing and knowing accurately and fully does, in fact, make us, as Pascal said, "wretched." Some of our greatest thinkers, like Descartes, because they begin with thinking and not with thinking something, are forced to examine the suspicion that we are simply deceived in all we do. But if it were true that we are deceived in our very faculties, in all we know, we wonder why then we can consider the proposition that "it is true that we are deceived"? Descartes's grandiose insight carries with it an implicit contradiction. Why are we not deceived about being deceived? Is it because, in fact, we are not deceived about basic things unless we choose to be? "There are things and I know them," is the truth Gilson taught us adamantly to affirm in the face of every sort of skeptic, including Descartes.

In what then does our wretchedness consist? Surely it does not consist in knowing the truth of our condition, in knowing what John Paul II called "the whole truth about man." Nor does our wretchedness consist in knowing and in delighting in knowing. For when we know and delight in knowing, we are least wretched and most ourselves. Again to know that we are wretched is itself, like all knowledge, a good. Aristotle said that the greatest of our crimes do not come from hunger, but from a lack of philosophy, or perhaps from the wrong philosophy. The pagans knew of the mystery of our wretchedness. The Jews knew of the Fall. We know of original sin and are surprised that it pertains to us, even when we know that it does. Perhaps the greatest perplexity of philosophy is its inability to propose a solution to the evil that we keep encountering in our souls, generation after generation.

Pascal, aware of these issues, said that what little we could know through genuine curiosity could subsequently be lost by our pride.[4] What did he mean here? He did not mean that we could not know some things, even the proof for God. He knew that there were proofs that, in themselves, did hold water, however difficult the holding. Pascal meant that, at some point, we could impose ourselves on the world as its cause, as the source of its order or at least its potential order. He understood that it was possible for us to want to rival God Himself and to want to set out to do so. This is what pride, *superbia*, meant. It meant reversing the order of our knowing by making our artistic or creative capacities, legitimate in their own order, to be superior to our knowing capacities that themselves required something else not themselves to flourish, that is, reality itself. Our temptation is to be like gods, not merely in establishing by ourselves the distinction of good and evil, to recall Genesis, but in formulating the distinction between *what is* and what is not. We wanted to say, in Plato's sense, of *what is*, that it is not, so that we would not be ourselves dependent on *what is* in what we do.

Our ultimate wretchedness consists, then, in mis-understanding what we are, in refusing to live what we are. Hell, thus, is not directly a consequence of God's judgment or of the structures of the world, but of our own choice to define what we, and hence the world, are. The worst thing that could happen to us, Plato told us, would be freely to accept a lie in our souls, knowingly to say of what is not, that it is; and of *what is*, that it is not. But this mis-understanding of what we are, to repeat, is a chosen mis-understanding. It does not happen apart from our willing. It is not neutral or innocent. Here is the source of the real wretchedness that afflicts us, the condition of our wills. Our God, in pride, is, to recall Pascal, without a mediator. Our communion with God, we claim, bypasses revelation. We affirm our own happiness. Our own minds are our only mediators with divinity.

We exchange *what is* for what it is we choose to think. And how exhilarating it is! The first chapter of Nietzsche's *Beyond Good and Evil* is entitled, "On the Prejudices of the Philosophers." In it, Nietzsche wrote, excitedly yet ironically, "when a philosophy begins to believe in itself, it always creates the world in its own image; it cannot do otherwise. Philosophy is this tyrannical drive itself, the most spiritual will to power, to 'creation of the world,' to *causa prima*."[5] It is interesting to observe that this philosophy that "creates the world" begins, in Nietzsche's view, precisely when "it begins to believe in itself." It begins not in power but rather in a "spiritual will."

And this claim of self-mediation, of creating in "its own image," in the actual order of things, invariably leads to pride, to making ourselves to be gods, *causa prima*, to the freedom to misinterpret, in our own imaginings and wishings, everything *that is*. It must lead in this direction because we implicitly deny something necessary in ourselves and about ourselves that enables us to know, after our limited manner of knowing, the truth about the real God. It is at this point where philosophy is important. Something evidently also philosophical is presupposed to enable us to know what God might want us to know about His inner life were it freely to be presented to us. The communion, Pascal says, is with the God known without a mediator. But who is this "God known without a mediator?" Surely it is the God of pride.

Pascal hints that it is the God without the Cross; that is to say, our theories require another kind of God than the one *that is*. "Come down from the Cross and we will adore you!" were words shouted at the Crucifixion, words that, had their taunts been actually carried out, would not have resulted in the said adoration of the shouters (Mark, 15:32). These words again hint at the ultimate temptation, namely, that those who "know" God in some sense as philosophers, that is, without a mediator, refuse to accept the way God in fact deals with men when they begin to suspect, even as philosophers, what this way is. The Word made flesh who dwells amongst us establishes the communion with the God *that is*, with He *who is*. The knowledge of our wretchedness, of our inability to know what we truly want to know, is, however, precisely what enables us to know God who in fact takes on our wretchedness. The mystery of suffering, of the Cross, even in the philosophic order, is the beginning of wisdom. "Man learns by suffering," as Sophocles wrote.

III

If we wonder and if we are puzzled, it is because we seem to encounter an order, the structure of which we do not yet understand. We can, to be sure, impose our order on things. We can claim that our order is identical with the order of things or, more likely, establishes the only order they have. This is what ideology and pride are all about. We can impose an explanation on things that does not arise from things themselves but from ourselves. It arises from ourselves because we despair of finding reason in things or because we refuse to admit that there is an order addressed to us, an order of which we are not the cause. We see that an order alien to us, that is, an order we did not make, may require of us, since we are part of that very order, to reorder how we live. There exists a tension between our order and *what is*. We notice this tension when something in our own explanation does not square with what is not ourselves, with *what is*. The very fact that we must revise our theories indicates that they are subject to testing from outside ourselves. But it also suggests that we do know something. The most important thing about us is not our curiosity or our wonder, but what we conclude as a result of their incentives in us.

We are, it is said, question-forming animals. Some would even suggest that this is our highest definition of ourselves—man, the animal who questions, *animal quaerens.* Linus is scrunched down in his bean-bag seat reading a book. Lucy, his usually petulant sister, is standing placidly behind him. "You don't care anything about anybody!" he admonishes her out of his book. Suddenly steamed up, he leaps out of the seat, points his finger at her, and yells, "You never show any interest in what anyone else is doing. . . . You never ask questions." In the next scene, he carries on eloquently, more soberly, "You never ask me what I'm reading, how I'm doing in school, where I got my new shoes."

Looking right at Lucy who retains her unmoved expression, Linus's rhetorical embellishment again grows, "You never ask me what I think about something, or what I believe, or what I know, or where I'm going, or where I've been, or anything!" Finally, having said his piece, Linus walks away, still muttering, "If you're going to show interest in other people, you have to ask questions." In the next to the last scene, Lucy is standing all by herself, looking rather contrite but bemused. In the final scene, Linus is back on his bean-bag seat reading. She walks up to him, bending toward him familiarly. As he turns slightly around, obviously with some consternation in his eyes, Lucy asks him, "How have you been?"[6]

If we reflect on these amusing scenes, we find all the great questions there—even, above all, the fact that there are questions, puzzles, wonderments. Questions are expected, questions about what we think, about what we are, about what we believe. Interest in people means asking them questions. Lucy's question—"how have you been?"—is, of course, in context, the most difficult question of all for us to answer, even more difficult than what one believes or knows or does. Lucy asks Linus the "being" question. It could mean, "how did you come to be?" Or more probably, "give me an account of your inner self, of the state of your being." One suspects that to answer Lucy's question adequately we need to be ourselves divine. This is why, after all his flourish, Linus is not prepared for it.

IV

What do we believe? What do we know? These are indeed philosophic questions, but, as Linus shows us, questions that are fundamental for everyone, even nonphilosophers. St. Thomas says that one of the reasons for revelation was the general condition of men in this present life, the difficulty of knowing, the limited time we have to know, the busyness of life that makes knowing so distracting and difficult. Chesterton says that Christianity is "democratic" in this sense that recognizing the rarity of good philosophers, it did not leave everyone else in the lurch when it came to ultimate things. Yet, Christianity is also directed to the philosophers, to the limitations of their knowing, to the wretchedness that envelops even the philosophers.

Faith and the intellectual life of man are often posed as if they were in conflict with each other, as if we had to choose one or the other. We could not be both philosophers and believers. We must, it is said, walk by faith or by reason, but not by both. Kierkegaard, in a famous phrase, itself designed to recall St. Augustine's famous phrase, when asked why he believed, responded, "*credo quia absurdam.*" St. Augustine had explained, "*credo ut intelligam.*" Christian thought in particular, and this is what is perhaps most unique about it, has always juxtaposed the two ideas "*fides quaerens intellectum*" and "*intellectus quaerens fidem.*" They belong together. If we believe, we are still to use our minds; indeed, we use them better. If we think, we wonder about what it is that we cannot seem to figure out even with the best of our own powers and efforts. Knowing also leads to wondering.

In all of this back and forth between reason and faith, we are mindful of St. Thomas's phrase that "grace builds on nature." He assures us that "nature and grace are not contradictory." The proof of his assurance is to show us one case in which they are. If things of God appear to be "absurd," or if, to use St. Ignatius's phrase, "what is black is said (by faith) to be white," we are aware that the black and the absurdity are never understood to indicate chaos or disorder or lack of intelligence. What is absurd turns out, after long examination, to lead to something that makes sense, something that we would not otherwise have known without wondering about, examining what is revealed. If grace builds on nature, nature is something that must be attended to in its own order, for its own sake, even if it is finite or imperfect. Even the philosophical denial that there is a nature, an order of secondary causes, is a philosophic statement that can and must be examined with the same reason that proposes and justifies the denial.

If we are going to have an intellectual life at all, therefore, it is necessary, to recall Linus's admonitions, to pose questions to oneself and to others, to pose and to listen to and examine the answers given to the questions. Those who merely question with no expectation of or concern for answers are not really questioning. They have already taken a view of the world that sees it as intrinsically chaotic or irrational. Revelation is not designed to destroy reason, though it may indirectly have the effect of revolutionizing reason, especially a reason proud in its own independence. The status of reason addressed by revelation is in fact to become more, not less, reasonable. No doubt, it will seem unjust to the philosopher to learn that his lack of belief, his serene autonomy as a philosopher, may in fact be what most prevents him from being a philosopher, assuming that a philosopher is not someone who refuses to look at or think about something simply because it is said to be revealed. The refusal to examine revelation is part of the refusal to examine *all that is*. The real philosopher remains someone willing to look at, think about *whatever is*.

V

What role does faith have in the intellectual life? The answer I will suggest here is that revelation will make the intellectual life more intellectual. At the same time, it will make it less prone to substitute its own speculations about unanswered questions for more plausible and sensible answers to the same questions presented by revelation. Both revelation and philosophy do claim to be, purport to be, explanations of reality. They cannot simply ignore or deny each other's claims on the grounds that their origins are different.

What is being said here? In Lecture Nine of "University Teachings," in *The Idea of a University*, Newman wrote: "Christian truth is purely of revelation; that revelation we can but explain, we cannot increase, except relatively to our own apprehensions; without it we should have known nothing of its contents, with it we know just as much as its contents, and nothing more. And as it was given by a divine act independent of man, so it will remain in spite of man."[7] Without the contents of revelation, Newman emphasizes, we should know nothing of its particular contents by ourselves. We would be thrown back on philosophy alone for an explanation of things. Once we know something of the contents of revelation, it is possible for us to examine what they might mean and how they might relate to things about which philosophers have thought. In other words, it is possible to compare what revelation has proposed to man with the claims of other religions and philosophies about these same issues. It is possible to make a rational judgment about the plausibility and superiority of one to the other on grounds that are, properly, philosophic.

What is revealed is given apart from any contribution of man and will remain what it is. Does this position mean that the nonbelieving philosopher is, by definition, unable to deal with revelation? Not quite, I think. In one sense, no doubt, philosophy can voluntarily seal itself off, once it knows something of what revelation says of itself—this is public knowledge, after all. This is why certain positions taken within philosophy make it impossible to believe the content of revelation. In this sense, the rejection of revelation stands on philosophic grounds whose premises can be examined for their truth.

The Christian faith, for example, is to some degree dependent for its credibility on miracles. We are long familiar with certain notions of science that are said to make it impossible to know or accept miracles or their possibility. Since this or that scientific theory is true, it is said, miracles are not possible.[8] One preliminary Christian response to this position would be that since miracles, on the basis of evidence, do happen, there must be something wrong with the "theory" that denies their possibility. Reductionism means, in general, that we can hold only what our methodology allows us to hold. Reality is a function of our methods, not of itself. The problem here, of course, is not with miracles but with methodology, hence, with philosophy.

Christianity in general and Catholicism in particular have been a religion in which philosophy played a special role. Christianity, unlike Islam and Judaism, was not a revelation of a law but of a teaching, a truth.[9] What mattered in Christianity was not primarily the observance of the dictates of a law but what was understood about God, man, and the world. Revelation was intended for everyone, including the philosophers. Indeed, in the Christian scheme of things, the philosopher performed a particularly important role. He was not, as Newman indicated, to change what was revealed, which did not properly fall under his jurisdiction or competency except to the extent that revelation did present itself as a coherent body of knowledge or understanding that could be fruitfully examined.

The Christian creeds and explanations of Christian beliefs and practices have long been reduced to orderly and intelligible concepts, themselves analogously or directly related to the subject matter they express.[10] They may yet be capable of more clarity or perfection but as they stand they represent a tremendous work of reason reflecting on, further explaining what was revealed. This corpus is not something the true philosopher, concerned with *all that is*, can simply ignore as if it did not exist. Any deliberate refusal to confront these articulated positions indicates a choice of intellect not to examine *all that is*, not to examine its own proper object.

It is said since at least Henry VIII that the British Crown bears the title *Defensor Fidei*. Whether it has done a good job at this noble task leads to remarkable reflections involving the papacy and the abidingness of doctrine over the centuries. It may even lead to the conclusion that the faith has not been adequately defended by this institution. Strictly speaking, the philosopher, unlike certain kings, would not want to be called a "defender of the faith." The faithful man who is also a philosopher does not admit that the two "sides" in him, reason and revelation, are incoherent (*Fides et Ratio*, #1). He does not wish to be an Averröist in any form. This rejection of any "two truth" theory wherein, within the same soul, contradictories could be true is typically Thomist in philosophy and theology.

That is to say, philosophy and revelation, since they reside in the same being, have an intimacy and coherence within the same person that allow for a retention of their distinction of origin and purpose and their inner relationship. The philosopher does not want to, nor can he, reason from his rational analysis to the truths of the faith such that he can assure us, by reason, that revelation is thinkable. The philosopher's own *modus credendi* cannot be the approval by his own reason of the truths of revelation, as if it were his reason that makes them thinkable. Some things the philosopher still must believe, even when he understands under the impetus of revelation.

Thomas Aquinas talked of certain philosophical truths that he called the "*preambula fidei.*" One of the shocks that medieval theologians, Christian, Muslim, and Jewish, got from the discovery of the Greek classics, particularly Aristotle and Plato, was that the human mind, on its own, as it were, seemed to be able to know much more about the highest things, including God, than they had ever anticipated from reading the Books of Revelation themselves. Many theologians even wondered if Plato in particular did not have some sort of private revelation that would have guided him to his great explanations of the Good and the Beautiful and the Just. They were reluctant to admit that his lofty knowledge was the product of mere reason.

Aquinas, looking at Aristotle, did not think that one needed to resort to revelation to explain the extraordinary power of the human mind as instanced in an Aristotle. Indeed, Aquinas thought rather that it was not to the glory of God to downplay the works of God, especially those lodged in man. What this means in practice is that the work of the philosopher is at its best a great work. One might even expect that the meeting of reason and revelation might require in some sense that the best in philosophy be articulated before we might appreciate fully what is revealed. It is a perfection of the natural intellect, as it were, to arrange itself before truth, before *what is*, in such a way that it can be prepared to receive revelation after the manner in which revelation can be received by philosophy. Revelation is never received by philosophy as if its conclusions must be accepted *by reason*. Rather, it is received by philosophy as if its conclusions are in fact at least possible or plausible answers to questions that reason has already asked itself but could not adequately resolve by itself.

The philosopher is said to seek a knowledge of the whole within which he himself exists. His questions, ever prodding, come from within the whole. They are his questions about his existence, his purpose. Even if he understood the whole, he would be aware that he is inside this same whole and not outside of it in a position to establish *what it is* in the way it is. If we speak of philosophy having limits, we do so against the background of the capacity of the mind to know, as Aristotle defined it, "all things." If philosophy is the love of wisdom, the love of truth, it does not want to deceive itself. It does not want to will what is not to be true merely to justify its own claim to know all things. This imposition of its own will on reality as its explanation would somehow skewer the mind's own direction toward *what is*.

Pride, we intimated earlier, means that we make ourselves the cause for the existence of and for the distinction in things. Perhaps it can be said that pride is the vice most dangerous to the philosopher. Surely Augustine and Paul thought this to be the case. On the other hand, the things that are most close to divinity are naturally the most delicate and, for that reason, the most dangerous. At the same time, they are the most glorious. The whole enterprise of creation as it is understood from the revelational side seems to intimate to us that the most dangerous creatures, both of men and of angels, are the most spiritual ones. This is why, most often, it seems that certain moral and philosophical positions need to be most stoutly defended. For, if they are refuted or shown to be inconsistent or contradictory, it means that the possibility at least of the truth of revelation is impossible. The struggles of the philosophers thus are not usually or simply philosophical quibbles. They are most often last-ditch stands that are openly or covertly seen to be the only remaining reasons why our lives as we have lived them are justified, why they ought not to be changed because of what is revealed to us.

VI

The intellectual life, no doubt, must be taken with some pleasantness if we are ever to see its relation to revelation. Evelyn Waugh recounts the story in his, for our purposes, marvelously titled autobiography, A Little Learning, in which he shows what a "dangerous thing" it is. He is in his college days at Hertford where the, to Waugh, distasteful subject of school spirit comes up. Waugh was suspected of a lack of said enthusiasm there. During a freshman rally, a young man to whom Waugh refers as a "tipsy white colonial"—which I suppose could be an American—invaded his rooms threatening him and demanding to know "what he (Waugh) did for the college?" "I drank for it," was Waugh's quick and witty reply.[11] Some questions thus have unexpected answers, answers that delight us. It is perhaps not too far-fetched to suggest that the relation of reason and revelation is like this, that our legitimate questions are given unexpected answers that delight us, or at least should delight us if we will to accept them. Be that as it may, the unexpected answers bear with them a delight that often contrasts with the despair or solemnity of the question as originally and frequently asked in philosophy, itself still arriving, in spite of its multiple proposals, at no proper or feasible solution from reason alone.

If we look at revelation as philosophers, we cannot simply pretend that it does not exist, that some articulated, orderly presentation of its content is not a presence in the world for our consideration. It is present as something handed down, something that is consistent, coherent, unchangeable in its foundations, something that did not originate in philosophy and did not claim to do so. Whatever our final judgment about it may be, not to ac-knowledge its inner coherence and the terms of its self-understanding is to deny our philosophic vocation to consider *all that is*. While it is true, from the revelational point of view, as Newman noted, that this content and the fact of revelation's existence in the world have nothing to do with human initia-tive, nonetheless, it is addressed to human understanding and intellect in the sense that it can be understood and reflected on by philosophers who are not also believers in the revelation, though by the latter too.

Just as Christians can understand something of Judaism or Islam or Hin-duism, so philosophers can understand something of the teachings or under-standings offered by the great religions explaining themselves. Christianity in particular has been attentively reflected on by philosophers so that, for this reason alone, it does not stand without inherited philosophic depth. Contrariwise, believers are not free simply to ignore the claims and methods of the philosophers. This is not to deny that there may, in principle, be things in philosophy or in the human explanations of the revelational traditions that are not true. The philosophers and the theologians, taken as a group, do, on certain basic points, contradict each other.

Sorting out these contradictions is one of the essential aspects of the ad-venture of truth, one of the reasons why philosophy remains essential to rev-elation's complete mission in the world. These contradictions may well mean, indeed in some cases must mean, that certain positions are not true and must be identified as such. But the judgment that something is not true does not mean that the position at issue had no meaning, that it was not a "plausible" error, so to speak. As an exercise in thought and reflection, error is well worth knowing. Indeed, as Plato and Aquinas imply, we cannot really know the truth of things unless we can also account for the errors related to the articulated truth (1154a23–25). The real adventure of philosophy and theology is, in part, the understanding of positions that are "almost" true or that are true but only when seen in a whole context.

The link between reason and revelation cannot be, and is not presented to be, a necessary relationship such that human reason can "prove" the truths of revelation. For human reason to be able to do this "proving" would imply that this reason is, in fact, a divine reason. Nevertheless, human reason is a reason and as such capable of responding to the divine reason if in fact it is presented to it in some fashion. And while belief in the truths of revelation requires grace, what is revealed does not demand the denial of intellect, but fosters it. Since it is a fact of divine revelation that it need not have happened, human reason can find no "necessary" reason why it must have happened. This is why Aquinas will call many of his reasons for believing to be, on the philosophical side, "suasive," and not "necessary."

From the side of reason, however, itself looking for answers to its own legitimately formulated questions, revelation appears as but another possibility, or at least as another plausible answer to a perplexity that has remained unresolved by the philosophers. But it is a "possibility." In this lies the peculiar disturbance that all proper revelation gives to closed philosophic systems unwilling even to consider its possibility. And this refusal is what turns good philosophy into bad philosophy, into the embrace of contradictions it will not admit. The "bad conscience" of modern philosophy in particular consists in its unwillingness to admit that revelation appears as a response to its own best efforts. Nietzsche had it right: "Every profound thinker is more afraid of being understood than of being misunderstood. The latter may perhaps wound his vanity; but the former will wound his heart, his sympathy, which says always: 'alas, why do you want to have as hard a time of it as I have?'"[12] The "wounded heart" and the "hard time" are perhaps signs of the despair of the philosopher, the "profound thinker," who has not discovered the truth and yet knows, again in his heart, that the path is of his own making.

The philosopher, in rejecting the "reason" contained within revelation, moreover, can always find some kind of alternate reason to justify his rejection. His dismissal of revelation will necessarily result in a counterproposal or thesis to account for the original question. This philosophical alternative itself will be in some degree untrue. Hence it will have consequences within the order of reason itself, ultimately within the world, when its prescriptions are carried out in time and place in ways that the philosopher did not anticipate. This is why, in modernity, there is a close correlation between the rise of activist political ideology and the rejection of revelation or attenuation of faith. How is it that Voegelin put it?

"Great masses of Christianized men who are not strong enough for the heroic adventure of faith," Voegelin wrote,

> become susceptible to ideas that could give them a greater degree of certainty about the meaning of their existence than faith. The reality of faith as it is known in its truth by Christianity is difficult to bear, and the flight from clearly seen reality to gnostic constructs will probably always be a phenomenon of wide extent in civilizations that Christianity has permeated.[13]

Ideology bears with it not the simple unknowing of the philosopher but the deliberate refusal to accept one plausible explanation of valid human questions. Both Voegelin and Nietzsche seem to think that Christian or former

Christian thinkers are most susceptible to deviant or Gnostic philosophic alternatives.

The reason for this susceptibility may well be, as Strauss maintained, that the elevated expectations of faith remain even when faith itself becomes weaker.[14] Hence, philosophy strives desperately to discover alternatives to the rejected or forgotten answers provided by revelation to the legitimate questions of philosophy. Thus, while revelation directs itself to reason, it does not command or necessitate it without grace and consent. It does leave the lingering sense that things do in fact fit together somehow because philosophy is at its best when prodded by revelation. It is, as it were, better than itself. But it does not and cannot, even under the prodding of revelation, forget its own humble origins in its Socratic not knowing, in its Thomist negative theology by which, as Josef Pieper said, we know the perfections of God only by denying the limits of the perfections that we do know.[15]

The experience of our own existence causes us to wonder both about why we are and why anything at all is. Our curiosity can lead us to pride in which we close ourselves in ourselves. We cannot remain closed within ourselves without justifying ourselves, justifying ourselves to the world, to the whole, to reason. Reason can examine what revelation says of itself, what it says about God, about eternal life, about resurrection, about virtue, about politics, about evil. It can also see that its own ponderings lead it to a wondering about things that reason does not seem able to know or conclude. It can recognize that revelation's statements about itself are at least plausible answers to questions that arose independently of revelation.

Here lies the narrow gap, here is found the flickering light that philosophy can see, that can assure it that revelation is not totally implausible. The "heroic adventure of faith," as Voegelin called it, may be less tortuous than he postulated, however difficult it remains. "The flight from clearly seen reality," after all, is the very opposite of the trends and instincts both of Incarnation and of the philosophy of *what is* that it accepts from the philosophers and on which it bases itself. Revelation, in the end, is as much an affirmation of and concern for *what is* in all its human and material reality as it is a response to philosophy's own unanswered questions, questions that always arise from man's experience of existence in the world and from his unavoidable wonderments about its cause.

Notes

1. Blaise Pascal, *Pensées*, translated by W. F. Trotter (New York: Modern Library, 1941), 127.

2. R. Eric O'Connor, ed., *Conversations with Eric Voegelin* (Montreal: Thomas More Institute Papers/76, 1980), 8–9.

3. See James V. Schall, "On the Sum Total of Human Happiness," *The New Blackfriars* 83 (May 2002): 232–41; "The Problem of Philosophic Learning," *Logos* 5 (winter 2002): 103–119. See also Joseph Owens, *Human Destiny: Some Problems for Catholic Philosophy* (Washington, D.C.: Catholic University of America Press, 1985).

4. See Peter Kreeft, *Christianity for Modern Pagans: Pascal's Penseés* (San Francisco: Ignatius Press, 1993).

5. Friedrich Nietzsche, *Beyond Good and Evil: Prelude to a Philosophy of the Future,* translated by R. J. Hollingdale (Harmondsworth: Penguin, 1975), #9, 21.

6. Charles M. Schulz, *Dogs Don't Eat Dessert* (New York: Topper Books, 1987).

7. John Henry Newman, *The Idea of a University* (Garden City, N.Y.: Doubleday Image, 1959), 229.

8. See C. S. Lewis, *Miracles: How God Intervenes in Nature and Human Affairs* (New York: Macmillan, 1960).

9. See Leo Strauss, *Persecution and the Art of Writing* (Westport, Conn.: Greenwood, 1952), 7–21.

10. The most recent and easily available of these efforts is the *General Catechism of the Catholic Church* (Vatican City: Editrice Vaticana, 1994).

11. Evelyn Waugh, *A Little Learning: An Autobiography* (Boston: Little, Brown, 1964), 164.

12. Nietzsche, *Beyond Good and Evil,* #290, 197.

13. Eric Voegelin, *Science, Politics and Gnosticism* (Chicago: Regnery/Gateway, 1968), 109.

14. See Leo Strauss, *Thoughts on Machiavelli* (Glencoe, Ill.: The Free Press, 1958), 176.

15. See Josef Pieper, *A Guide to Thomas Aquinas* (San Francisco: Ignatius Press, 1986), 147–60.

~

CHAPTER EIGHT

Modernity: What Is It?

Modern thought reaches its culmination . . . in the most radical historicism, i.e., in explicitly condemning to oblivion the notion of eternity. For oblivion of eternity, or, in other words, estrangement from man's deepest desire and therewith from the primary issues, is the price which modern man had to pay, from the very beginning, for attempting to be absolutely sovereign, to become the master and owner of nature, to conquer chance.

—Leo Strauss, "What Is Political Philosophy"[1]

"Christian philosophy" is a label that may be given to what philosophers do when they deliberately relate their professional work to their religious or ecclesiastical commitments.

—Jude Dougherty, "Christian Philosophy."[2]

Summary: Modernity or "the modern project," as Strauss called it, needs to be understood as both a philosophical and a cultural phenomenon. The notion of "openness to the world" needs to be understood in the light of the ideas and principles that motivate the decisions and customs that are at the basis of human activity. The failure to understand modernity is the origin of efforts to reconcile philosophy and theology to a world whose operative principles of autonomy and freedom presupposed to no limits cannot be justified without abandoning what is essential to both metaphysics and revelation.

I

We are wont to classify the history of philosophy in the following manner: First, while not entirely forgetting the ancient empires such as Persia, Babylon, Egypt, and distant China and India, we have Homer and the pre-Socratics. These ancients were followed by Socrates, Plato, and Aristotle, not forgetting Thucydides, Sophocles, the historians and the dramatists, even the artists. Stoics, Epicureans, and Cynics in both Greek and Roman varieties succeeded the immediate post-Greek classical world. We do not overlook Polybius and Plutarch, nor the Jews, Josephus and Philo. The Romans imitated the Greeks but they had their own priorities. Cicero, in his *De Officiis*, tells us that "moral philosophy" is the most important branch of philosophy, something quite different from the contemplative priorities of Plato and Aristotle. Tacitus, Seneca, and Marcus Aurelius tell us much the same thing; we cannot forget Virgil or Horace. They all remain quite worth reading.

The corpus of Greek and Roman thought is what we know as "classical philosophy." Though ancient traditions of the gods and their dealings with men exist, something we find taken quite seriously in Plato, this classical philosophy is held to be the primary manifestation of what man, especially brilliant man, can know by his "unaided" reason. Classical philosophy characteristically retained a certain openness to a reality that it knew it did not fully comprehend. Socrates knew that he did not know, but he also knew that it was never right to do wrong. Plato made it possible for everyone to relive the trial and death of the philosopher, Socrates, at the hands of the best existing city, Athens. Aristotle, meanwhile, calmly examined all that was to be known. Philosophy began not with ourselves, but with wonder, with our curiosity about why things are, why things are as they are.

Into these natural or philosophic traditions came the revelational corpus that we know from the Bible. The Bible presents us with a history, an account of a people who are said to be directly presented with an understanding of the divine order, of what God, man, and the world were conceived to be in that continuous narrative account of Israel, of Jesus, and of the Church. Both philosophy and revelation, in their own ways, addressed themselves to the whole, to all of *what is*. Incorporated into cultural life itself, revelation reflected the ways of life of the Jews and Christians and later, with the Koran, of Islam. At first, the early religious communities tried to live solely within the parameters of their respective revelation, though eventually they found that, if they were going to deal with them, they had to explain themselves to each other as well as to the philosophers and to other citizens around them.

Augustine and Aquinas, among many others, are significant for the Christians as thinkers who forged a coherent reconciliation between reason and revelation. Neither denied the validity of one or the other.

The Jews and Islam evidently had more of a difficulty with philosophy than did Christianity, even though Maimonides, Averröes, and Avicenna faced these issues in their own ways. This intellectual obstacle of how revelation was to deal with reason was in part due to the fact that the way of life of the Jew and the Muslim had to do with conformity to a revealed Law. Living well meant living according to the Law, indeed according to the letter of the Law, hence the need for lawyers, not philosophers. The peculiarity of the New Law was that it did not prescribe in detail every action or thought, except to say that believers ought to be good and follow the general admonitions of Christ, who, unlike Socrates, was not usually conceived to be a philosopher. Christ, moreover, as Aquinas points out, recognized that external and political disorders arise originally from disorders of soul, from thought, something that Plato and Aristotle also understood.

Moreover, Christ was considered to be true man and true God, one Person, two natures, divine and human, both distinct, both real. That is to say, the very understanding of who and what Christ was found expression not merely in scriptural but also in philosophic terms. In its own way, this effort of clarification was revolutionary because it took seriously the truth of the mind about the gods. The early councils of the Church and the Patristic fathers had no scruple, when necessary and made for clarity, in finding philosophic terms for Christian doctrines. The classic example is the use of the word "Trinity" to express the inner life of God, a term not found in Scripture. Implicitly, Christian thinkers recognized that revelation was directed to reason, perhaps to challenge it, perhaps to make it more itself. Conversely, they understood that error had consequences in the real world; it was not merely an amusing foible. This attitude again was a sign that thought, especially thought about God, was a claim on truth and a claim that truth was grounded in *what is*.

Christian revelation was not merely concerned with external obedience or public order, though it did not neglect these areas—things were to be "rendered" to Caesar; the emperor was to be "obeyed"—but also it was concerned with the ordering of the soul and heart, with the correct definition of the truth about God, man, and the world. Christian revelation in particular seemed to maintain that right thinking, "orthodoxy," was not only possible when it came to the divinity but that it was a proper perfection of the human knowing power as such to seek to know what it could of the Divinity. Moreover, right action, "ortho-praxis," was itself usually dependent on orthodoxy.

In short, Christian revelation took reason seriously even while it recognized that human reason was not itself God, though it was proper to call it, by comparison, as Aristotle did, "divine" (1177b27–28).

We are accustomed, then, to depict classical philosophy as that knowledge that we can learn by the powers of reason operating solely by themselves. By the reflective openness of our intellect looking back on our own interior operations, themselves incited into act by reality, we can, with some effort, distinguish what belongs to our own powers and what arrives from outside of them, though not necessarily alien to them. The work of the philosopher, however lonely it may be, is to know what the human mind with its own resources can know, having first been stimulated by reality, by *what is*. In the beginning, the mind is only mind, a *tabula rasa*, as they say. But it always remains a mind open to *all that is*, so that its true functioning is to know what is not itself and to know itself only indirectly through knowing what is not itself. This power of knowing is what makes it all right to be a human being, to be oneself not a god but a finite being still open to all the things that return to us in knowledge. Plato says, in Book Five of *The Republic*, that truth is to say of *what is* that it is, and of what is not, that it is not. No one has said it better, though Aquinas's formulation, that truth is the conformity of mind and reality, is about as good and says essentially the same thing (I, 16,1–2). And Aristotle held that the mind is *capax omnium*, capable of knowing all things. Such a mind potentially exists in each of us and constitutes the ground of our dignity.

The advantage of studying Plato and Aristotle, in this sense, why no real education is possible without them, is said to consist in demonstrating what the "unaided" human mind can learn by itself. "Aided" human reason comes with the stimulus of revelation, which revelation, nevertheless, is said to be addressed to rational man insofar as he is rational, that is, insofar as he has actively asked questions of himself and of the reality that stands before him, the reality, no less than himself, that he did not himself constitute. Thus, revelation, with its grounding in its own sources, is nonetheless interested in what man does know by his own powers and encourages him to know it. Revelation does not stand against reason, but rather it is in the line of the unity of the truth of all things, including divine things. Christianity explicitly rejects any "two truth" theory that would allow the truths of reason and the truths of revelation to stand in a contradictory relation to each other. It does not "save" revelation by denying reason. In fact, it is deeply suspicious of any "revelation" that contradicts reason, due consideration to the issue involved. When revelation is said to "contradict" reason, it usually turns out, on closer examination, that something of a more profound reasoning is involved than reason at first sight suspected.

Christianity is, to be sure, concerned with the man who has no professional or articulated philosophy, as it were, with the common man, with his salvation. But it is consciously and explicitly also concerned with man the philosopher. Christianity knows that there are many souls and not so many articulate philosophers. But it also knows, with Plato, that in things of the spirit, numbers are of less importance than quality of ideas or genuineness of insight. Christianity, in a sense, addresses the question of whether philosophy, even if it be a good thing, is enough, whether it is possible to "save" both the philosopher and the nonphilosopher without denying the significance of the difference between them. Not everyone needs be a philosopher, even if we need philosophers for the good of our being what we are. It is not wrong to observe that some are more gifted than others; it is wrong to conclude that the less gifted cannot also think and are not destined to the Beatific Vision, which is presented to us initially both in intellectual terms and as a gift. It is also wrong not to be aware that there are philosophers who are not worthy of the name of philosophy. Philosophical errors are possible and are dangerous. This is why they have a necessary place in the philosophic enterprise itself.

This particular interest in philosophy seems to be what John Paul II was getting at in *Fides et Ratio*, in which he chided the Christian theologians and thinkers of recent decades for neglecting philosophy. He likewise questioned contemporary philosophers about the poor quality of their thinking, about their inability to get out of their own minds, as it were. Christianity in general was not hostile to what the philosophers could know, even though Tertullian asked, in a famous question, one echoed by Leo Strauss, "What does Jerusalem have to do with Athens?" Tertullian implied in fact that Athens was dangerous to Jerusalem, a position that turned out, in retrospect, to be something more characteristic of Jerusalem and Mecca than of Rome, though there were Jewish and Islamic philosophers who struggled with the challenge of the classic philosophers to their own revelation.

Likewise, we could find Christian thinkers who embraced philosophic systems, both ancient and modern, that, by their internal principles, could not manage to reconcile the given truths found in revelation—the Trinity, the Incarnation—with their own peculiar philosophic suppositions about reality. Cartesian and Kantian systems in general make the connection of reason and revelation mediated through the events of actual history in a real world to be most doubtful. This latter inability to connect mind and reality has ever been in Christian philosophic tradition a sign that something was aberrant with the philosophic system, not with philosophy as such, but with a peculiar system. Not all philosophic systems are equally true even if they claim to be genuinely philosophical. In this sense, revelation in its proper articulation is considered to serve as a guide for genuine philosophy even in the classical or natural order. This is why St. Thomas found Aristotle so compatible, not because he was Aristotle, but because of the truth of what he said. That the world is coherent is not only a doctrine presupposed by faith, but it is also the assumption of any philosophical quest.

II

What is called "medieval philosophy" is a philosophy that is open to more than bare philosophy, if I can put it that way, to more than can be known to reason by itself.[3] This position does not imply that there is anything wrong with philosophy provided it remains what it is, an openness to everything *that is*. Philosophy does not get itself into trouble if it admits that it does not know something. But it gets into enormous difficulty when it claims that the wholeness of reality is itself coterminus with what it actually knows by its own methods. In other words, if it "reduces" the content of reality from *what is* to what it can know only by means of human reasoning, then reason itself is limited to certain humanly organized methods. No freshness of being can intrude on a mind unable to get outside of itself.

In a famous quip, Chesterton once remarked that, in some strange way, men who set out to be natural or purely philosophic somehow invariably end up being unnatural and un-philosophic.[4] They come to deny that there is anything unnatural or un-philosophic. It is almost as if, from the beginning, men were not simply in a natural order, which is indeed the case. As St. Thomas says, in a memorable phrase, *homo non proprie humanus sed superhumanus est* (*De Virtutibus Cardinalibus*, 1). If this orientation to an end higher than is open to human nature by itself be so, as revelation indicates it is so, it would mean that every effort to limit oneself to what is merely human or natural would leave an emptiness in our restless souls. Indeed, more ominously, it would lead us to intellectual error and moral disorder, something that, in Book Ten of his *Ethics*, Aristotle himself seems at least to have suspected. The very metaphysical structure of our souls implies that we have an openness to all things. The intellect is open to *what is*. That is to say, the very direction of the intellect is somehow transcendent to any limited thing that the same intellect can present to itself as an object of its mind for its own satisfaction or curiosity.

Medieval philosophy, then, is that body of reflection that is aware that something from outside reason's own limited confines is challengingly addressed to reason itself. But it does not know this quality of itself "being-addressed" in some Pelagian manner that would propose that we are the architects of our own destiny both as to its content and as to its acquisition. We do not only know what we make. Reason does not construct what is addressed to itself. Rather, genuine philosophy knows that something is addressed to it by its own insufficiencies, insufficiencies that are themselves the products or results of the mind's own legitimate searchings to explain *what is*. The very questions that any intellect must address to itself—"Why is there something rather than nothing?" "Why is this thing not that thing?"—cannot fail to indicate to our intellects that we do not cause in being either ourselves or what is not ourselves.

What-it-is-to-be-man, just as little as the product of two times two, is not then something we ourselves make or create, but something, after the manner of intellect, we discover as already in being. That is, self-reflective intellect knows certain questions that it has itself formulated that it cannot answer by itself, even when it has tried diligently to answer them, as it should. But it can understand that reason does pose questions to the human intellect that this same intellect does not answer with any adequacy even when it does come up with some sort of answer. What surprises human intellect is not so much that there is a claim in revelation to truth, but that the very questions that reason cannot seem to answer adequately do appear to have from revelation strangely plausible even if not absolutely certain answers. Faith, itself possessing its own philosophic articulation, remains necessary in the essential answers of revelation, answers that of their nature are grounded in the divine, not human, intellect. This unexpected congruity with reasons's questions, however, is what makes revelation ever provoking to intellect, to philosophy.[5] This curious relationship is what in fact causes philosophy to be more itself, more philosophy.

The end of medieval philosophy occurs when the questions that revelation addresses to pure reason are no longer asked, answered, or even paid attention to. Medieval philosophy in this sense becomes not merely a question of historic time but of perennial philosophy that will always be present whenever the human mind thinks of *what is* and its relation to the whole. It is, of course, quite possible for the human intellect to stop seeking answers for valid questions. It does not follow from this voluntary cessation that the questions do not remain central to an understanding of what-it-is-to-be-man. It is quite possible, indeed, to choose not to consider this strange coherence that arises from the revelational answers to questions that reason can pose but which it cannot answer by itself. Revelation does not necessitate reason, but it does challenge it to be itself.

Revelation likewise remains itself, free and beyond the powers of human intellect directly to fathom. But revelation does agitate reason, does make it look outside of itself, which is indeed the purpose of reality before reason as well as the purpose of revelation before reason. But the human being can and does at times will or will not to accept certain truths of what it is. It makes this choice not because there is not some guidance from revelation but because there is. That is to say, that most of our intellectual problems are moral problems. We do not want to know the truth because we see where it might lead us and what it might entail in our way of living. We "protect" ourselves from truth by looking away first from revelation then from reason. We find we must more and more choose a philosophic position that entails a world that presupposes no objective revelation or no coherent metaphysics.

III

The two founders of modern philosophy are Machiavelli and Descartes. Both explicitly reject what has gone before them. Note that they do not so much "disprove" what went before but rather they "reject" it. They claim that they start anew. The central problem of modernity is in the will, not in the reason, except insofar as reason itself is "will" based or will controlled as to the intellect's freedom to see *what is*. As for newness, most of Machiavelli was already in Book I of *The Republic* of Plato, while the premises of scepticism, as it was already conceded in ancient philosophy, themselves demanded some nonskeptical truth. That is, if it is true that all things must be doubted, then one thing must not be doubted. It was Augustine, that most fascinating of men, who first said *"fallor, ergo sum."* Both Machiavelli and Descartes affirm what appears to them to be a "new" method of considering reality.

Machiavelli rejects "ideal kingdoms" to concentrate on a "what men 'do' do." He prescinds from the distinction of good and evil that had been found both in the philosophers and in revelation. He is interested in success not morality. Descartes was so hesitant about ever getting outside of his own mind that he began all things in doubt, not in wonder, as did Aristotle. As a result, he had to provide a philosophic argument of sorts, beginning with the famous "ontological" proof for the existence of God, to establish that the world really existed and existed as it appeared to do so in his own mind and sensation. He needed a proof for the existence of God to demonstrate how his own senses did not deceive him about the existence of the tree in front of his house. No theology has ever demanded so much and, at the same time, so little of human reason.

Modernity, as I call it, is the product of Machiavelli and Descartes, further spelled out in philosophers from Hobbes to Locke to Rousseau to Kant to Hegel to Marx to Nietzsche and to Heidegger. The essence of modernity, and even of what is called "post-modernity," lies in the claim that man is himself, both in morals and in metaphysics, "autonomous." That is, all the rules of reality, including the rules or standards of his own being and acting, are to be found in his own reason, but in that reason insofar as it is not guided or ruled by anything from outside of itself. Ever since Occam and Hobbes, the will is supreme over reason. In nature, it came to be said in modernity, we cannot find any "order." Especially, we cannot find any order or standard in ourselves for our acting, for acting for a purpose that we do not give ourselves. Therefore, we are "free." Freedom is not the liberty to do what is right, since with no connection between nature and reason, there can be no criterion of right. Rather, we have the freedom to declare what is right, whatever that right might be. Any order, whatever it be, will stem from us, not from nature or nature's God.

We are thus beings that do not even presuppose what we are, for that would imply that what we are has some structure or basis for its being *what it is*. The result of this thesis again is that we are free, absolutely free. All our world is to be the result of a freedom that signifies no being, no order, that presupposes anything but freedom. In the beginning was not the Word, nor even the Deed, but the Choice. Needless to say, we are not surprised that the classic definition of democracy was precisely this sort of freedom that allowed us to do what we want, whatever it is that we wanted to do (1317a40–b16). The social world was ruled by a maximization of groundless "freedom" that brooked no limits that came from nature. The purpose of our social being was to maximize whatever it was we wanted to do. There were to be, somehow, laws but no commandments. There were to be "rights" but no obligations. Hobbes, in this sense, remains a principal architect of modernity.

Perhaps some of the flavor of this modernity can be found in the following passage from Flannery O'Connor, a writer ever suspicious of modern things:

> I don't think you should write something as long as a novel around anything that is not of the gravest concern to you and everybody else and for me this is always the conflict between an attraction for the Holy and the disbelief in it that we breathe in with the air of the times. It's hard to believe always but more so in the world we live in now. There are some of us who have to pay for our faith every step of the way and who have to work out dramatically what it would be like without it and if being without it would be ultimately possible or not.[6]

That is to say, we already have a culture of secularized explanations or habits within our souls. We find it difficult even to imagine what a world with faith, a world in which faith addressed itself to a reason that could know *what is*, might be like. The best thing seems alien to us. We not only do not recognize it if it exists, but we consider it to be an aberration

The Sixteenth Stanza of Robert Browning's poem, "Youth and Art," reads as follows:

> Each life unfulfilled, you see;
> It hangs still; patchy and scrappy.
>
> We have not sighed deep, laughed free,
> Starved, feasted, despaired,—been happy.[7]

We have not, in other words, known what we are, only what we made ourselves to be over against what *we are*. Modernity's claim of mastery of nature eventually came to include its mastery over human nature through science's ability to imagine and reconstruct the human corpus and psyche itself. Man is what he "might" be, not what he is. Freedom was no longer limited freedom but autonomous freedom that found in nature no footprints but its own.

Socrates, in *The Apology*, spoke of the "unexamined life." He said it was not worth living. That is to say, there were lives that were not worth living. But why should we "examine" our lives if there is no standard of what it is to be human? If our culture defines what is human not from what we ought to do but from what we "do" do or what we might do with no limits on ourselves, from whence might we acquire standards with which we might criticize the way we live as inhuman? And if we cannot know anything, even ourselves, if the failure of modernity leads us back not to the nature and revelation we rejected in forming modernity but to an isolated intellectual cage out of which we cannot escape, then the end of modernity has led us to something worse than we might have expected, though where we have been led has a certain "logic" to it.

The final question I want to consider in this chapter is whether the culture of modernity can really adapt itself or be adapted to permit a Christian life or presence in its world? What modernity is, is a will-centered autonomy that has no criterion but itself. This same will-thesis finds itself incapable of justifying any relation to others through any reference to nature or revelation except through a self-interest theory that, as Nietzsche maintained, is a position of pitiable weakness. Modernity and post-modernity really do not differ except, as Nietzsche also saw, for the reluctance to carry out to their logical conclusions certain premises about what we can or cannot know. We can only "baptize" what is capable of being baptized. Certain ideas and certain habits must be understood as intellectual positions but they must firmly be rejected as ways of life.

What I want to suggest here is that the direction of modernity and post-modernity, taken as a whole, follows a logical progression because they refuse to allow themselves to be addressed by revelation. Or to put it more bluntly, such positions cannot be addressed by revelation because within their intellectual horizons, they allow no room for any intelligence from outside of themselves. What we see being played out in genetic studies, in moral life, in international politics and economics, is the visible result of ideas that were articulated because revelation was rejected as itself directed to reason. This rejection naturally forced reason to discover some alternative to truth. What was ultimately put forth was a theory that evaporated any reason in things, human or divine. What is being built is a counterculture, as it were, a closed world in which the mind under the control of autonomous will systematically prevents any opening of evidence or reason that would allow the classic suspicion that revelation was in fact addressed to the reason found in things and especially in human things.

In conclusion, let me recall an old *Peanuts*. Charlie Brown is sitting slouched in his Bean Bag Chair watching TV. Sally comes up behind him to tell him, "I have to do a book report on *Treasure Island*—Do you know what it's about?" Charlie looks up a bit to inform her, "It's about pirates." Looking at her notebook, Sally looks pleased with this sparse information. "That's all I need to know," she replies. Then she turns away, to a totally confused Charlie, to add, "I can fake the rest of it . . . (United Features, 1988). Perhaps it would not be too much of an exaggeration to think that modernity has "pirated" reality away from us. What we have left is a fake world, a world into which, every time we look, we see only ourselves, only our wills that could always be otherwise. The "newness" that our culture finds within itself is a newness that is faked or concocted because we do not want to consider the possibility that our reason could be saved if we would consider that revelation was indeed directed at its own legitimate but unanswered questions. The modern world is not the result of a truthful examination of the order of being. Rather, it is a continued effort to find alternatives that do not lead it to the truth of things, to the truth that is directed to and completed by revelation.

Notes

1. Leo Strauss, "What Is Political Philosophy?" *What Is Political Philosophy and Other Studies* (Glencoe, Ill.: The Free Press, 1959), 55.

2. Jude Dougherty, "Christian Philosophy: A Sociological Category or an Oxymoron?" *Western Creed, Western Identity: Essays in Legal and Social Philosophy* (Washington, D.C.: Catholic University of America Press, 2000), 27.

3. See James V. Schall, "On the Point of Medieval Political Philosophy," *Perspectives on Political Science* 28 (fall 1999): 189–93.

4. "The only objection to Natural Religion is that somehow it always becomes unnatural." G. K. Chesterton, *Orthodoxy* (Garden City, N.Y.: Doubleday Image [1908], 1959), 77.

5. See Charles N. R. McCoy, *The Structure of Political Thought* (New York: McGraw-Hill, 1963), 41–51.

6. Flannery O'Connor, "Letter to John Hawkes," September 11, 1959, in *Letters of Flannery O'Connor: The Habit of Being*, edited by Sally Fitzgerald (New York: Vintage, 1979), 345–46.

7. Robert Browning, "Youth and Art," in *Poems of Robert Browning*, edited by Donald Smalley (Boston: Houghton Mifflin, 1956), 299.

CHAPTER NINE

~

Revelation, Political Philosophy, and Morality

Philosophy demands that revelation should establish its claim before the tribunal of human reason, but revelation as such refuses to acknowledge that tribunal. In other words, philosophy recognizes only such experiences as can be had by all men at all times in broad daylight. But God has said or decided that he wants to dwell in mist. Philosophy is victorious as long as it limits itself to repelling the attack which theologians make on philosophy with the weapons of philosophy. But philosophy in its turn suffers a defeat as soon as it starts an offensive of its own, as soon as it tries to refute, not the necessarily inadequate proofs of revelation, but revelation itself.

—Leo Strauss, "The Mutual Influence of Theology and Philosophy."[1]

(Theology is about) created reality seen in the light of divine revelation, and God himself before everything else. This is why every theology worthy of its name ends by stopping itself, not short, but stumbling and bumbling before the essential ineffability of God. St. Thomas possessed this sense of mystery in the highest degree, but since he was, at the same time, imbued with boundless admiration for the intellect—for the two great wonders are that there can be both being and knowledge—he often sets us to grappling with positions that consist in defining exactly the intelligible shape of a mystery whose complete philosophical elucidation is impossible.

—Étienne Gilson, Letter to Henri de Lubac, June 21, 1965[2]

Summary: The Roman Catholic understanding of the relation of revelation and philosophy is one of appreciating the relative autonomy of both reason and faith, but it posits that men have both as directed to their understanding. They are not hostile to, nor are they isolated from one another. The sense of mystery and the sense of understanding are not opposed to each other. Yet, revelation claims to have an effect on the inner and exterior lives of those who practice it, be they sinners or saints. Classical philosophy understood the things of virtue, but not the full path to virtue. Roman Catholicism in its practical living out, in morality, is concerned with both the philosopher and the ordinary man, while it conceives its moral teaching as directed to and demanding of both.

I

The focus of this chapter is on the relation between religion, political philosophy, and the generation of morality. Revelation, politics, and morality deal with high goods. They relate to such goods each in a specific way. Because of their very reality, each is related to the other. The world of morality, of revelation, and of politics is not three "worlds." They constitute one world contained within the further question of what the world itself is. The separation of any of these three areas from each other implies a kind of "two truth" theory associated with Averröism, a division of mankind at its highest levels of reality. Revelation and reason, in this view, were said to be both true even if contradictory to each other, a position that divided the human understanding in two realms with no theoretical way to resolve the difference.

Morality, moreover, is not simply given. It must be "generated," that is, virtue must be achieved through the powers given to each person in and by nature. Neither politics, religion, nor morality makes man to be man. All three are interested not in the question of the givenness of man but, presupposing his givenness, they are interested in his goodness, in what causes him to pass from being merely man to being good man, to being good man who has achieved what being man is for in the first place. This achievement must in some sense be self-caused but it is not self-isolated. To be good means to choose to be good and to choose to recognize and to do what is good, wherever this good appears in reality. If man is a political being, it is because his good includes the good of others. If man is a religious being, it is because his good includes God who is good.

The assumption present here is that if morality, that is, right acting, is to be achieved, then certain ideas, techniques, practices, or institutions aid or hinder this generation. The question is asked in particular whether revealed religion can contribute to virtue and morality, whether revelation might not be useful, if not necessary, for human beings to act rightly both as individuals and in their political organizations? Presumably, if it cannot, revelation is irrelevant in most basic human enterprises. Religion itself becomes a kind of "opium," as a now discredited philosopher once derisively held.

The implication was, of course, that revelation must be false if it cannot contribute to the generation of morality. No doubt there is some considerable truth to this eminently practical feeling. For worldly or moral success must itself be a result of religious faith and action for us to take it seriously, provided, of course, our understanding of "success" can itself stand the test of truth. True thought, true virtue, true religion, it is suggested, must go hand-in-hand as if they belonged together in a coherent whole.

For many thinkers, even in antiquity, religion was a kind of substitute for philosophy in the masses. Few people could bear the loneliness of philosophy or have the courage to adhere to its consuming demands. Religion with its myths or doctrines was designed to serve the greater numbers of people who could not, because of a lack of virtue or talent or time, be themselves philosophers. The polis could not contain only philosophers without destroying itself. All polities needed craftsmen, lawyers, and poets even though these sorts of men were also the very politicians who killed Socrates, the philosopher.

Those ordinary people, by far the majority, who could not be the few intellectuals who saw in reason the dimensions of right action, would be given instead stories, "myths," or accounts of gods and their dealings with men. Most people would catch but hints and images of the highest things that the philosopher held in such awe. They would do the right things without knowing exactly why they were right. Even the Commandments were precisely "commands" and not conclusions from a practical syllogism. They kept order without explaining in great detail why this order should be kept in the first place or what its real origin was.

II

The philosopher hovered over religion as its higher self. Philosophy allowed no fantastic myths between itself and *what is*. Most people most of the time, however, were guided in their practical activity by religion, not philosophy. Religion was thus presumed to be a kind of substitute for philosophy, but it was not perceived to be a challenge to philosophy's own incompleteness. The incompleteness of philosophy was hinted at by Aristotle in the last book of *The Ethics*, when he told us not to listen to those who told us, being human, to listen only to human things (1177b33).

Philosophy was the "love" of wisdom, not wisdom itself. The philosopher was ever engaged in search, in perplexity, in questioning those who were said to be wise. Philosophy could easily get lost in its own questions. The philosophers, however, were the authentic representatives of our kind. They alone, it was said, grappled directly with the highest things. They spent their lives preparing for death, such was the seriousness of what they were about. They expected no other reward but virtue itself. They rejected with some contempt those selfish rewards or nasty punishments that most people needed to generate virtue.

Religion, like parenthood, however, seemed in classic thinking under the name of *pietas* or piety to be rooted in a certain kind of imperfect justice. *Pietas* suggested that there were some debts that could not be fully repaid. This strange debt, in turn, hinted that there were things beyond justice. The world, the city, seemed to proceed by justice, yet justice somehow could not account for all that was in the world. Aristotle himself devoted more space to a discussion of friendship than to a discussion of justice. St. Thomas made the startling statement (1, 21, 4) that the world itself, even though created in justice, that it is this very justice that presupposes mercy. This mercy hints that philosophers reach not merely reason but willed reason when they seek the explanation of the reality to which they claim to be committed.

In his *Conversations* in Montreal in 1980, Eric Voegelin, reflecting on St. Paul's "faith, hope, and charity," along with St. Augustine's *amor Dei*, in the light of Bergson's "openness of the soul to transcendence," remarked that "we all experience our own existence as not existing out of itself but as coming from somewhere even if we don't know from where."[3] If our existence is experienced as not coming from ourselves, we cannot help but wonder whether this existence is intended to have a kind of order that we can discover and pursue? Is the generation of morality, in other words, a command as well as a reasoned discourse?

In his "Treatise on the Law" (I–II, 91, 4), St. Thomas asked whether, in addition to reason, we needed, most of us, any revelation in order that we might be *what we are*? He recalled that the civil law cannot penetrate to our thoughts from which most of our disorders arise. Then he pointed to those passages in the New Testament that command us rightly to order even our thoughts, even our desires, lest the great evils that proceed out of the human soul be not effectively interrupted at their very core. Religion in the light of revelation seemed to result not only in a proper relation to God but, indirectly perhaps, in a proper ordering of the polity itself.

More basically, Aquinas suggested that even though the philosopher might come to some knowledge of God or a First Cause, we, in our self-insufficiency, could not help but wonder what this cause might be like. We wondered whether our self-reflective realization that we are not self-complete might not suggest that this origin of all being, of especially our own being, might not also be intelligent and desire to communicate with us? Somehow, right thinking and right acting were not totally disparate, even for the nonphilosopher.

What seemed even more startling was that it was not only the philosopher who seemed to be made for the highest things. The young Augustine, in the first pages of his *Confessions*, affirmed, in the name of all of us, that "our hearts are restless until they rest in Thee." He was not just addressing the philosophers. He was closer to Voegelin's awareness of our own nonself-caused grounding in reality.

In a way, it almost seems that Chesterton was right in his reflection on St. Thomas, that revelation was strangely democratic, that it was concerned that the nonphilosopher did not miss the highest things.[4] Even if he were not a philosopher, the ordinary man could know how to act rightly, even if he chose not to do so. The other side of revelation was that morals, when generated, had a transcendent end. It was possible, even for the insignificant, to refuse to live rightly, a possibility that grounded the drama of each individual human life. On the other hand, the inner drive to a virtuous life seemed not wholly sufficient to itself since man wanted to know the origin or meaning of why there was virtue in the first place.

And what of the philosopher? He had himself to contend with. "I am become a puzzle to myself," Augustine reflected (*Confessions*, X, 33). The very act of philosophy seemed to lead to a kind of proud self-sufficiency that isolated the philosopher within his own mind. The philosopher often seemed quite foolish, as St. Paul told the Corinthians (1 Corinthians, 1, 23). Could it be possible that the philosopher needed revelation as much, perhaps more, than the nonphilosopher? Plato had already hinted that the worst aberrations we experience come from the philosopher who has chosen himself over *what is*.

III

Christian revelation did not tell the philosopher not to philosophize. But it did tell him to listen, to recognize that his thoughts at their most perceptive led him to formulate certain questions. Many of these questions, when accurately formulated, seemed to be responded to in revelation. Thus, revelational religion appeared designed to address the points at which the philosopher in all existing societies seemed to undermine the very society in which religion served as a guide for civil peace.

Revelation served the generation of morals first in presenting a right order of commandment for action. This revealed order could be compared with the moral teachings of Aristotle or Cicero. It also moderated the philosopher so that he did not turn on society with his own inner speculations, themselves rooted in nothing but himself. Religion, thus, did not formally make everyone a philosopher. With Plato, revelation recognized that everyone had something different to contribute so that the good of the whole required a great diversity of contribution from its parts. In a sense, it recognized the validity of the world, the fact that there were "things of Caesar" (Matthew, 22, 22). Nor did it suggest that the destiny of the philosopher and the non-philosopher was not the same Kingdom of God. What it did suggest was that the danger to the polity of the aberrant philosopher was real.

What the philosopher held did make a difference both to the polity and to philosophy, as well as to the philosopher himself. Even the philosopher's existence "comes from somewhere, even if he does not know where." The function of religion in the generation of morals is not merely that we act rightly, though it is at least this. It is first that we, even if we be philosophers, know our final end. In this, I think, revelation and the First Book of *The Ethics* of Aristotle meet.

In a classic debate, Aristotle is said to have disputed the Socratic notion that virtue is knowledge. Aristotle held that there must be an intellectual component to every human action. This is what ultimately prudence meant. But it was possible nevertheless to "know" what was right without doing it. Indeed, a knowledge of the difference between right and wrong or good and evil was at the heart of any ethical discussion. The generation of morality does include the understanding of human actions in their essential distinction of good or bad. To prescind from this distinction is to avoid the most essential element in any human action. The praise or blame due to each action is rooted in the reality of the action in terms of its objective goodness or badness, something that inheres in the action itself and not merely in the subjective feeling of the observer.

Historically, the great shock to the religious world of the Middle Ages was precisely the encounter of a religious society with Plato, Aristotle, and other Greek thinkers. The question arose: how did these thinkers who did not depend on revelation knew what they did? Some writers thought there must be other sorts of revelation besides that attributed to the Old or New Testaments. Others thought that Plato or Aristotle had encountered Isaiah or Jeremiah. The fact is that there seems to have been no direct encounter. The thesis about private revelation to a Plato or Aristotle seems most dubious. Indeed, this double source of knowledge about human action, from reason or revelation, seems to be one of the major sources of dynamism in Western culture, the fact that things diverse or apparently contradictory need to be reconciled.

The late medieval problem of the "two truths" was, as we have seen, offered as a solution to this problem.[5] That is, it was held in this view that truths of reason and revelation could be contradictory. No doubt, this attacked the unity of human nature and human existence but it was designed to save what appeared impossible to reconcile. The best result of this encounter of reason and revelation, as in the case of St. Thomas, is that great care was suddenly needed to establish just what in particular reason or philosophy did say and what exactly revelation maintained. The results of this effort were first to engender humility in representatives of both reason and revelation. It became clear that, while many perplexities might remain, the claim that reason had nothing to say to revelation, or the claim that revelation made no sense even in terms of philosophy, had to be rejected.

Philosophy and theology might in fact be more intimately related than Strauss had implied when he suggested that the best we could do was to establish that one could not, on its own grounds, exclude the other. The theologian's use of philosophical tools did need critical attention, while the philosopher could not himself know the whole as he was only part of the whole. He too knew that he was not the origin or explanation of his own being. The philosopher could not prove that revelation had happened. To do so would imply divine power in the philosopher. But he could not prove that it had not happened either. If God chose to dwell in "mist," to use Strauss's phrase, this did not necessarily mean that He meant to dwell in or perpetuate confusion.

If we read the Trial of Socrates, he was accused of atheism and of corrupting the youth. In the case of the Trial of Christ, He was accused of claiming a divine position.[6] The men in charge of killing Socrates were a poet, a craftsman, and a lawyer. To perform each of these tasks, each had to devote most of his time to his profession and in addition each was a politician in Athens. Both the Jewish high priests and Pilate were busy men suddenly confronted with a most extraordinary man who claimed to be the Son of God but who did not seem to desire any real political power. Pilate tried every way he could to figure out how to avoid having to condemn the man. The issue in both cases was: how is it possible to cause enough real virtue in the actual politician so that he will recognize virtue when he sees it before him and have the strength to act on it? Whether by proper education and music or by earnest discourse, it seemed necessary to prepare oneself to recognize the good even if one did not fully understand what it was.

In *Centesimus Annus*, John Paul II, to recall, remarked that "there can be *no genuine solutions of the 'social questions' apart from the Gospel*, and . . . the 'new things' can find in the Gospel the context for their correct understanding and the proper moral perspectives for judging them" (#5). What this passage seems to affirm, when sorted out, is that more genuine solutions to social questions are possible with the Gospel. It means the Gospel is in part addressed to genuine social questions that need to be first correctly formulated. Understanding the nature of old and new questions, furthermore, itself requires some attention to revelation, while the proper judgment of what goes on in human society itself requires, for its full understanding, teachings or virtues presented in the Gospel. It also suggests that believers themselves ought to have an intimate realization of the worth of philosophical reflection.

The mood of this passage, at first sight, is merely factual. It is no doubt a challenge to the notion that the social sciences are complete and autonomous in themselves. But it does not contest the true nature of such disciplines as themselves related to man's highest end and to his place in *what is*. It is today somewhat of a scandal even to hint that our natural reason is not sufficient by itself to answer all the highest questions or even to enable us to choose the things normally understood to be good. It remains, nevertheless, true to our experience that even if we do achieve the good we all recognize, it is increasingly difficult to agree on any common understanding of what any particular good might in fact be.

Gilson, in speaking of St. Thomas, recognized that we are fascinated with the relation of thought and action. Granting the mystery of God, we can still make a pretty good case that science, politics, morality, and revelation belong coherently to the same world. The fact that this case is made increasingly rarely is, paradoxically itself, a problem of will and not of intellect. The effort of modernity to establish the complete autonomy of man on a planetary basis involves refusing precisely to consider any philosophical question that might suggest reason's own natural incompleteness.

IV

In this context, it is interesting to note interest in contemporary Gnosticism, a theme familiar in political philosophy for fifty years largely through the influence of Eric Voegelin.[7] Giandominico Mucci wrote that "Modern Gnosticism, which prescinds from the concept and from the reality of sin and of grace and makes the salvation of man to depend on man himself, leads back to the error of Pelagius. This is the inevitable consequence of the 'humanization' of religious experience, especially that of Christianity."[8] If man is so good by nature that no sin is possible, if grace is not needed, it is difficult to deny the Gnostic position about the adequacy of the human intelligence before all reality. What this observation suggests is that the encounter of Christianity with modernity is no longer one of seeking what in the modern world is good, after the manner of Genesis which saw that creation itself is good. Rather it is to understand that structures of culture and of human life are found that exclude those elements of Christianity that are peculiar and exclusive to revelation, the things that were in fact addressed to genuine philosophy. In the aftermath of the demise of marxism, it is important to realize that the modern philosophy, which gave rise to marxism, remains vigorous and alive.

The essence of this view is that man saves himself through his own intellectual, spiritual, and political efforts. The object of this salvation is inner-worldly and consists in removing all the objects given by nature, first, by denying the possibility of any sin and hence responsibility to God and, second, by redefining, usually as "rights," all disorders in social and political terms. These objects are said to be capable of being removed by imposing on the world a man-made reformation of all human needs in global terms. In the end, there is to be nothing but man.

Christianity and classical morality would expect that what this mentality would invariably produce is still another tyranny on even a more massive scale. Furthermore, as Plato had already intimated, this tyranny would call itself and expect to be called "good." It would want to be praised in its standards of order and virtue, a praise that would implicitly or explicitly deny at each point the basic elements of classical virtue and of the Christian understanding of man with the sort of redemption that he is promised.

V

In this context, to conclude, the articulation of a coherent relation between revelation, politics, and morality remains the first intellectual task. In this effort, the proper questions are asked and all responses are taken into consideration, including the results of ideology as itself something that can be philosophically known and accounted for. There can be no surprise that religion, even sectors of revelational religion, is increasingly stated in Gnostic terms, in terms of an inner-worldly political agenda, as religion's only proper presence in the public forum. The symbol of this Gnosticism is no doubt abortion, for Catholicism in particular, because more than any other topic, we have here the startling fact that there is no real scientific evidence that what is being killed is not human. This result leaves us only with will as a justifying rationale, the raw political will to kill simply because it is so legislated and wanted by a political majority of the people. This is the imposition on human reality of an idea that can only be "willed" to be true. It has no other standing.

Revealed religion, then, is basic to morality because it does "command" what is right. Such command is not to be obeyed only because it is "commanded," however. It is addressed to beings who are invited to think even about revelation's commands, to see if in fact they do cause men to live well. If for the most part, we are not sufficient unto ourselves to define either what our proper end might be or to discover in ourselves the strength of character to do what we understand to be right, we must acknowledge the insufficiency of natural sciences and of political institutions. Once we have acknowledged both of these points, we are then finally in a position to recognizing both science and politics for what they are.

Notes

1. Leo Strauss, "The Mutual Influence of Theology and Philosophy," *Independent Journal of Philosophy*, 3 (1979): 116.

2. Étienne Gilson, *Letters of Étienne Gilson to Henri de Lubac*, translated by M. Hamilton (San Francisco: Ignatius Press, 1988), 91–92.

3. R. Eric O'Connor, ed., *Conversations with Eric Voegelin* (Montreal: Thomas More Institute Papers, 1980), 9.

4. G. K. Chesterton, *St. Thomas Aquinas* vol. 2 in Collected Works (San Francisco: Ignatius Press, 1986), *Collected Works*, Vol. II, 499.

5. See Josef Pieper, *Scholasticism: Personalities and Problems of Medieval Philosophy* (New York: McGraw-Hill, 1964).

6. See James V. Schall, "The Death of Christ and Political Theory," *The Politics of Heaven and Hell: Christian Themes from Classical, Medieval, and Modern Political Philosophy* (Lanham, Md.: University Press of America, 1984), 21–38.

7. Eric Voegelin, *The New Science of Politics* (Chicago: University of Chicago Press, 1952), chap. 4.

8. Giandominico Mucci, S. J., "La Gnosi Moderna," *La Civiltà Cattolica* 143 (January 4, 1992): 16.

~

CHAPTER TEN

Worship and Political Philosophy

What mankind has so far considered seriously have not even been realities but mere imaginings—more strictly speaking, lies prompted by the
bad instincts of sick natures that were harmful in the most profound
sense—all these concepts, "God," "soul," "virtue," "sin," "beyond,"
"truth," "eternal life."—But the greatness of human nature, its "divinity," was sought in them.—All the problems of politics, of social organization, and of education have been falsified through and through because one mistook the most harmful men for great men. . . .

—Nietzsche, "Why Am I So Clever?" *Ecce Homo, #10*[1]

Creation was created for the Sabbath and therefore for the worship and
adoration of God. Worship is inscribed in the order of creation (Genesis 1:14). As the rule of St. Benedict says, nothing should take prece-
dence over the "work of God," that is, solemn worship. This indicates
the right order of human concerns.

—*General Catechism of the Catholic Church, #347*

*Summary: For classical philosophy, particularly in Plato, there has been an aware-
ness that we are ordained to the highest things. Revelation, likewise, teaches that in
creation, God does not "need" the world, so that the rational beings in the world,
in particular, exist not out of some necessity in God, but because of a freedom and
abundance. Political philosophy is aware that at its highest, the polity points to a life
of leisurely contemplation of what is in its causes. Revelation is addressed to this*

side of the nature of political things. Catherine Pickstock's "the liturgical consummation of philosophy" points to the final direction of political things, even by being political things.

I

Is it possible to discover that what is really "new" is something about which we have already known, but perhaps just did not notice? And can what is "really new" be totally devoid of grounding in *what is*? I ask these questions, in the beginning, because of a striking remark that Eric Voegelin made in Montreal in 1980. Voegelin's words, in fact, point to an intellectual cul-de-sac, to a dead-end into which he held that modern thought had driven itself—driven itself, for granted the premises of modern thought, there would be no one else but itself to drive it anywhere. The essential issue can be briefly stated: why has philosophy not been able to think itself out of its own theoretical problems? Why has the optimism of the Enlightenment ended with the skepticism of post-modernism? Voegelin's comments thus seem particularly appropriate for the third Millennium.

"We can observe, for the last two hundred years, that every possible locale where one could misplace the ground (of being) has been exhausted," Voegelin pointed out.

> This expresses itself in the fact that we have, since the great ideologists of the middle and late nineteenth century, since Comte, Marx, John Stuart Mill, Bakunin (and so on), no new ideologist. All ideologies belong, in their origin, before that period; there are no new ideologies in the twentieth century. Even if one could find a new wrinkle in them, it wouldn't be interesting because the matter has been more or less exhausted emotionally. We have had it.[2]

The twentieth century, in its turn, was resigned in its pride to explore all the relatively insignificant ideological "locales" and "wrinkles" because the great theses had already been largely expounded by the time it began. We do seem to have encountered the boredom of the "relatively insignificant." The mind exhausted itself pursuing one humanly grounded explanation after another, now a "locale," now a "wrinkle," each of which contained some truth and had a curious logical connection with the others.[3]

Without knowing where else to turn to resolve problems presented by these ideologies and their "wrinkles," we, the public, to use Voegelin's graphic expression, "have had it." And we ask: "what is it that is 'exhausted?'" It is the modern hypothesis, the effort exclusively to explain ourselves to ourselves by ourselves with no need of anything but ourselves. It is the "modern project," to use Strauss's term, that exhausts us.[4] But even more than that, what confuses and tires us is the insufficiency of the responses to that project, the insufficiency even of the revived classical reconsiderations that were proposed to remedy modernity's most obvious errors and deficiencies. It is not so much that "God is dead," but that the alternatives to God are likewise even, so to speak, more dead. What can these two symbolic "deaths" possibly imply about the nature of political philosophy? Are the "culture of death" and the boredom of the "end of history" included in the original design of our being?[5] Are they perhaps indicators that there is no design, even in a world apparently full of design?[6]

II

One hundred years ago, the philosopher who, almost with a certain sad disappointment, most mocked our public and religious explanations of reality, who most chided us for not seeing what we had chosen to become, was, of course, Nietzsche. He is still with us, still shocking us. The most "harmful men," in Nietzsche's view, are those who speak of such "concepts" as "God," "soul," "virtue," "sin," "beyond," "truth," and "eternal life." These very words recall Machiavelli's fifteenth chapter of *The Prince*, wherein he speaks derisively of the "imaginary kingdoms" of the ancient philosophers and theologians.[7] These moral and transcendent words, for Nietzsche, refer not to realities but to "imaginings." Even worse, they are simply "lies" that arise from "bad instincts of sick natures." "Imaginings" might be innocent; lies are deliberate deceptions. The solutions for mankind's ills were said, by the same men whom Nietzsche called "harmful," to be found in these very lying "concepts." "Great men," however, knew that in seeking something there—in "lies," that is—political life was thereby "falsified." This falsification is what Nietzsche chastised. He was himself a new kind of "great man." His prince could "lie" because there was no transcendent truth whereby a lie was anything more than a legitimate tool to stay in power. He seemed vaguely aware, to be sure, that in a world full of liars, there could be no "lies," which is why the traditional morality was kept for all but the prince.

For Nietzsche, as for Plato, the actual disorder of politics was itself reflective of a disorder of soul. Nietzsche never forgave Socrates, just after he took the hemlock, for having asked Crito to offer a cock in sacrifice to the god of healing, as if in dying he could be cured. In dying, Nietzsche thought, Socrates revealed his sickness, not his strength.[8] To Nietzsche this much-admired Socratic piety was a sign of monstrous cowardice, an antipolitical act. Evidently, political life could best be itself without all these "imaginings." That is to say, politics becomes something else, something absolute, something of pure will, something "modern," when it is not seen in the light of these supposedly transcendent and corrupting realities, these lies. Politics is, finally, "what it is." It has no limitation, no competition from revelational or metaphysical theories. It becomes itself, in effect, a substitute for revelation and metaphysics. It becomes, by a kind of logical necessity, the highest of the sciences, not just the highest of the practical sciences, as Aristotle held (1141a20–22). Nietzsche wrote these things in a book called *Ecce Homo*. This title, to recall, contains the ironic Latin words of the Roman governor, Pontius Pilate, when, convinced that He was not guilty, he exposed Christ to the screaming crowds in his vain attempt to gain their sympathy and free Christ instead of Barabas (John, 19, 6). Thus, there is a new kind of man we have been "beholding" in the last three hundred years. He is first rationalist man, then man of iron will, the man who has the courage to make his own laws for himself. But we have "had it" with him too; we are exhausted. But do we have a place to turn that is not another self-constructed reality that, on trial, proves yet again its inadequacy? What are we missing? Are we culpable for missing it?

III

The occasion, or perhaps the inspiration, for these reflections comes from the subtitle of Catherine Pickstock's book, *After Writing*.[9] Her subtitle is unabashedly bold: "The Liturgical Consummation of Philosophy." Indeed, the phrase "after writing" itself implies that writing is perhaps not enough, even deceptive.[10] Not merely is it true that neither Socrates nor Christ wrote anything, but that the most important thing about them was not something precisely "against" writing, virtue, ideology, or intellectual argument but rather something "beyond" them without denying them.

On first coming across *After Writing*, we would not be surprised, I think, if this particular subtitle read, "The Liturgical Consummation of *Theology*." That subtitle would not shock us or pique our interest. In that form, it would speak of a presumably normal topic of theological training and study. Rites would be where they were "supposed" to be, in theology, not in philosophy. We could, presumably without penalty, ignore them. It would cause no further interest or, as it were, raised eyebrows. We are not prepared to "hear" or "sing" the liturgy as a worthy philosophic exercise, to reflect on what it might mean to "worship," though we do recall that the "ancient city" was not complete without its civic worship.[11] We think such rites merely private occupations of the easily distracted. The obvious implication of Pickstock's subtitle, however, suggests that something is "wrong" or "incomplete" about philosophy. And this title refers not to "bad" or erroneous philosophy, but to philosophy itself.

Moreover, what is bothersome in that subtitle is not merely the word "philosophy" but also the word "consummation." Consummation implies that some connection exists between liturgy and philosophy.[12] We have so separated reason and revelation that we cannot "imagine," to recall Nietzsche's word, how they might, without contradiction, be related to each other.[13] Was it possible that something was incomplete or unfinished in philosophy so that it could not consummate what it proposed by itself to itself? Is philosophy, by itself, the *search* for the "whole" or the *finding* of the "whole"? If it is the latter, it verges into divinity. If it is the former, the search, as our tradition (Plato, 486a) suggests against the "modern project," does this mean that we are left, in the end, with experiences and questions that we have not resolved because we cannot resolve them in philosophy? And if we cannot resolve them, are they therefore unresolvable in principle or merely unresolvable by us?

To juxtapose "worship" and "political philosophy" is no doubt deliberately provocative, if not downright rash. Already in Plato, we are aware of a certain "divine madness" or "enthusiasm" that lies just below or just above the surface of the political life, almost as if something is waiting to burst forth. "The Deity is the truly active source from which something happens to man," Josef Pieper writes in his commentary on Plato's *Phaedrus*, a dialogue central to understanding the Pickstock book:

> For this very reason we cannot speak simply of *madness* or *frenzy* without further qualifying the words. If the word *enthusiasm* were not so debased in English, it would in fact most fittingly describe what Plato intended, and indeed he himself uses it in the sense of "being filled with god." In the middle of the *Phaedrus*, he speaks of a man thus possessed by *mania*. "The multitude regard him as being out of his wits, for they know not that he is full of a god [*enthousiazon*]."[14]

These words imply that it is quite possible to call things that have higher purpose "insane" or "mad" not because there is no point to them but because we refuse to accept them or we are not given understanding—the problem of grace. Is it possible that the relative incompleteness of human things is intended? Deliberately challenging? On the philosophical and political levels, it is well to recall that in a classical democracy, the fool and the philosopher are indistinguishable because there is no principle of truth in the regime. This lack of ability to distinguish was why Socrates could live for seventy years in Athens. To most, he appeared odd, a fool. Will grace and revelation appear to reason as madness or *mania*? Does that mean that they contradict reason or do they stimulate it to be more reason?

Plato also tells us that, comparatively speaking, compared to divine things, that is, human things are not particularly important (417c; 804b). Aristotle similarly admonishes us in Book Ten of his *Ethics* not to listen to those who tell us to devote our lives to "human" things, the highest of which are economic and political things. We are rather to strain ourselves to know, even if it be little, the highest things, the truths of the contemplative life, the things that cannot be otherwise (1177b30–78a2). If human affairs are not really "serious," not really important, what is? What are the things beyond politics to which we ought to spend our lives, even if what we learn about them is very little? Plato says in his *Laws* that we should spend our lives not in politics but in "singing, dancing, and sacrificing" (803e). If we smile at this proposal, is it because we are moderns? Singing, dancing, and sacrificing would seem to indicate that we need some object worthy of such activities.

In the fifth chapter of the Acts of the Apostles, moreover, Peter and John are forbidden to preach by local political authorities. They respond by asking, not entirely rhetorically, whether they should "obey God or men?" (Acts, 5:29). They knew what Socrates already knew, namely, that the men in power could kill them if they wished. But they also knew that death was not the worst evil. Obedience to God may well result in death at the hands of men, political men, even as, in this case, of religious men who were also political men. Yet if violent death and its fear are, as Hobbes was later to maintain, the worst evils, then the politician could control all ideas, religious and philosophical, that opposed him. He did have the power of death with its consequent Machiavellian freedom, the freedom to use either evil or good means, to achieve his purposes.

Even Pontius Pilate, anticipating Hobbes, said ominously to Christ at His trial, "Surely you know that I have the authority to release you, and I have the authority to crucify you?" (John 19:10). There is every indication that Christ did know this fact. Notice again that Christ did not piously reply to Pilate, "all capital punishment is wrong." Rather, He said that "you would have no authority over me were it not given to you by God." Plato, Aristotle, and Luke in *Acts* are in agreement that the polity does not itself define the highest things, even though it has legitimate authority when used properly in human affairs. Christ does not deny that Pilate, the Roman governor, has authority. When the threat of death by the state causes us to change our minds, the state rules all things through ruling our minds. When we die affirming our beliefs, however, the state is limited to what it is in the very act of claiming to be more than it is.

IV

"The noble type of man feels *himself* to be the determiner of values, he does not need to be approved of, he judges 'what harms me is harmful in itself,' he knows himself to be that which in general first accords honor to things, he *creates values.*"[15] These prophetic words of Nietzsche near the end of the nineteenth century define what modern man thinks he is, the creator of his own "values." They remind us of the dangers of apparently good words like "values." If we are creators of our values, of our reward, then what is accorded "honor" is nothing less than ourselves. What gives the "honor" is also ourselves. We create it and distribute it by the movement of our will subject to nothing other than ourselves.

"Rights" and "values" are modern, not ancient or medieval, words. They are rooted in this idea that we can "create" them literally from "nothing." Rights come from Hobbes. Values come from Max Weber.[16] They both indicate the same thing about the modern project, that we have a "right" to everything, that we can have only "science" about means. Values are what we "create" and choose to live by, with no rational ability to determine why one value is better than another. Rights and values are both understood in modern philosophy to be rooted in will, in arbitrary will. If God becomes pure arbitrary will, from Duns Scotus and Occam on, as Catherine Pickstock has shown, then so is his image.[17] On this basis, *what is* could always be otherwise. No objective ground exists. The foundation has no foundation.

Man thus is not measured; he measures, even himself. When he examines reality, he finds only himself. His scientific methods allow him to see only what such methods, constructed by himself, allow him to see. On defining himself by declaring his "rights" and his "values," he constructs a polity that excludes all but himself. Nietzsche was right to see the weakness of a polity built on the collective will of weak men willing only themselves. Nietzsche was not wrong to wonder about "greatness." Man is not only to live but to live "well," as Aristotle said. Since man does not ground his own being, it seems strange, if not impossible, that he could give greatness to himself even when he does great deeds and speaks great words.

It is my thesis here that Voegelin is right. We have had presented to us, in effect, all the intellectual "wrinkles." The twentieth century did not produce anything new. Reason will not by itself find its way out of what will has chosen to construct for itself. Is there a conceivable alternative? Recently, a student sent me via e-mail the following definitions of justice, mercy, and grace. I do not know where he found them, but they are, when read together, both insightful and amusing. In a sense, they collectively make the point that I wish to propose in this chapter about worship and political philosophy, namely, that the highest things may not come to us by our own reasonings and our own makings, but they still may come to us in another form if and only if we choose to accept them. Political philosophy, in reflecting on political things, naturally comes to queries, to questions that it cannot resolve. That is to say, its very being and status require it to acknowledge an openness that it cannot close by its own efforts. Why after all did the best existing states kill Socrates and Christ?

Justice, so the explanation went, is when "we get what we deserve." Mercy, on the other hand, is when "we don't get what we do deserve." And grace is when we unexpectedly do "get what we don't deserve." All in all, these are pretty sound definitions. We live in a time when the churches seem to be primarily interested in "justice," not grace. At times, they seem to think it their primary function to make the state work better by its own means. And, as Augustine showed, grace does have this effect.[18] Modern religious leaders often add "faith and justice," but rarely "faith, justice, freedom, and mercy." Even rarer do we hear about "grace," though this is the most profound reality of them all. This is why creation and redemption are both "graced" topics; neither the one nor the other is "deserved," though mercy and forgiveness have the added notion of the response of grace to injustice, even political injustice. The end of the famous "Prologue" to the Gospel of John even speaks of "grace upon grace," as if to imply a certain unanticipated superabundance in reality (John, 1:16).

What I am concerned about here, then, is in fact the First Commandment—"I am the Lord thy God; thou shalt not have strange gods before me." Are the "strange gods" that we have before us related to the "liturgical consummation of philosophy"? If we start from within the world, within philosophy, it is indeed quite possible that we will arrive, at best, at a "first mover." This step is not to be minimized, of course. But if there is a proper way to "worship" God, it seems quite clear that lack of this worship would send the members of any existing polity off into myriads of directions, into ever new "locales," seeking the reasons why their explanations are insufficient or even corrupting. Thus, I do not propose beginning from reason to see what kind of answers that it can come up with, though there is nothing wrong with this beginning. Rather I propose, at least as an noninvestigated alternative, beginning from proper worship as found in revelation, to explain why it is that personal and public lives are disordered to the extent that they lack its presence.

Political philosophy, needless to say, has, on the face of it, little to do with mercy and grace. Its realm is justice—legal, distributive, and rectificatory, as Aristotle described the various kinds of justice. Rarely do political things seem to cross these higher notions, though perhaps it happens more frequently than we might guess. Revelation itself admonishes us to be at least just, a fact that itself makes us wonder about how these two are related. Just why are some things found both in reason and revelation?[19] To be sure, the notion of clemency is related to mercy. Governors and executives can grant pardons in the name of some greater good. And benefactions, free giving, is known in human affairs. Compassion is likewise known, though it has frequently become not just a means of understanding another's suffering but a tool to deny the wrongness of certain things classically considered to be evil. Justice, moreover, is never so perfect that the world has no need of things like punishment, let alone things like fraternity, grace, and mercy to allow us to live with our faults and sins, having acknowledged them. Hannah Arendt, I believe, said that the most politically important of the Christian virtues was forgiveness.[20] Without forgiveness, justice would lead to recurring vengeance. No polity could rest with its actual situation, with the city composed of many less than perfect men if justice, the terrible virtue, were the sole element present within its exchanges.

V

What has particularly intrigued me is the notion that modern ideology is the result of an effort to explain things in a manner other than that set down in reason and revelation. When in modernity revelation ceased to play an intimate, active role, we have seen arise the situation that Voegelin described, that is, a gradual, increasing exhaustion of reasons that would ground our "being." Voegelin, like Nietzsche, actually thought that the reason for the rise of ideological, rationalist explanations of reality was, in fact, the practical loss of faith of Christians in their own understanding of the world order.[21] Notice that ideology here is not conceived as a first order explanation but as a substitute for something that is lost—faith, to be precise. Since the modern human being cannot rest with the reality before him unexplained, unexplained even by himself, he seeks some alternative, some "wrinkle" as it were, that would finally close off any explanation not totally under the control and guidance of the human will and mind.

But the human will is only creative in the sense of art, not of reality itself. *What is*, including the human will itself, is not the product of its own making. Human action is action having been first acted upon. Even our knowledge, to be active, depends in the first instance on something that is not ourselves. We do not first think, then discover reality; we first see things, then we begin to think. This awareness leads naturally to the question of the relation of theoretical and practical intellect. It questions the primacy of practical intellect that resulted when the will knew no limitations other than its own values, choices, or rights. Morality, how we ought to act, cannot begin with our wills but with our understanding of how things are apart from our will, with theoretical intellect. This is not to deny the possibility of our willing not to see.

In order to understand where we are, would it be possible to re-propose political philosophy in such a manner that the "queen of the social sciences" (political philosophy) and the "queen of the sciences" (theology) be approached from the side of the latter? Here I do not propose an artificial "faith" on the part of the unbeliever, but I do propose an intelligent understanding of what is proposed in revelation, if nothing else as an intellectual consideration that has some relation to issues not found satisfactorily answered in reason. The question that I want to propose is whether political philosophy has sought autonomy for itself, has sought to elevate itself as the queen of the social sciences, and ultimately of the sciences themselves because it, unwittingly perhaps, provided an alternate object of worship of sorts, when the true object of worship was either unknown or rejected? I take seriously, in other words, Augustine's "city of man" because his "city of God" contains so many answers that ought not to be there solely on the basis of accident.[22] Augustine's political realism, in the *City of God*, lists several hundred different possible ideas of the gods.

How does one even go about posing this question in the modern intellectual world so that it will be intelligible and not simply ridiculous? No doubt, Catherine Pickstock's acute analysis of the classic Tridentine Mass of the Roman Rite provides an immediate occasion for this consideration. Her approach is through a minute analysis of the post-modern philosophers whose theories of language, objectivity, and interpretation have locked them not merely into themselves but into a kind of vast unknowability about themselves and reality. They have sought a kind of reassurance of freedom in professing the inability of the mind to know things and what other minds might think. It is not merely that in knowing themselves they know something of reality. Rather, since they cannot know themselves or others, they cannot know reality. This unknowing is taken to be a guarantee of freedom, almost the opposite of the classic meaning of freedom as the capacity to learn from and know what is not oneself.

We have here not merely the dead end of modernity, but the dead end itself. I have the impression that this dead end was reached, a dead end that included the fall of communism because of a refusal to return back to the original sources that were rejected in the formation of modernity. There is no place, no "locale" to which we can turn if we follow the logic of the premises on which the modern mind was built. The argument is not whether this dead end exists, nor whether it is the result of a logical progression of modern thought from modernity to post-modernity through the great constructs of political ideology. It is whether there is an alternative, even if that alternative does not come directly from reason.

As we will see in the final chapter, John Paul II has drawn our attention to philosophy and reason, *Fides et Ratio*. Those who know St. Thomas are familiar with the idea of grace building on nature, of reason not contradicting faith and faith not destroying reason. This implies a certain intrinsic connection between reason and faith. It is important to state this relationship properly. We cannot conclude to certain truths about God as given to us in revelation on the basis of our reason alone. Otherwise we would be gods ourselves, in fact the great temptation of modernity. But it is possible to attempt to understand the order of things revealed and to ask whether they relate in any fashion to what we know in reason. It is possible to become more "philosophical" because we seek better to understand what is revealed. We do not in principle exclude what makes some sense even if it does not come from reason.

Lucy lies on her back, her head propped up against the piano while Beethoven is playing. She muses out loud, "if you really liked me, you would give me presents." To this, Beethoven rises up on his piano bench with hauteur, "if you really liked me, you wouldn't expect any presents."[23] In the third scene, he returns to playing the piano while she is on her side with a quizzical look. Finally, with Beethoven indifferently playing, she reflects, "Either way, I end up not getting any presents." In the end, do we end up our theological-philosophical problem by getting no presents? The notion of "present," of gift, of grace is the essence of what I want to say here about worship and political philosophy.

No state, consisting as it does of a multiplicity of citizens bound together in some defined relationship, is a proper subject or object of worship. Only individual persons, properly speaking, worship. If they worship themselves, we call it properly pride, *superbia*. The being of human beings is good, but it is not itself worthy of worship. Human beings also, normally, worship together—the singing, the dancing, and the sacrificing. In the abstract, many varied rites might be proposed as ways to properly worship God. The question that the history of classic, medieval, and modern philosophy presents is whether the central act of worship proposed in revelation is so fundamental that it "consummates" philosophy, that is, resolves its unanswered questions in a fashion that the coherence of reason and revelation, if not necessary, is certainly intelligible. But this intelligibility must always carry the proviso that it would not have been arrived at unless the impetus of revelation had not been somehow addressed to it.

VI

Josef Ratzinger, in a remarkable address to Italian bishops, recounts a thousand-year-old story, perhaps apocryphal, of certain Russian envoys from Kiev who were sent by Prince Vladimir in search of a proper religion for their kingdom. As they probably did not know of Buddhism, Hinduism, or China, with Protestants not yet around, they examined Islam in Bulgaria, Judaism, and Catholics among the Germans.[24] Finally, they went to Santa Sofia in Constantinople. There they were struck with wonder by the liturgy and its beauty. Ratzinger uses this occasion to reflect on the nature of liturgy, of worship. I emphasize this passage in the light of Aristotle's notion of the highest things being for their own sakes.

The Byzantine liturgy, Ratzinger pointed out, is not primarily "missionary"; it is not directed to nonbelievers. Its roots were entirely "within the faith." What goes on is the "acclamation of faith." The liturgy presupposes "an 'initiation,' only someone who has entered into the mystery with his life can participate in it."[25] "The Byzantine liturgy," Ratzinger goes on, "was not a way of teaching doctrine and was not intended to be. It was not a display of the Christian faith in a way acceptable or attractive to onlookers. What impressed onlookers about the liturgy was precisely its utter lack of an ulterior purpose, the fact that it was celebrated for God and not for spectators, that its sole intent was to be before God and for God." Essentially, Catherine Pickstock stresses the same quality in the Tridentine Mass. If there is a point within the world where men contemplate and worship God, the city can consequently find its proper dimensions. The highest things came among us; they are not initially humanly made or constructed, however much they are, like the Byzantine and Tridentine Mass, open to the "creative" genius of artists, poets, and musicians.

In this sense, worship has much to do with political philosophy. We are little prepared, I admit, to grant the fact that already existing among us, with origins in revelation, not directly in philosophy, though with certain intimations from it, a proper, though to us improbable, way to worship God is established. We are loathe to admit, furthermore, that the neglect, corruption, or unknownness of this way has consequences even in the political order through the restless souls of men unable or unwilling to find a proper object of their striving in any locale or wrinkle. Aristotle constantly refers to the theoretic mind in its seeking of things "for their own sakes." Such are the very words that Ratzinger uses when explaining the reaction of the Russian officials to beholding the liturgy of Byzantium. It utterly lacked "an ulterior purpose" beyond its own doing. It is the First Commandment, the "I am who am" of Exodus (3:13–15).

Worship, no doubt, presupposes doctrine and right living, but that is not its own purpose. It looks outward from its depth in inwardness, not to the city, but through it. Why is this such an important point? Are we not to worry about the later rigidity of the Byzantine state and church, about the widespread rejection of the Mass as the central human act of worship? Has not the Roman rite suddenly gone over to the very missionary and social concerns that Ratzinger warned about, so that the Mass no longer causes this awe that he and Pickstock understood? Much of the Protestant world gave up some or all of this full liturgy at the Reformation. The rest of the world barely heard of it, if it did hear of it at all. Thus, the proposition that the existence of a mode of worship that derives from revelation and is intended to celebrate the unbloody Sacrifice of the Cross as the central act of worship will seem if not unecumenical, at least impractical.[26]

VII

To conclude, I want to inquire whether, once the outline of the act of worship is set down in revelation, whether the reason why modernity has been in such turmoil is because it sought and could not find an alternative to it? It exhausted the "locales" and all the "wrinkles" that might propose something else. The orthodox position, no doubt, at least insofar as it has not itself imitated this same modernity, is that no alternative is to be found. A "reason" exists for this mode of worship that goes to the very heart of the sort of beings we are created to be, supernatural, not natural, from the beginning. "God," "soul," "truth," "eternal life"—Nietzsche's "lies"—are the ground of our being.

What is proposed here is not proposed in any defiant or triumphant manner, but rather sadly, with a sense of loss at what might be, of what ought to be. If one examines the vast effort that the current Holy Father has given to conversation with other branches of Christianity, with other religions, with philosophers, with anyone really, it is clear that the spirit of the endeavor is honestly to see what truths are held in common, whether many or few. With regard to those in which there is difference, we must continue to see the other's point of view. Likewise, this same consideration accepts the principle that faith is a free gift. If one does not have the "gift" of faith, why on earth talk about it except to those who have it?

Why would worship have universal significance? Those who reject the faith or who never have heard of it remain human beings and members of some existing polity. It is true that the faith is to be preached to all nations, as if to suggest that there is something about it that is pertinent to all nations whatever it is they now hold as the structural principle of their living together as this or that nation, their "foundation myth," to recall Plato.

This reflection on worship and political philosophy thus brings us back to the question of "the liturgical consummation of philosophy." Catherine Pickstock does not say "the liturgical consummation of political philosophy" because she understands that it is not "the state," though it is the political philosopher and the politician, who can worship. If the order of polity is a reflection of the order of our souls, as the classical writers taught us, we can suspect that the completion or "consummation" of philosophy comes about when a proper object of worship is "given" to us with a proper indication of how it is we are to worship. Once this order is in existence, all other idols, including the state when we make it an idol, will fail. We, who are readers of Plato, cannot be too surprised at this.

At the end of his discussion of "classical philosophy" in "What Is Political Philosophy?" Leo Strauss warns us not to be charmed either by mathematical certainty or by the "humble awe" engendered by "meditating on the human soul and its experiences." Philosophy must mate "courage and moderation" to resist these charms. Sometimes philosophy seems to produce very little. Like Sisyphus and his burden, its achievements and goal are very different. Out of frustration, philosophy can appear "ugly," though Strauss seems to admit, unlike the analogy with Sisyphus, that something of the "goal" is seen. Philosophy must be "sustained, accompanied, and elevated by *eros.*" It is, he concludes in an evocative phrase, "graced by nature's grace."

Does indeed "nature" have a "grace"? If nature has a "grace," is it still grace? And what might a philosophy be that is precisely "elevated" by "eros," the noble Platonic word? Strauss, at the same time, seemingly both denies and intimates more than he implies. The Russian envoys were, perhaps, more perceptive, or at least, more awe-struck, not by meditating on their own souls but by beholding the worship in Santa Sofia. The "mating" of courage and moderation may well require, not the "lowering," but the raising of our sights.

If philosophy is "consummated" in liturgy, it does not mean that philosophy ceases to be philosophy. It means that it is all the more important that philosophy remain itself. Nietzsche's "imaginings" and "lies" are precisely what we most need, as even he intimated in his disappointment at those who really do not believe. Nor does it mean that the city ceases to be the city. It does mean that we are open to gifts that complete what we are, that we do not look to the city for what it cannot do, however tempted it always seems to be to propose itself as an object of worship. It does mean that our natural limits are not in vain. It does mean that, as philosophers and political philosophers, we can recognize that answers are posed in revelation to questions we legitimately ponder but are unable to resolve in our own contemplations. "The Deity is the truly active source from which something happens to man." Justice means getting what we deserve. Mercy means not getting something we do deserve. Grace means getting something that we don't deserve. Grace upon grace.

Notes

1. Friedrich Nietzsche, *Ecce Homo*, translated by Walter Kaufmann (New York: Vintage, 1969), 256.

2. *Conversations with Eric Voegelin*, edited by R. Eric O'Connor (Montreal: Thomas More Institute Papers, 1980), 16.

3. See Étienne Gilson, *The Unity of Philosophical Experience* (San Francisco: Ignatius Press [1937], 1999).

4. "According to the modern project, philosophy or science was no longer to be understood as essentially contemplative and proud but as active and charitable; it was to be in the service of the relief of man's estate; it was to be cultivated for the sake of human power; it was to enable man to become the master and owner of nature through the intellectual conquest of nature." Leo Strauss, *The City and Man* (Chicago: University of Chicago Press, 1964), 3–4.

5. The expression "culture of death" comes from John Paul II and the boredom of the "end of history" from Francis Fukyama, *The End of History and the Last Man* (New York: The Free Press, 1992).

6. See Michael J. Behe, *Darwin's Black Box: The Biochemical Challenge to Evolution* (New York: Simon & Schuster, 1996); Patrick Glynn, *God: The Evidence: The Reconciliation of Faith and Reason in a Post-Secular World* (Rocklin, Calif.: Prima Publishers, 1997); E. F. Schumacher, *A Guide for the Perplexed* (New York: Harper Colophon, 1977).

7. Niccolò Machiavelli, *The Prince*, translated by Leo Paul S. de Alvarez (Irving, Tex.: University of Dallas Press, 1980), 93.

8. See Friedrich Nietzsche, *Twilight of the Idols*, "The Problem of Socrates," no. 12, in *The Portable Nietzsche*, translated by Walter Kaufmann (Harmondsworth: Penguin, 1959), 479.

9. Catherine Pickstock, *After Writing: The Liturgical Consummation of Philosophy* (Oxford: Blackwell, 1998). See John Milbank and Catherine Pickstock, *Truth in Aquinas* (London: Routledge, 2002).

10. I note what I call the three "after" books: Alasdair MacIntyre's *After Virtue* (Notre Dame, Ind.: University of Notre Dame Press, 1981; David Walsh, *After Ideology* (San Francisco: Harper, 1987); and Catherine Pickstock, *After Writing*.

11. See the famous study of Fustel de Coulanges, *The Ancient City* (Garden City, N.Y.: Doubleday Anchor, 1956).

12. See Dietrich von Hildebrand, *Liturgy and Personality* (Manchester, N.H.: Sofia Institute Press, 1993).

13. John Paul II's *Fides et Ratio*, in *The Pope Speaks*, no. 1 (1999): 1–63, is but the latest complete and authoritative endeavor to show just how they might belong together. See also Robert Sokolowski, *The God of Faith and Reason* (Washington, D.C.: Catholic University of America Press, 1995); James V. Schall, *Reason, Revelation and the Foundations of Political Philosophy* (Baton Rouge: Louisiana State University Press, 1987); John Hittinger, *Liberty, Wisdom, and Grace* (Lanham, Md.: Lexington Books, 2003); Peter Augustine Lawler, *Aliens in America: The Strange Truth about Our Souls* (Wilmington, Del.: ISI Books, 2002).

14. Josef Pieper, *"Enthusiasm and the Divine Madness: On the Platonic Dialogue Phaedrus,"* translated by Richard and Clara Winston (New York: Harcourt, 1964), 50.

15. Friedrich Nietzsche, *Beyond Good and Evil*, translated by R. J. Hollingdale (Harmondsworth: Penguin, 1975), #260, 176.

16. See Leo Strauss, *Natural Right and History* (Chicago: University of Chicago Press, 1953), chaps. 2 and 5; Eric Voegelin, *The New Science of Politics* (Chicago: University of Chicago Press, 1952), 13–22, 152–62; E. B. F. Midgley, *The Ideology of Max Weber* (Aldershot, Hants.: Gower, 1983).

17. Pickstock, *After Writing*, 123–36. See also Josef Pieper, *Scholasticism: Personalities and Problems of Medieval Philosophy* (New York: McGraw-Hill, 1969), 136–52.

18. See Charles N. R. McCoy, "St. Augustine," in *History of Political Philosophy*, edited by Leo Strauss and Joseph Cropsey (Chicago: Rand-McNally, 1963), 151–59.

19. See Ralph McInerny, *St. Thomas Aquinas* (Notre Dame, Ind.: University of Notre Dame Press, 1982), 145–61. See Ralph McInerny, "John Paul II and Christian Philosophy," in *John Paul II—Witness to Truth*, edited by K. Whitehead (South Bend, Ind.: St. Augustine's Press, 2001), 113–25; Germain G. Grisez, "The 'Four Meanings' of Christian Philosophy," *The Journal of Religion* 42 (April 1962): 103–18.

20. Hannah Arendt, *The Human Condition* (New York: Doubleday Anchor, 1959), 212–18.

21. Eric Voegelin, *Science, Politics, and Gnosticism* (Chicago: Regnery, 1968), 109.

22. See Pierre Manent, *The City of Man*, translated by Marc Le Pain (Princeton, N.J.: Princeton University Press, 1998).

23. Charles Schulz, in Robert Short, *The Parables of Peanuts* (New York: Harper, 1968), 310–11.

24. Josef Ratzinger, "Ratzinger on the Eucharist," *Inside the Vatican*, January 1998, 43.

25. Ibid., 44.

26. See John Paul II, "Ecclesia de Eucharistia," *L'Osservatore Romano*, English edition, April 23, 2003.

27. Leo Strauss, "What Is Political Philosophy?" *What Is Political Philosophy?* (Glencoe, Ill.: The Free Press, 1959), 40.

~

CHAPTER ELEVEN

Roman Catholic Political Philosophy

Philosophy could be employed, not indeed as a principle allowing one to pass judgment on the truth or falsity of Revelation, but as a tool with which to probe its meaning and counter any attack that might be leveled against it in the name of reason.

—Ernest Fortin, 1996[1]

Revelation clearly proposes certain truths which might never have been discovered by reason unaided, although they are not of themselves inaccessible to reason. Among these truths is the notion of a free and personal God who is the Creator of the world, a truth which has been so crucial for the development of philosophical thinking, especially the philosophy of being. There is also the reality of sin, as it appears in the light of faith, which helps to shape an adequate philosophical formulation of the problem of evil. The notion of the person as a spiritual being is another of faith's specific contributions: the Christian proclamation of human dignity, equality and freedom has undoubtedly influenced modern philosophic thought. In more recent times, there has been the discovery that history as event—so central to Christian revelation—is important for philosophy as well.

—John Paul II, *Fides et Ratio*, 1998, no. 76[2]

The emperor of the visible empire, "sol invictus," the invincible sun, has as his opponent and successor the vicar of the invisible empire, "servus

servorum Dei," the servant of the servants of God. . . . We never understand more than the half of things when we neglect the science of Rome.

—Pierre Manent, *The City of Man*, 1998[3]

Summary: The Encyclical Fides et Ratio *of John Paul II has a particular interest to
political philosophy. In it, the failure of much theology to attend to the movements in
modern philosophy, movements that undermine the possibility of genuine philosophy
and, hence, a valid understanding of revelation, are noted. Political philosophy in
particular has, at least in some of its leading thinkers, remained open to classical philosophy but is curiously closed to revelation. Once political philosophy is open to
"more than half the things" that burst forth in the ordinary and intellectual world, it
regains and deepens the direction toward* what is *that is found within its own experience and to which it points by its own awareness of what it lacks within the polity.
By recognizing why political things are not the highest things, political philosophy
serves both to protect the highest things to be themselves and to free the polity to accomplish what it can do in this world by its own judgments and experiences.*

I

At first sight, "among the heathen," so to speak, if not also among believers
themselves, the very idea of a "Roman Catholic political philosophy," as I
have indicated, is rather quaint, if not actually shocking.[4] To hint that an inner and coherent relation exists between the core of Roman Catholic thought
and political philosophy requires a "secret writing." Roman Catholicism, of
course, prides itself on distinction, forthrightness, and clarity in the service of
a knowledge of the whole. St. Thomas's refusal—his careful distinctions—to
let intellectual confusion reign is central to its identification of itself. "Grace
builds on nature; it does not contradict it."[5] Both grace and nature, while remaining what they are, can be intellectually explicated and, if necessary, both
defined and defended. Therefore, reason, to be helpful to revelation, must be
what it is, namely, reason acting according to its own exigencies on its proper
object, on *what is*. Reason itself is found in human nature as a real property or
faculty not itself constructed or given to this same nature by man himself.
Man possesses this capacity but does not himself "invent" it.

But not just anything that calls itself "reason" is reasonable. Even "chaos"
theory presents itself as reasonable, as does every form of skepticism. Claims
to truth or to doubt can be tested. We must add, if it is not a tautology, we
are concerned with "*true* reason," with reason that seeks to know the truth
even when it denies, paradoxically, that truth can be known by reason. Thus,
when some philosopher, implicitly or explicitly, denies, say, the principle of

non-contradiction, we do not, as Aristotle said, have to believe him, even less, agree with him. We just have to watch what he does to see that implicitly he upholds in practice this basic principle he denies in theory. He invariably opens the door before he walks through it; he assumes that it cannot be there and not there at the same time and in the same place. And yes, we have to trust our senses when we see him open the door. Our minds and our sensory powers are connected.

Thus, we ask one last time: what is Roman Catholic political philosophy? I deliberately use the term "Roman Catholic," as in previous chapters, to distinguish it, benignly not polemically, from a more Protestant view as found in, say, Glenn Tinder's excellent *The Political Meaning of Christianity*, or Reinhold Niebuhr's famous *Moral Man and Immoral Society*, or C. S. Lewis's *Mere Christianity*. Lewis sought admirably to concentrate on those things all Christians hold in common. I also distinguish Roman Catholic thought formally from an Orthodox view as in Nicholas Berdyaev's *The Destiny of Man* or Solzhenitsyn's Harvard Address.[6] The things that are uniquely Roman Catholic are part of the argument I make, however much or little other branches of Christianity might agree with them. Or, perhaps I should say that I am interested in the whole that it stands for. Still, I acknowledge that some of the most provocative incentives to Roman Catholic thought on political philosophy come today from outside its immediate circles. I emphasize again the enormous influence of Strauss and Voegelin, each of whom I hold of particular importance for any consideration of reason, revelation, and political philosophy.[7]

Of increasing importance is the work of Oliver O'Donovan, George Grant, Catherine Pickstock, Hadley Arkes, Robert Song, Henry Veatch, and others, such as those associated with "Christians in Political Science."[8] On the Catholic side itself, we find a surprising number of scholars doing political philosophy with full awareness of the import of revelation.[9] This later flourishing in serious considerations of revelation and political philosophy owes much to an earlier generations of whom many of the newer thinkers are students.[10] I am concerned in this final chapter with what I would call basically mainline positions—say those who can read the *General Catechism of the Catholic Church* with no major dissenting problems. Movements such as "liberation theology," in its varied incarnations, while interesting, I would consider mostly aberrations.[11]

Philosophy and theology are both legitimate; both can establish their foundations. The intelligible content of each is at least comprehensible to the other, even when not agreed upon. But they are *not* related to one another as reason to unreason, respectively. Revelation is a grounded claim to truth, not to some higher irrationality. Things can be beyond the power of particularly human reason fully to know without necessarily being beyond reason as such. We are the lowest, not the highest, of the intellectual beings.[12] "Man is the best of animals . . . [but] there are other things much more divine in their nature even than man," as Aristotle put it (1141a35–b2).

Revelation addresses itself to the same reason that philosophy considers. *Fides quaerens intellectum; intellectus quaerens fidem.* Indeed, the very fact that reason brings up questions, legitimate questions, that it cannot fully answer on its own terms means, as we have seen, that it is not a complete account of all things, of the whole, even when it is *capax omnium*, even when it wants to know all things. This awareness of a desire to know the whole is the valid, if negative, insight of Strauss in his famous essay, "On the Mutual Influence of Theology and Philosophy."[13] Roman Catholic sources in theology and philosophy would put closer together what Strauss separated so dramatically, without denying, indeed while affirming, the difference between the way of the philosopher and the way of the theologian. These approaches may indicate different ways of seeking the truth, but they do not find different truths. John Paul II puts it this way: "Philosophy must obey its own rules and be based upon its own principles; truth, however, can only be one. The content of revelation can never debase the discoveries and legitimate the autonomy of reason. Yet, conscious that it cannot set itself up as an absolute and exclusive value, reason on its part must never lose its capacity to question and to be questioned" (*Fides et Ratio*, no. 79).[14] Roman Catholic theology, at least, has a vested interest in the validity of philosophy as such.

Human reason does not "explain" everything. It explains, having first encountered what is there not caused by itself, what needs to be explained. It is "philo-sophia," the friendship with or the love, not the cause, of wisdom. It therefore remains open to what it does not yet know, even, with Socrates, knowing that it does not know everything when it does know something. "It is owing to their wonder that men both now begin and at first began to philosophize" (982b13). And they began this effort, Aristotle notices, only "when almost all the necessities of life and the things that make for comfort and recreation had been secured" (982b23–24). The most important things are beyond comfort and necessity, even though, as Aristotle also said, an adequate amount of material goods is needed for must of us to practice virtue. Both faith and authority in revelation rest not on themselves but on someone who does know, who does see, who does hear. In this sense, faith is not blind, and reason can reflect on itself.[15]

II

By any objective analysis, revelation appears to be much more conscious of reason than most philosophical reason is of revelation, though there are always Plato and his followers to caution us here. Philosophy has to be proper philosophy to hear revelation. An inadequate philosophy is deaf to the voice of revelation. Revelation, rather frequently, has to defend philosophy itself from itself. This is, in fact, what *Fides et Ratio* is about, that philosophy be philosophy. "Christian doctrine is primarily concerned with offering salvation, not with interpreting reality or human existence," Josef Pieper has written. "But it implies as well certain fundamental teachings on specifically philosophical matters—the world and existence as such."[16] Reason that illogically proclaims its own autonomy can, however, consciously and voluntarily choose to make itself into a closed system incapable of any openness to *what is*. Philosophy, and this is the dark side of its mystery, can choose to deny itself, deny its openness to truth, and still call itself "philosophy." Political systems can be built on this theoretical denial. Political philosophy seems inordinately susceptible to corruption by an ill-grounded philosophy. This propensity is why political philosophers must also know philosophy.

This possibility of philosophy denying itself is no doubt at the origin of St. Paul's famous impatience with the philosophers: "Where is your wise man now, your man of learning, your own subtle debater—limited, all of them, to this passing age? God has made the wisdom of this world look foolish" (1 Corinthians, 1:20). Much of modern philosophy, which surely considers itself as "the wisdom of this world," can best be understood as the intellectual and logical consequences of this choice of denying to itself, frequently indeed "foolishly," some basic element of the proper "range of reason," to use Jacques Maritain's phrase.[17]

The Bible, to be sure, is not immediately a "political" or "philosophic" tract. It is primarily an account of a way, indeed the way, as it maintains, of salvation, itself a word related to the "happiness" discussions of the philosophers and the political philosophers. Yet, for philosophers, if they set their mind to it, the Bible is neither incoherent nor unintelligible; it is not lacking in its own philosophical profundity.[18] "The Bible, and the New Testament in particular, contains texts and statements which have a genuinely ontological content. The inspired authors intended to formulate true statements, capable, that is, of expressing objective reality" (no. 82). Scripture can be intelligently read by philosophers, believed by the politicians, without making either philosopher or politician any less profound or, in spite of Machiavelli, any less competent or practical. Theologians and believers can likewise philosophize; they have in fact done so. *Ex esse sequitur posse* ("From the fact of being the possibility of being follows"). To deny this possibility is itself unphilosophic, an unwillingness to consider *all that is*. The notion that philosophy and theology are two "contradictory" ways of life does not explain the fact that at least a few men, perhaps more than a few, are legitimately both the one and the other without confusing the one for the other.

Philosophers and believers, moreover, must, like everyone else, live in cities in this world, even when they call Augustine's "City of God" their true home. They are both aware—if we pass over certain types of utopians over the centuries—that we "have here no lasting city." The New Testament in particular has very little to do, directly, with politics.[19] In fact, it frankly acknowledges that the things of Caesar and the things of God are not the same (Matthew, 22:22–23). Almost for the first time, we have here a revelational source affirming the validity of the state in its, the state's, own terms. The "things" of Caesar, however, still need to be explicated philosophically to show why it is "natural" that man is a "political animal."[20] Without a polity, he cannot "flourish," cannot practice all the virtues he discovers in himself, cannot have the leisure for things beyond politics.[21]

When Paul told Christians to be "obedient to the Emperor" (Romans, 13:1–7), the emperor was Nero, a tyrant, as Tacitus graphically tells us in his *Annals*. Paul was not, however, approving tyranny, nor denying its obvious possibility or dangers. Nor was he an advanced Nietzschian who saw in "turning the other cheek" a sure sign of political ineptness and betrayal of worldly power. He was rather pointing out, something already found in Aristotle, that man was by nature a political animal, but one who often revealed his own inability, or better, unwillingness, to rule himself. Interestingly, revelation seems to have more to do with our inability or unwillingness to live the virtues than with our more successful efforts to define them.[22] But, to keep priorities straight, "I would rather feel compunction than know how to define it," as Thomas à Kempis remarked in a famous phrase in the *Imitation of Christ*. Therefore, at times, indeed often, Paul acknowledged that the ruler also possess "the sword . . . to punish wrong-doing" (Romans, 13, 3–4).

Aristotle indicated much the same thing at the end of his *Ethics* when he spoke of the transition to *The Politics* (1179b31–80a4), about the need of law and coercion. Neither philosophy nor politics, however, could quite explain why this abiding wrongdoing, this "wickedness," as Aristotle called it (1263b23), persisted in all human polities. This very perplexity was something to which revelation addressed itself in the account of the Fall. There, the problem of human disorder is located not in things, nor in institutions, nor in human faculties as such but in the operation of the will, and therefore in personal choice (Genesis, 3:1–24). The Philosopher, as Aquinas called him, did notice, without revelation, that human nature was in a kind of "bondage" (982b29). Philosophy had questions it could not quite answer.

This "unansweredness," as it were, was theoretically bothersome. It caused many a good philosopher to wonder if the world was not created "in vain," with no purpose or meaning, hardly a consoling alternative. Paradoxically, it was revelation's odd answer to this enigma that charged the universe, particularly the human universe to which all else seemed ordained, with risk, drama, uncertainty, and, yes, the possibility of love and glory. Such things are possible only if our choices make some ultimate difference, if we really do choose between right and wrong. The tractates on evil, thus, are aspects of the tractates on free will.

III

Evidently, as we suggested earlier, there should no more be Roman Catholic politics than there should be Roman Catholic physics. The methods and subject matter of politics and physics, and, yes, of theology, differ. "It is the mark of an educated man," Aristotle tells us, "to look for precision in each class of things just so far as the nature of the subject admits; it is evidently equally foolish to accept probable reasoning from a mathematician and to demand from a rhetorician scientific proofs" (1094b25–27). Modern sociology, by its own "methods," investigating issues of faith or grace, is thus replete with irony. Yet, perhaps it makes a difference what our philosophy is, what our understanding of the world is, before we can have either physics or politics.[23] Both physics and politics at some level claim to deal with reality. A politics without a metaphysics can itself be, and usually is, an unacknowledged metaphysics. Moreover, political science is itself a valid, but limited "practical science." It elucidates a certain range of reality, that is, the reality of free human beings in active exchange about what they are and choose in this world. Without bad will, political philosophy cannot refuse to consider revelation's insight into political things when politics does not solve its own problems in its own terms about its own subject matter.

"Although the teachings of Jesus as recorded in the Gospels have little to say about the proper attitude for Christians to adopt toward the social order and the state," Herbert Deane has written,

> certain fundamental principles are clearly established. On a number of occasions, Jesus warned His disciples against thinking of His kingdom as an earthly kingdom, to be established by a revolt of the Jews against Roman rule and maintained by ordinary political instruments. . . . Jesus not only insisted that

His kingdom was not of this world and so discouraged his followers from thinking of Him as a Messiah who would be the temporal ruler of the Jewish people,
but He also endeavored to draw His followers' attention away from interest in
worldly matters such as the attainment of wealth or power over other men.[24]

Roman Catholic political philosophy would, thus, agree that the ultimate
destiny of each human being, the political animal, is not located in politics.
Here it agrees with Plato and Aristotle. It would also recognize that in leav-
ing politics relatively free, Christianity implied that the political order had
its own worth and, indeed, its own dangers. It accepted, in other words, the
teaching in Genesis that nature, including angelic and human nature, was
good in its fundamental being. The origin of evil—the lack of something that
ought to be present—was neither in God nor in nature as such. It was in a
good and free faculty that could cause things to be otherwise—in brief, in the
human free will.

The early Christians were primarily city dwellers, though some of the
more pious ones began to flee the city's corruption into the desert.[25] Cities,
if left to themselves, could and did, at times, become morally unliveable. A
certain "exodus," individual or collective, always remained a possibility.[26]
The founding of America itself, with its Old Testament overtones among the
Puritans, is not unrelated to this sentiment. The city was, however, the scene
within which the positive things that Christians were commanded to do—
forgive, love, serve their neighbor, keep the commandments—were to be vis-
ibly carried out in a real, not abstract, world. The dictates of faith and charity, as well as the practice of the natural virtues, were expected to bear fruit
in the world—the Good Samaritan was to be a real citizen, as was Paul of
Tarsus a Roman citizen, as he insisted (Luke, 10:29–37; Acts, 25:8–13).[27]
This is why Christian metaphysics has always insisted on defending the reality of the world itself, the reality of being. Augustine could thus argue that
Christians were good citizens, good soldiers even.

The city was also the arena wherein Christians found themselves, in their
own way, in the predicament of Socrates. They were tried by the state for telling
the truth and living as they were commanded—something as well true in the
present century as in the first century A.D.[28] Christians were often seen, however, as apolitical, as not believing in the gods of the city. Again like Socrates,
they were considered to be "atheists." When they first appeared in any numbers,
they were in one of the most powerful and indeed in one of the most decent of
historical states, one that, to reform itself, thought, as did someone like the Emperor Diocletian, that it should demand full allegiance to the city's gods. In spite
of this aberration, much about Rome was worth saving and was saved.

IV

Thus, we can ask again: what is Roman Catholic political philosophy? The things that are uniquely Roman Catholic are part of the argument. I am interested in the whole that it stands for. However esoteric or strange it may sound, the consideration of Roman Catholicism and political philosophy together, keeping the proper distinctions, is itself a worthy endeavor that betrays the deepest cultural and intellectual purposes. Lest there be any doubt about claims to truth, let me add these words of caution from *Fides et Ratio*: "To believe it possible to know a universally valid truth is in no way to encourage intolerance; on the contrary, it is the essential condition for sincere and authentic dialogue between persons" (no. 92). It is more philosophical, indeed more "ecumenical," to take important intellectual differences seriously since they too are arguments about the truth itself. Unfortunately a presumed fear of political "intolerance" or "fanaticism" has become a justification for intellectual skepticism.

Roman Catholic political philosophy is obviously not simply "political theology," a description of exactly what Scripture may say about political things, however important the little that is said may be. It is not a discussion of civil religion. Nor is it an effort to compete with, say, Aristotle or political science about its own subject matter. Indeed, if anything via St. Thomas, it claims Aristotle as its own, even knowing his non-Christian origins and certain problems connected with his thought, like that of the eternity of the world, also happily resolved by St. Thomas. *Fides et Ratio*, the 1998 Encyclical of John Paul II, is not itself, as was, say, his *Sollicitudo Rei Socialis* (1987) or his *Centesimus Annus* (1991), more directly social, economic, or political in content or inspiration. Yet, I wish to suggest, more than almost any other specifically Roman Catholic document, *Fides et Ratio* addresses itself to the broad background questions that have surged through political philosophy in what is called modernity and even in what the pope himself calls "postmodernity" (no. 91).

We thus do not call *Fides et Ratio* a tractate in political philosophy, but what it says about philosophy is pertinent to political philosophy:

> The Church has no philosophy of her own nor does she canonize any one particular philosophy in preference to others. The underlying reason for this reluctance is that, even when it engages theology, philosophy must remain faithful to its own principles and methods. Otherwise, there would be no guarantee that it would remain oriented to truth and that it was moving toward truth by way of a process governed by reason. A philosophy which does not proceed in the light of reason according to its own principles and methods would serve little

purpose. At the deepest level, the autonomy which philosophy enjoys is rooted in the fact that reason is by its nature oriented to truth and is equipped moreover with the means necessary to arrive at truth. A philosophy conscious of this as its "constitutive status" cannot but respect the demands and the data of revealed truth. (no. 49)

Among the academic disciplines, political science departments are the only ones with their own specific subdivision devoted to "philosophy." These same principles and admonitions apply in their own way to all endeavors claiming philosophical pertinence, including political philosophy. It is worth adding that if we look at the number of doctoral theses in academic departments of philosophy devoted to what has to be called "political philosophy," as indicated in the annual review of theses published in the *Review of Metaphysics*, it is clear that political philosophy represents a large segment of philosophic studies.[29]

The peculiarities and strengths of Roman Catholicism relative to political things are that it does not, following Scripture, have a specific political program or philosophy, something explicitly reaffirmed in *Fides et Ratio* (no. 49). Politics, as it were, is not one of the things revealed in Scripture, but it is not taken less seriously for all that. If, as we should, we are to know political things, we must largely rely on reason and experience, both of which can go wrong. It is necessary to read the philosophers and consult the constitutions, laws, and practices to know how peoples succeed and fail in political history. No doubt, certain scriptural passages and teachings can and should have political meaning. Christians were supposed to live in this world, "quietly," if they could, as "sojourners and wayfarers" (1 Peter, 2:11). But perforce, they could never quite be completely passive. They were commanded to do too many things that related to others.

The fact that Scripture does not contain a systematic political teaching modeled on *The Republic* of Plato or *The Politics* of Aristotle—or even on Hobbes or Locke or Rousseau, who in fact spend a good deal of time on Scripture—does not imply that something is lacking in revelation. Not a few good books in political affairs, both ancient and modern, no doubt, have been written by Roman Catholics—perhaps the most pertinent these days is de Tocqueville's *Democracy in America*. But Scripture's, especially the New Testament's, lack of treatment of political affairs rather indicates that much is to be learned from Plato and Aristotle, from the philosophers ancient and modern, even for the sake of Scripture. The lack of attention to politics in Scripture implies that politics is, for the most part, adequate unto itself, unless perhaps politics claims something more than it is in itself or unless the personal lives of citizens in any given polity fall into moral chaos.

Christ says to Pilate, "you would have no authority over me at all were it not given to you by my Father" (John, 19:11) That is, to draw an indirect principle, the Roman governor has authority, but neither he nor his polity invented what authority is. Its discovery and definition may be something reason could, and more importantly, should figure out by itself. Not everything, in other words, was necessary to be revealed. Human reality had the relative autonomy of its own finite being. But what was revealed had the indirect effect of freeing politics from the burden of answering certain higher questions that cannot be answered by politics, even though it is tempted to do so. To burden politics with responsibility for answering questions that are more than political is a sure way to corrupt politics itself.

The first step in politics is to think of its form, that is, of its limits, of what makes it to be politics and not something else. A politics that conceives itself to have no limits is the main rival to revelation in any age, including our own, a view, ironically, already found in Scripture itself.[30] Politics is the highest practical science, not the highest science as such, as Aristotle also noted (1141a20–22). When it claims to be the highest science, as it often does, it strives in effect to take the place of both reason and revelation, to become itself a metaphysics defining by itself a will-based "what is."

Early Christians first met politics when politicians wanted to get rid of them as being threats to the state, as they thought. They were even, as Augustine recounted at the beginning of the City of God, accused of being the cause for the decline of Rome—a perennial theme that later became famous with Gibbon and Nietzsche. The Augustinian answer to Rome, interestingly enough, was not to deny in principle legitimate political authority to Rome. Rather it was to point out, in the very name of its greatest minds, Varro and Cicero, that Rome itself did not observe its own philosophic standards which themselves were quite valid. It does not take revelation to identify and observe moral and political corruption. Revelation, in other words, said to political reason that it was not reasonable enough.

V

Fides et Ratio barely speaks of what would ordinarily be called political things. It speaks of philosophical things, of what is revealed, of how and why there is a relation between the one and other. Theology, in the Christian sense, does not begin with, but presupposes, reason directed to reality, to what is. It begins with what is revealed. However, it soon discovers that to understand and render in intelligible order what is revealed, it needs to turn to issues of human knowing, human experience, to philosophy. "The chief purpose of theology is to provide an understanding of revelation and the content of faith" (no. 93). What is characteristic of Roman Catholicism is this "understanding," this effort to make clear and available to the human mind as such, in a coherent whole, what is revealed in the myriads of narratives in Scripture. Likewise, it endeavors to relate this knowledge to what we know by our experience and reason, among which latter are political things. It does not see this elaboration as a violation of the explicit words of Scripture, which it must respect as given. It sees it as an obligation to illumine the intelligibility that is found there. And this endeavor does not imply that God was rather sloppy in not revealing Himself in a concise form that would not require, over the centuries and even today, much human theological and rational effort.

Rather, what Catholicism suggests is that we are intended to use our minds even in revelation, or more exactly, we are to use them better because of revelation. It implicitly grants the possibility of a human historical order in which revelation never happened, even though such an order is not the actual one in which we live. In using mind to reflect on revealed things, the mind itself becomes more mind. "The Word of God is addressed to all people, in every age and in every part of the world; and the human being is by nature a philosopher" (no. 64). Not only is this sentence a delicate statement about the universality and equality of all men, but it is even more an affirmation of the primacy of Chesterton's "common man," of the fact that everyone can know basic truths. This position that "the human being is by nature a philosopher," but not a philosophic relativist, is the true basis of Catholicism's advocacy of "democracy" as a good regime. This preference is not a denial of the worth of excellence and talent, which are also recognized as worthy. But it is a deep-seated Christian and Catholic sentiment that each person does have the faculties and insights to enable him consciously to know his own meaning and destiny. The doctrines of eternal life, sin, resurrection of the body, and beatific vision, among others, have about them a definite communal flavor, that is, at the same time, anticollectivist.

Strauss, among others, often stresses that philosophy is a "knowledge of the whole," a knowledge rooted in the capacity of human reason. This same reason cannot arbitrarily exclude what is understandable and claims intelligible content, particularly when revelation itself has turned to philosophy precisely to explain more fully what is revealed.[31] "It is necessary therefore that the mind of the believer acquire a natural, consistent and true knowledge of created realities—the world and man himself—which are also the object of divine revelation," John Paul II writes. "Still more, reason must be able to articulate this knowledge in concept and argument. Speculative dog-

matic theology thus presupposes and implies a philosophy of the human being, the world and, more radically, of being, which has objective truth as its
foundation" (no. 66).

The point here is not that the nonbeliever, presumably closed off from this
revelational knowledge, must live only in philosophy and therefore be un-
concerned about these revelational questions. Rather, it is to maintain that
even the nonbeliever, genuinely aware of unanswered questions he shares
with others, including believers, can appreciate that revelational arguments
and positions can be seen as responses to genuine philosophic questions and
enigmas. Even though such revelational responses be rejected, it cannot be
denied in some uncanny sense that they do present answers to philosophic
questions as asked. The pope has taken great pains in this encyclical fairly to
present the case of various other religions and philosophies, even those most
hostile to his enterprise. It is on philosophic, not revelational, grounds that
he invites reciprocity and mutual respect.

Roman Catholic political philosophy, thus, does not think, whatever the
distinction of faith and reason, that the subjects of political life and those
who receive revelation live in different physical or political worlds. The
"knowledge of the created universe" is also "the object of divine revelation."
We must take the knowledge of the whole seriously. "It may well be," Josef
Pieper has remarked, with some irony, "that at the end of history the only
people who will examine and ponder the root of all things and the meaning
of existence, e.g. the specific object of philosophical speculation—will be
those who see with the eyes of faith."[32] It is not insignificant in the twenty-
first century that it is the pope, the "Philosopher-Pope," as the New York
Times called him when Fides et Ratio was published, who speaks of the legitimacy and necessity of philosophy, who speaks of its own condition, a condition that is, often, antiphilosophical. It is not, after all, the pope but the
Supreme Court, in the Casey decision, that embraces the antimetaphysical
position that each one's happiness and understanding of the universe is for
him to define for himself, a position that implicitly denies any human common good, indeed, any common world.

Contrary also to what we might expect, Fides et Ratio is not primarily concerned to relate philosophy to revelation, though it is quite frank about revelation's interest in and need of a sound philosophy. Its main purpose is to address itself to philosophy and its contemporary condition. Indeed, it argues
that it is in the strongest possible interest of revelation for its own integrity
that philosophy be itself. "It is an illusion to think that faith, tied to weak
reasoning, might be more penetrating; on the contrary, faith then runs the
grave risk of withering into myth or superstition. By the same token, reason

which is unrelated to an adult faith is not prompted to turn its gaze to the newness and radicality of being" (no. 48). "Weak reasoning" is not an ally of revelation. The pope is at equal pains both to reject a fideism that distrusts reason in the name of faith and to reject a skepticism or nihilism which, as it were, distrusts reason in the name of reason (nos. 52–55; 87–89)

Revelation thus does not hesitate to engage the philosophic mind and examine its own proposed validity. This might annoy philosophers who want to claim the exclusive turf of reason for themselves. But they cannot maintain this position if the object of the mind is not the mind itself but *what is, all that is*. Philosophy cannot pretend or prove that revelation does not exist and exist as something also directed at itself. Catholicism takes the condition of the philosophic mind seriously because it sees clearly that its own truths depend for their integrity on the validity of a philosophy that can know, and know *what is*. That is, revelation defends both the mind's own introspective powers and the fact that those powers do not simply turn on themselves. They reach the world, reality. They can speak or judge the truth of things.

John Paul II sees the necessity to clear the air, filled as it with the predominance of what might be called "tolerance theory," which tolerates everything but efforts to state the truth (no. 92). The notion that tolerance is the first principle of political philosophy and not a practical principle for setting the ground rules for engagement in the highest things is itself a product of philosophic modernity. This "dogmatic tolerance," for fear of "fanaticism," must deny, it is said, the possibility of "universally valid truth." In other words, the very claim of a "universally valid truth" is said to be "fanatic," and thus not worthy of serious examination. This position is itself the product of philosophy that must be examined for its philosophical integrity. It takes no genius to comprehend that if the principle of "dogmatic tolerance" is true, it is, by its own definition, false.

The pope draws out the consequence of this contradiction, namely, that it is itself intolerant to refuse to examine a philosophy or doctrine that claims to be true on the sole ground that it does claim to be true. Moreover, there are conditions in which this examination can and should take place—in "sincere and authentic dialogue between persons"—that is, in circumstances the very opposite of fanaticism or intolerance. This is something already found in Plato, of course. That widespread discussion of reason and revelation is not taking place, on the grounds that revelation has nothing to talk about or no opening to reason, is already, as it seems to many, a sign of unacknowledged "fanaticism." The truth condition of the contemporary polity is itself the result of ideas proceeding from the "lowering of the sights" of virtue (Machiavelli) on which much of modernity was originally built. The political order is already shot through with dubious philosophical underpinnings.

Clearly, classical political philosophy pointed to and in a sense brought human beings to friendship which itself depended on "the sincere and authentic dialogue among persons." Roman Catholic political philosophy cannot be unaware that the link between reason and revelation is most graphically attested to by St. Thomas's use of *amicitia* as the natural analogate for *caritas* (II–II, 23, 1). That is to say, tolerance at its best is a condition of manners and friendliness that enables the highest things to exist in conversation.

VI

John Paul II does not use the expression "Roman Catholic political philosophy." He does speak of "Christian philosophy," which is a reference to earlier discussions in neo-Thomism (no. 76). In this sense, he does not ask about the relation to philosophy of the various Christian denominations such as Luther's famous hostility to Aristotle. Christian philosophy refers to the fact that the content of revelation does address itself to truth and philosophy. It is clear that not every philosophy can sustain the realism that Christian theology requires if it is to defend the reality of its content. Moreover, certain questions, such as the dignity of the person, the meaning of evil, or the significance of history, have come to the fore through the influence of revelation. Once posed, these philosophic questions remain active in philosophy itself.

This is how the famous and much-discussed notion of a "Christian philosophy" appears in *Fides et Ratio*:

> Christian philosophy therefore has two aspects. The first is subjective, in the sense that faith purifies reason. As a theological virtue, faith liberates reason from presumption, the typical temptation of the philosopher. . . . The philosopher who learns humility will also find courage to tackle questions which are difficult to resolve if the data of revelation are ignored—for example, the problem of evil and suffering, the personal nature of God and the question of the meaning of life, or more directly, the radical metaphysical question, Why is there something rather than nothing. (no. 76)

It is worth remarking here that these "metaphysical questions" that are asked here and are often repeated by John Paul II, are similar to the ones that Eric Voegelin employs in his efforts to ground philosophy in being.

"The quest for the ground . . . is a constant in all civilizations," Voegelin likewise observed: "The first question is, 'Why is there something; why not nothing?' and the second is, 'Why is that something as it is, and not different?' (If you translate those into conventional philosophical vocabulary, the first question, 'Why is there something; why not nothing?' becomes the great question of *existence*; and 'Why is it as it is and not different?' becomes the question of *essence*.")[33] These metaphysical questions that John Paul II and Voegelin ask are the very ones that first establish the grounding of philosophy and the questions that it must ask of *what is*. The fact that there are both metaphysical and revelational answers to these questions, however complete or incomplete, itself prevents political philosophy from claiming an autonomy it does not possess. When the politician's will decides also the content of the metaphysical questions, political philosophy, in justifying such an aberration, itself claims to be its own metaphysics.

The second understanding of "Christian philosophy," John Paul remarks, is "objective" because it concerns "content." What is meant here?

> Revelation clearly proposes certain truths which might never have been discovered by reason unaided, although they are not of themselves inaccessible in reason. Among these truths is the notion of a free and personal God who is the Creator of the world, a truth which has been so crucial for the development of philosophical thinking, especially the philosophy of being. There is the reality of sin, as it appears in the light of faith, which helps to shape an adequate philosophical formulation of the problem of evil. The notion of the person as a spiritual being is another of faith's specific contributions: The Christian proclamation of human dignity, equality, and freedom has undoubtedly influenced modern philosophical thought. In more recent times, there has been the discovery that history as an event—so crucial to Christian revelation—is important for philosophy as well. (no. 76)

Notice that these ideas, or many of them, are, in the pope's mind, indeed open to reason, but they were not in fact discovered by reason without the prior impetus of faith. This correlation or coincidence is itself a curious intellectual event of the first order. History, evil, equality, freedom, dignity—these are subjects of philosophy which are also addressed in revelation as if they were both investigating the same reality and the same notions on which it is based.

Strauss, in *Persecution and the Art of Writing*, moreover, had made an important point about the relation of Christianity to philosophy, something that made it distinct from the law emphasis of Islam and Judaism.

> For the Christian, the sacred doctrine is revealed theology; for the Jew and the Muslim, the sacred doctrine is, at least primarily, the legal interpretation of the Divine Law. The sacred doctrine in the latter sense has, to say the least, much less in common with philosophy than the sacred doctrine n the former sense.

It is ultimately for this reason that the status of philosophy was, as a matter of principle, much more precarious in Judaism and in Islam than in Christianity: in Christianity philosophy became an integral part of the officially recognized and even required training of the student of the sacred doctrine.[34]

In *Fides et Ratio*, John Paul II spends a considerable amount of time reaffirming the importance of philosophy to students of theology.

Interestingly enough, the pope's strongest words in criticism of the failure to study philosophy in the modern world are not directed at the professors but at theologians. "I cannot fail to note with surprise and displeasure that this lack of interest in the study of philosophy is shared by not a few theologians" (no. 60). He warns them that their own methods invariably contain philosophical suppositions which they ignore at their peril. Many of the aberrations in theology have arisen from precisely philosophical sources. "I wish to repeat clearly that the study of philosophy is fundamental and indispensable to the structure of theological studies and to the formation of candidates for the priesthood. It is not by chance that the curriculum of theological studies is preceded by a time of special study of philosophy" (no. 62). Strauss, in other words, had it right.

The most evident way that Catholicism might differ from Strauss's hesitation to say anything more than that theology could not disprove philosophy and philosophy could not disprove theology can be seen in the pope's effort to reunite the two "ways" through what is in effect the basic principle of metaphysics. "This truth which God reveals to us in Jesus Christ is not opposed to the truths which philosophy receives. On the contrary, the two modes of knowing lead to truth in all its fullness. The unity of truth is a fundamental premise of human reasoning, as the principle of non-contradiction makes clear" (no. 34). Granting the contingency and freedom of political and moral affairs, there is still an awareness that moral truth, of which political life is an aspect, is open in a coherent and noncontradictory way to both reason and revelation.

VII

Fides et Ratio is an explicit argument about why Roman Catholic understanding of itself needs philosophy. Reason and faith are everywhere directed at each other in such a way that they correct or better illuminate each other, without ceasing to be themselves. The biblical scholar who knows no philosophy is a dangerous man. The scientist who is unaware of the higher dimensions of philosophy locks himself into an autonomous ideology. The pope is particularly concerned with metaphysics, a concern that is of immense indirect importance to political philosophy.

> Here I do not mean to speak of metaphysics in the sense of a specific school or a particular historical current of thought. I want only to state that reality and truth do transcend the factual and the empirical, and to vindicate the human being's capacity to know this transcendent and metaphysical dimension in a way that is true and certain, albeit imperfect and analogical. In this sense, metaphysics should not be seen as an alternative to anthropology, since it is metaphysics which makes it possible to ground the concept of personal dignity in virtue of their spiritual nature. In a special way the person constitutes a privileged locus of the encounter with being, and hence with metaphysical inquiry. (no. 83)

Ever since his own philosophical studies long before coming to the papacy, Karol Wojtyla concentrated his attention on the central place of the person as the ground on which both nature and grace stand firm.[35] It is to the special dignity of the human person that political philosophy is particularly attuned.

In *Fides et Ratio*, John Paul II directly but briefly touches on contemporary political philosophy by noticing the changes in the meaning of "democracy," changes that tend to relativize the special dignity of the human person. Speaking of "pragmatism," John Paul writes,

> There is growing support for a concept of democracy which is not grounded upon any reference to unchanging values. Whether or not a line of action is admissible is decided by the vote of a parliamentary majority. The consequences of this are clear: In practice the great moral decisions of humanity are subordinated to decisions taken one after another by institutional agencies. Moreover, anthropology itself is severely compromised by a one-dimensional vison of the human being, a vision which excludes the great ethical dilemmas and the existential analyses of the meaning of suffering and sacrifice, of life and death. (no. 89)

This understanding of "democracy," the pope observes, does not arise so much from political philosophy as from certain epistemological and metaphysical aspects of modern philosophy itself. This understanding of democracy is itself, like historicism, a consequence, not a cause (no. 87). What is of particular interest in this passage is how this relativist theory about democracy is seen to deprive us of genuine philosophical questions that stand behind all political life, those of ethics, suffering, sacrifice, life, and death.

Strauss, to recall, in a solemn address, explained the importance of Jerusalem and Athens to *political* philosophy, the background in which all discussions about the relation of reason and revelation are set. "It is a great honor, and at the same time a challenge to accept a task of particular difficulty, to be asked to speak about political philosophy in Jerusalem," Strauss began.

> In this city, and in this land, the theme of political philosophy—"the city of righteousness, the faithful city"—has been taken more seriously than anywhere else on earth. Nowhere else has the longing for justice and the just city filled the purest hearts and the loftiest souls with such zeal as on this sacred soil. . . . The meaning of political philosophy and its meaningful character is evident today as it always has been since the time when political philosophy came to light in Athens.[36]

The theme of political philosophy—"the city of righteousness, the faithful city"—and its relation to the best regime in fact and in speech comes from revelation, yet Athens is present. No one in a Catholic tradition, of course, can read these lines without recalling Augustine and his location of "the City of God."

The pope has his own reflection on the relation of Jerusalem and Athens—perhaps a "Roman" view, to recall Pierre Manent's remark cited in the beginning of this chapter. John Paul II pointed out the difference of method between Eastern and Western theologians and philosophers. "Consider Tertullian's question," Wojtyla writes in a manner redolent of Strauss's "Jerusalem and Athens":

> "What does Athens have in common with Jerusalem? The academy with the Church?" This clearly indicates the critical consciousness with which Christian thinkers from the first confronted the problem of the relationship between faith and philosophy, viewing it comprehensively with both its positive aspects and its limitations. They were not naive thinkers. Precisely because they were intense in living faith's content they were able to teach the deepest forms of speculation. It is therefore minimalizing and mistaken to restrict their work simply to the transposition of the truths of faith into philosophical categories. They did much more. In fact they succeeded in disclosing completely all that remained implicit and preliminary in the thinking of the great philosophers of antiquity. As I have noted, theirs was the task of showing how reason, freed from external constraints, could find its way out of the blind alley of myth and open itself to te transcendent in a more appropriate way.[37] (no. 41)

Several things are worth remarking about John Paul II on "Jerusalem and Athens." First, faith was not an accident to, but an essential element in a consideration of the "deepest forms of speculation." Second, he not only includes Jerusalem and Athens but the academy and the Church. This calls to mind Voegelin's thesis that after Athens, the city of philosophers, betrayed philosophy in killing Socrates, philosophy fled to the Academy. It also touches Dawson's thesis that the ancient civic culture was kept alive in the monasteries.[38] 3) Third, the pope specifically relates revelational responses to the completion of philosophical, not theological, questions. What was implicit or uncertain was "completed." That is, reason and revelation were not seen to be at impossible loggerheads. The deepest forms of "speculation" could be pursued further. "Purified and rightly tuned, therefore, reason could rise to the higher planes of thought, providing a solid foundation for the perception of being, of the transcendent and of the absolute" (no. 41). The "perception of being" became the key metaphysical grounding that was needed to keep track of "the whole."

VIII

When I suggest, in conclusion, that *Fides et Ratio* grounds "Roman Catholic political philosophy," what I have in mind is that, in almost an uncanny way, it addresses the very theoretical problems that were urged by philosophers like Strauss and Voegelin. I am not suggesting, of course, that the Holy Father intended to take up their profound works in any specific way. But the similarity of concern and topic is striking and ought to be reflected on. Indeed, *Fides et Ratio* includes, as does Voegelin in particular, a relationship with the ancient religions, particularly Hinduism (no. 72). While classical Greek and Roman philosophy does hold a special place for both intrinsic and historical reasons, revelation is conceived to be addressed to all men, granted its historical dimensions. All men, naturally described as philosophers in *Fides et Ratio*, are capable of understanding revelation's essential core and the common sense philosophy that is implicit in it if its content can be made clearly.

The renewed consideration of philosophy is not a "political proposal" in the sense that it implies some particular political regime. But it is addressed to political philosophy in the sense that it seek the opportunity to present the highest things to be open for consideration within any polity, no matter what its configuration. As the history of martyrdom, among other things, shows, revelation is not absent from history's worst regimes. The essential argument is that in fact, a personal or human in-completeness exists in every historical polity. This "in-completedness" is rooted in the transcendent destiny of each human being who has a right and duty to know what is revealed and how it relates to his reason. This revelation can personally be rejected, of course, and modern ideology is, in many ways, the political form of this rejection. Insofar as ancient and modern religions also reject central points of revelation, they share in this ideological rejection.

The central events in political philosophy are the deaths of Socrates and Christ. In his *Crossing the Threshold of Faith*, John Paul II remarked that "Christ is not simply a wise man as was Socrates, whose free acceptance of death in the name of truth nevertheless has a similarity with the sacrifice of the Cross."[39] The question of political philosophy is how to prevent the politician from killing the philosopher. When Socrates' death comes up in *Fides et Ratio*, the pope remarks that "It is not insignificant that the death of Socrates gave philosophy one of its decisive orientations, no less decisive now than it was more than 2,000 years ago" (no. 26). The question of death can be avoided by neither "philosopher nor the ordinary person." What is at issue?

> The answer we give will determine whether or not we think it possible to attain universal and absolute truth; and this is a decisive moment of the search. Every truth—if it really is truth—presents itself as universal, even if it is not the whole truth. If something is true, then it must be true for all people and all times. Beyond this universality, however, people seek an absolute which might give to all their searchings a meaning and an answer—something ultimate which might serve as the ground of all things. In other words they seek a final explanation, a supreme value, which refers to nothing beyond itself and which puts an end to all questioning. (no. 27)

To such searching, political philosophy is surely related. It does not itself substitute for metaphysics or for revelation. But it does, as Strauss intimated, need to know enough about both to render the politician—hopefully better educated and better willed than Callicles who loved philosophy but only in his youth (485a)—sufficiently benign that the pursuit of the highest things, including the light given by revelation and our response to it, be a legitimate presence in any polity of our kind.

Notes

1. Ernest Fortin, "Faith and Reason in Contemporary Perspective," in *Classical Christianity and the Political Order: Reflections on the Theologico-Political Problem*, edited by J. Brian Benestad (Lanham, Md.: Rowman & Littlefield, 1996), 299.

2. John Paul II, "*Fides et Ratio: On the Relationship between Faith and Reason,*" *L'Osservatore Romano*, English edition, 14 October 1998, no. 76. Also in *The Pope Speaks* (no. 1, 1999).

3. Pierre Manent, *The City of Man*, translated by Marc A. LePain (Princeton, N.J.: Princeton University Press, 1998), 206.

4. "It is not sufficient for everyone to obey and to listen to the Divine message of the city of Righteousness, the faithful city. In order to propagate that message *among the heathen*, nay, in order to understand it as clearly and as fully as is humanly possible, one must also consider to what extent man could discern the outlines of that city if left to himself, to the proper exertion of his own powers." Leo Strauss, *The City and Man* (Chicago: University of Chicago Press, 1964), 1. (Italics added.)

5. "This also confirms the principle that grace does not destroy nature but perfects it." *Fides et Ratio* (no. 75).

6. Glenn Tinder, *The Political Meaning of Christianity: The Prophetic Stance* (San Francisco: HarperCollins, 1991); Reinhold Niebuhr, *Moral Man and Immoral Society* (New York: Charles Scribner's Sons, 1960); C. S. Lewis, *Mere Christianity* (London: Fontana, 1961); Nicholas Berdyaev, *The Destiny of Man*, translated by N. Duddington (New York: Harper, 1960); Alexander Solzhenitsyn, *Solzhenitsyn at Harvard*, edited by R. Berman (Washington, D.C.: Ethics and Public Policy Center, 1980), 3–22. See also on C. S. Lewis and politics, Josef Sobran, "Happy at Home," in *Single Issues* (New York: Human Life Press, 1983), 156–89.

7. See James V. Schall, *Reason, Revelation, and the Foundations of Political Philosophy* (Baton Rouge: Louisiana State University Press, 1987); *At the Limits of Political Philosophy* (Washington, D.C.: Catholic University of America Press, 1996).

8. See Ernest Fortin, "Rational Theologians and Irrational Philosophers: A Straussian Perspective," in *Classical Christianity and the Political Order*, 287–96; James Rhodes, "Christian Faith, Jesus the Christ, and History," in "Eric Voegelin's *The Ecumenic Age*—a Symposium," *The Political Science Reviewer* 27 (1998): 44–67; "Philosophy, Revelation, and Political Theory: Leo Strauss and Eric Voegelin," *The Journal of Politics*, 49 (1987): 1036–60; Oliver O'Donovan, "Behold the Lamb!" *Studies in Christian Ethics* 11 (1998): 91–110; Hadley Arkes, *First Things: An Inquiry into the First Principles of Morals and Justice* (Princeton, N.J.: Princeton University Press, 1986); Hadley Arkes, *Natural Right and the Right to Choose* (New York: Cambridge, 2002); Catherine Pickstock, *After Writing: On the Liturgical Consummation of Philosophy* (Oxford: Basil Blackwell, 1998); John Milbank and Catherine Pickstock, *Truth in Aquinas* (London: Routledge, 2001); Robert Song, *Christianity and Liberal Society* (Oxford: Clarendon, 1997); Henry Veatch: *Swimming against the Current in Contemporary Philosophy* (Washington, D.C.: Catholic University of America Press, 1990); Mortimer Adler, *The Difference of Man and the Difference It Makes* (New York: Holt, 1967).

9. See Robert Kraynak, *Christian Faith and Modern Democracy: God and Politics in the Fallen World* (Notre Dame, Ind.: University of Notre Dame Press, 2001); David Walsh, *The Third Millennium: Reflections on Faith and Reason* (Washington, D.C.:

Georgetown University Press, 1999); Daniel J. Mahoney, *DeGaulle: Statesmanship, Grandeur, and Modern Democracy* (Westport, Conn.: Praeger, 1996); Peter Augustine Lawler, *Aliens in America: The Strange Truth about Our Souls* (Wilmington, Del.: ISI Books, 2002); Patrick Buchanan, *The Decline of the West* (New York: St. Martin's Press, 2002); John Hittinger, *Liberty, Wisdom, and Grace* (Lanham, Md.: Lexington Books, 2002); Frederick Wilhelmsen, *Christianity and Political Philosophy* (Athens: University of Georgia Press, 1980); Aidan Nichols, *Christendom Awake: On Reenergizing the Church in Culture* (Grand Rapids, Mich.: Eerdmans, 1999); Thomas Molnar, *Politics and the State* (Chicago: Franciscan Herald, 1980); Susan Orr, *Jerusalem and Athens: Reason and Revelation in the Work of Leo Strauss* (Lanham, Md.: Rowman & Littlefield, 1995); *Shakespeare as a Political Thinker* (Durham, N.C.: Carolina Academic Press, 1981); Robert Royal, *The Virgin and the Dynamo: Use and Abuse of Religion in Environmental Debates* (Washington, D.C.: Ethics and Public Policy Center, 1999); Tracey Rowland, *Culture and the Thomist Tradition* (London: Routledge, 2003).

10. I am thinking of the works and teaching of scholars like Gerhart Niemeyer, Alasdair MacIntyre, E. B. F. Midgley, Heinrich Rommen, Charles N. R. McCoy, Francis Canavan, Ernest Fortin, John Hallowell, Charles de Koninck, Clifford Kossel, I. Th. Eschmann, Yves Simon, Jacques Maritain, Etienne Gilson, John Courtney Murray, Russell Kirk, Mary Nichols, Francis Slade, Francis Graham Wilson, Waldemar Gurian, Morehouse F. X. Millar, Jerome Kerwin, Josef Ratzinger, John Finnis, Josef Pieper, Charles Taylor, Germain Grisez, Henri de Lubac, Dietrich von Hildebrand, Robert Sokolowski, Hans Urs von Balthasar, G. K. Chesterton, Hilaire Belloc, Christopher Dawson, and a number of others.

11. See James V. Schall, *Liberation Theology* (San Francisco: Ignatius Press, 1982).

12. See E. F. Schumacher, *A Guide for the Perplexed* (New York: Harper Colophon, 1977), 27–39.

13. Leo Strauss, "On the Mutual Influence of Theology and Philosophy," in *Faith and Political Philosophy*, edited by P. Emberley and B. Cooper (University Park: Pennsylvania State University Press, 1993), 217–34.

14. See Robert Sokolowski, "The Method of Philosophy: Making Distinctions," *The Review of Metaphysics* 51 (March 1998): 515–32.

15. See Josef Pieper, *Problems of Faith in the Modern World*, translated by J. Van Heurch (Chicago: Franciscan Herald, 1985).

16. Josef Pieper, "Philosophy out of a Christian Existence," *Josef Pieper—an Anthology* (San Francisco: Ignatius Press, 1989), 165.

17. See Jacques Maritain, *The Range of Reason* (New York: Charles Scribner's Sons, 1952).

18. On the curious philosophic order in Genesis itself, see Leo Strauss, "On the Interpretation of Genesis," in Susan Orr, *Jerusalem and Athens: Reason and Revelation in the Works of Leo Strauss* (Lanham, Md.: Rowman & Littlefield, 1995), 209–26.

19. "The most striking feature of Christianity, as distinguished from the other great religions of the West, Judaism and Islam, is its almost complete indifference to questions of a properly political nature." Ernest L. Fortin, "Natural Law and Social

Justice," *Classical Christianity and the Political Order: Reflections on the Theologico-Political Problem*, edited by Brian Benestadt, Vol. II of *Ernest L. Fortin: Collected Essays* (Lanham, Md.: Rowman & Littlefield, 1996), 226.

20. The best explication of this philosophic reasonableness of political authority is still Yves Simon, *A General Theory of Authority* (Notre Dame, Ind.: University of Notre Dame Press, 1980), 31–49.

21. For a discussion of the term "flourish," see John Finnis, *Natural Law and Natural Rights* (Oxford: Clarendon, 1980), passim.

22. "Classical philosophy had failed, not because—by its stubborn refusal to take into account the all too deplorable human character of man's behavior—it makes unreasonable demands on human nature, but because it did not know and hence could not apply the proper remedy to man's congenital weakness." Ernest Fortin, "St. Augustine," in *History of Political Philosophy*, edited by Leo Strauss and Joseph Cropsey, 3rd ed. (Chicago: University of Chicago Press, 1987), 182.

23. See William Wallace, *The Modeling of Nature: Philosophy of Science and Philosophy of Nature in Synthesis* (Washington, D.C.: Catholic University of America Press, 1996).

24. Herbert A. Deane, *The Political and Social Ideas of St. Augustine* (New York: Columbia University Press, 1963), 5.

25. See Christopher Dawson, *Religion and the Rise of Western Culture* (Garden City, N.Y.: Doubleday Image, 1958).

26. "The rise of monasticism in the fourth century was no accident. It was rather an attempt to escape the Imperial problem, and to build an 'autonomous' Christian Society outside of the boundaries of the Empire, 'outside the camp.' On the other hand, the Church could not evade her responsibilities for the world, or surrender her missionary task. Indeed, the Church was concerned not only with individuals, but also with society, even with the whole of mankind." Georges Florovsky, "Empire and Desert: Antinomies of Christian History," *Cross Currents* 9 (summer 1959): 237.

27. See Charles N. R. McCoy, *The Structure of Political Thought* (New York: McGraw-Hill, 1963), 117–18.

28. See Paul Marshall, *Their Blood Cries Out* (Dallas: Word, 1997); Robert Royal, *The Catholic Martyrs of the Twentieth Century: A Comprehensive World History* (New York: Crossroad, 2000).

29. See *The Review of Metaphysics* 52 (September 1998): 221–48.

30. See Oscar Cullmann, *The State in the New Testament* (New York: Scribner's, 1956), 71–85; Heinrich Schlier, "The State in the New Testament," *The Relevance of the New Testament* (New York: Herder & Herder, 1968), 234–38.

31. "Philosophy, as a quest for wisdom, is quest for universal knowledge, of the whole." Leo Strauss, "What Is Political Philosophy?" *What Is Political Philosophy? and Other Essays* (Glencoe, Ill.: The Free Press, 1959), 11.

32. Josef Pieper, "The Possible Future of Philosophy," ibid, 184. Consider the following lines that conclude G. K. Chesterton's *Heretics*: "Everything will be denied. Everything will become a creed. It is a reasonable position to deny stones in the

street; it will be a religious dogma to assert them. It is a rational thesis that we are all in a dream; it will be a mystical sanity to say that we are all awake. Fires will be kindled to testify that two and two make four. Swords will be drawn to prove that leaves are green in the summer. We shall be left defending, not only the incredible virtues and sanities of human life, but something more incredible still, this huge impossible universe which stares us in the face. We shall fight for visible prodigies as if they were invisible. We shall look on the impossible grass and the skies with a strange courage. We shall be of those who have seen and yet have believed." (New York: John Lane [1905], 1914), 305.

33. R. Eric O'Connor, ed., *Conversations with Eric Voegelin*, edited by R. Eric O'-Connor (Montreal: Thomas More Institute, 1980), 2.

34. Leo Strauss, *Persecution and the Art of Writing* (Westport, Conn.: Greenwood, 1973), 19.

35. See John Paul II, *Person and Community: Selected Essays*, translated by T. Sandok (New York: Peter Lang, 1993).

36. Leo Strauss, *What Is Political Philosophy? and Other Studies*, 9–10.

37. Strauss's famous essay on "Jerusalem and Athens" can be found in Orr, *Jerusalem and Athens* 179–208. It is also in Leo Strauss, *Studies in Platonic Political Philosophy*, edited by T. Pangle (Chicago: University of Chicago Press, 1983), 147–73.

38. See Eric Voegelin, *Plato and Aristotle*, vol. 3, *Order and History* (Baton Rouge: Louisiana State University Press, 1957), 3–23; Dawson, *Rise of Western Culture*, 44–66.

39. John Paul II, *Crossing the Threshold of Hope*, edited by Vittorio Messori (New York: Knopf, 1994), 43.

~

Conclusion

(Socrates to Adeimantus) But I mean that to lie and to have lied in the soul about the things that are, and to be unlearned, and to have and to hold a lie there is what everyone would least accept; and that everyone hates a lie in that place most of all.

—Plato *The Republic*, 383b.

We want no lies in our souls about *the things that are*. To deceive oneself about the most important things is what we should least want in our own souls. "Surely no one wishes to lie about the most sovereign things," Socrates had just said to Adeimantus. This rhetorical question makes us suspect that some people do in fact lie to themselves in their own souls and we wonder why. Yet, in our souls we want the truth about *what is*, particularly about what causes us to stand outside of nothingness. We seek the truth of things from whatever sources that truth presents itself to our souls. We can, to be sure, distinguish reason and revelation. What we should not do, if we seek the truth in our own souls, is to reject a truth because we do not like or accept its source or the way it comes to us. The spirit of this book has, in this sense, been Socratic—the spirit that does not wish to have a lie on our souls about the highest things, the things *that are*.

To summarize these considerations of "Roman Catholic" or "Catholic Christian" political philosophy, let me cite Pascal who never, to put it mildly, liked the Order to which I belong: "The Jesuits have not made the truth uncertain, but they have made their own ungodliness certain. Contradiction has always been

177

permitted, in order to blind the wicked; for all that offends truth or love is evil.
This is the true principle" (no. 901).[1] One might hope, with some piety, that
these pages do not reveal one's "ungodliness," nor make the truth "uncertain."
Contradictions are permitted not merely to "blind the wicked," but, as intellectual tools, to guide us to *what is*. Pascal is right, of course, "all that offends truth
or love" is indeed "evil." Such is indeed the "true principle."

To conclude initially, it is useful briefly to recapitulate the principles on
which a sensible case for a "Roman Catholic Political Philosophy" might be
understood:

a) The New Testament is not a book in political science or philosophy.
   This means that Scripture itself, by its silence and selectivity on the
   topic, suggests that to understand political things, we must go to the
   philosophers and the men of experience. Yet, on this very basis, when
   Scripture does mention politics, it is good to pay careful attention to
   what is said. And both philosophy and Scripture, in the seminal cases
   of Socrates and Christ, tell us what can happen when philosophy and
   revelation meet the world of politics.

b) Political philosophy is not the description of the workings of actual
   polities, though it must be vividly aware of what goes on in them. It is
   the higher understanding of political things insofar as these things account for what pertains to and rises out of political living, insofar as political things are included in the explanation of man, *what he is*.

c) Political philosophy is also a dialogue between the politician and the
   philosopher to convince the politician to allow within the city the
   things of philosophy and the higher truths. Likewise, it is also the acute
   realization of the politician that sophists, intellectuals with their dubious philosophy, can undermine any existing city.

d) Revelation is itself a coherent body of understanding that is found in
   the Scriptures. Political theology is the description of how these documents treat of political things, insofar as they do directly or indirectly
   deal with them.

e) Roman Catholic political philosophy is the intellectual endeavor to inquire about the relation of political things and the things of revelation,
   to ask whether their relationship is plausible or contradictory. This relationship, insofar as it exists, takes the form of questions and answers
   that each presents to the other.

f) Political philosophy does not "necessarily" lead to revelation; nor does
   revelation necessarily clarify things of reason in the sense that the two
   sources are interchangeable. In principle, there is no necessary relation

of the two orders such that we can or must "deduce" revelation from political philosophy, or political philosophy from revelation. The fact is, however, that a relationship of intense curiosity exists between them precisely because the unanswered questions arising in political philosophy do meet the proposals that revelation makes to reason. These proposals would often seem merely "interesting" were there no unanswered questions in philosophy or political philosophy.

The freedom to reject revelation is inherent both in the fact of free will and in the fact that other possible answers might and do exist to the questions that political philosophy makes central. The fact of "other answers" requires that we examine their truth. Though not necessarily happily, revelation itself can live in any polity, even the worst. The history of martyrdom is testimony to this latter point, though not every martyrdom took place in the worst of regimes. Revelation's principal concern is the salvation of souls, in whatever polity, good, mediocre, or deviant. Man, the political animal, transcends politics without denying its importance even in his higher concerns.

Yet, indirectly, revelation has the effect of confirming or strengthening philosophy and political philosophy by providing answers that, when sorted out, make philosophy to be more philosophic and politics to be more "politic," each in its own order. Much of what is called political philosophy, especially modern political philosophy, though this would include the position of other religions also, consists in answering otherwise than Catholicism does the central questions that political philosophy inevitably raises about or within itself about what the rational being is "for."

Indeed, one of the main purposes of this book has been to make it known that there is a sensible position arising within and articulated by Catholicism regarding the valid questions of political philosophy. It is not necessary, at this level of analysis, to agree with or accept this response. What is not permitted in intellectual integrity is to deny that such a response exists or to maintain that it is not plausibly related to what political philosophy is. At a personal level, issues of grace, virtue, understanding, or integrity, issues that can deflect or obscure such answers as individual options, may remain. It is not the purpose here to deal with these issues. I accept the fact that, for a number of reasons, truth can be rejected, even when its validity is at least suspected. No one, lest of all the present writer, can in principle exclude himself from this latter danger. The factual, even widespread, acceptance or rejection of a position is not, as such, an argument against its truth or validity.

In this book, I have included two chapters, those on modernity and on pride, in order to identify the real alternatives to granting a coherent relation between revelation and political philosophy. I have suggested that political philosophy is, in a manner peculiar to modern times, at the cutting edge of the deepest questions about *what is*. Very often theology has, as Eric Voegelin noted, in spite of its own relation to philosophy, tended to imitate the political ideologies of the modern era. In part, this turn is, contrary to its own tradition, due to an inadequate philosophic training within Catholicism. But more likely it is due to a weakness of faith, the result of which over-emphasis, the things of this world are portrayed as a more plausible meaning of or justification for revelation than that to which revelation actually points.

Revelation does, as Aquinas held, have an indirect relation to politics. Those who live virtuous and Christian lives do advance any decent public order, even any distorted one. But the transcendent questions remain, even in the best regime, either in the regime in speech or in any existing regime. What limits politics to be politics is, ultimately, the adequate description of the highest things, of what is beyond politics. Without this description, as I have suggested, the perennial modern temptation is to itself create all its own forms and values, nothing presupposed to the human will conceived as autonomous freedom. While this alternative might sound like the epitome of "liberty," in fact it misses the point of the *what is* of human beings.

Obviously, I maintain that classical philosophy is still alive among us. Its so-called "rejection" does not satisfy, does not explain things, especially the things that have followed upon this very rejection. Nietzsche correctly saw the inability of modern thought to discover any real alternative. If we will begin to study political things, we will still begin with Thucydides, Plato, and Aristotle. And after we have seen where their heritage has led us, even to revelation, we will come back to them with new eyes.

In his essay on *King Lear*, in *Shakespeare's Politics*, Harry Jaffa wrote the following memorable lines:

> If there is a single philosophical doctrine which we may, without hesitation, ascribe to Shakespeare, it is that intellectual beauty is the condition of the existence of the beauty we apprehend with our senses. It would be an absurdity unworthy of his greatness to suppose that, though it was given to him to move us with the images of the senses, as it has perhaps been given to no other man to do, he was for this reason less concerned with intellectual beauty which was its cause. . . . The vividness of the sensual world presented to us by Shakespeare is a pallid thing compared to that other world which was his ultimate concern.[2]

This is Platonic, neo-Platonic, even Augustinian. It is Thomas Aquinas also. And yet, what is characteristic of Catholic philosophy takes its beginning from the Incarnation. Beauty, and there is beauty, as we see it, begins with incarnate beauty. The reflection of eternal beauty in the cities of men is, in part, the reason for their existence. This reflection of divine beauty is most vivid, however, in the life, face, and reality of man, the being that transcends the city by "what is best in him," as Strauss put it.[3]

But reflection of the divine beauty does not stop there, at simple transcendence. The conclusion of Catherine Pickstock's *After Writing: The Liturgical Consummation of Philosophy* is as follows:

> So while Plato intimates that the lover and the beloved will be together in eternity, there persists an element of sacrifice of the body for a greater spiritual gain. There is here no resurrection of the body, but instead a becoming "light and winged." The Eucharistic difference is therefore more radical. Since every Eucharist is an essential repetition of the incarnation . . . our attempt to "return" to our divine origin is not so much a journey towards God, as a journey toward God's entry into our body. . . . Thus, with Christianity, the optimum of meaningfulness and the optimum of living subjectively coincide *within* the world—with all its temporality, space, and embodiment. And whereas in Plato the body is ultimately left behind, in Christianity the spirit and the body are sacrificed together in order that the spirit and the body together might be received back again on the eschatological morning.[4]

These are solemn, indeed joyful words. John Paul II remarked that we are to know "the fulness of the truth" about ourselves. "Faith and reason are like two wings on which the human spirit rises to the contemplation of truth, and God has implanted in the human heart a desire to know the truth."[5]

That the lover and the beloved should be together in eternity is indeed something hinted at in Plato. That their friendship includes their bodies, that we would not want our friends, even in eternity, to be other sorts of beings than we are, is something we learn from Aristotle. Such is what we learn in the political and philosophical books. What we learn in the revelational books is that this is indeed the case. We find out that any religious, philosophical, or ideological alternative we might conceive, and many, many have indeed been conceived, is by no means as exalted, reasonable, or satisfying as the alternative presented in the revelational books. It was Augustine in the *Confessions* who, as a young man and still our most fervent guide, enthusiastically recounted reading the books of the Platonists to find there the "Word," but not "the Word made flesh" (VII, 9). The direction of our minds and experience is not to the perfect kingdoms of this world, nor to ourselves as purely spiritual beings

I have long been curious about the remark in Leo Strauss's discussion of Thomas Aquinas about the natural law wherein he argues that the "presumption" of revelation was placed into classical political philosophy and theoretical contemplation by Aquinas. It did not, it was said, arise within philosophy or politics itself.[6] Strauss implies, therefore, that the reason that he himself did not follow Aquinas was that this natural desire for revelation was artificially injected into philosophy by Aquinas on the basis of his understanding of revelation. The fact that Aristotle did not specifically "anticipate" revelation indicated to Strauss that Aristotle's system was open to nothing other than itself.

It is the thesis of this book that this understanding is not the proper reading of Aquinas. Aquinas did not "read" revelation into philosophy. Rather, he read philosophy as philosophy. The exigency toward or the unsettlement of the soul was not "caused" by first discovering revelation. It was already there. Revelation itself discovered philosophic questions that already existed. Though it had "answers" to propose, it did not implant the questions. The rejection of any coherent relation of reason and revelation is more of a reluctance to see the relationship and where it goes than it is a necessary conclusion from the realities of philosophy and revelation each taken in themselves.

This conclusion, finally, brings us back to Plato. The sacrifice of the body, the lack of resurrection in Plato—together with Aristotle's uncanny insistence on the fact that human reality includes both body and soul—recalls the notion that beauty is not to be understood only as "spiritual." It is, after all, this same Plato who tells us in The Laws, that we should spend our lives "singing, dancing, and sacrificing" (803e). These are not the actions of bodiless beings. Finally, it seems quite clear that the end of politics, that to which it points, to being itself, is contemplation, while the end of contemplation is what is for its own sake.

What the human race lacks is not so much the "best regime," but rather it lacks the proper way not just to know the truth but a way to respond to it once it is known. The proper way to worship God is not some way that we create ourselves. It is something given to us, something that involves the sacrifice of the body to reunite body and soul in the singing and dancing. We cannot help but wonder whether, perhaps, it is true, even on philosophical grounds, that political things point to philosophy and both point to transcendence. Revelation, for its part, points to the rational creature that is, the being that "desires to know the truth," the being that seeks, once encountered, to respond, as he is, body and soul, to the truth, to what is.

Notes

1. Blaise Pascal, Pensées, translated by W. F. Trotter (New York: Modern Library, 1941), 315.

2. Harry Jaffa, "The Limits of Politics," in Allan Bloom and Harry Jaffa, *Shakespeare's Politics* (Chicago: University of Chicago Press, 1964), 137.

3. Leo Strauss, *The City and Man* (Chicago: University of Chicago Press, 1964), 49.

4. Catherine Pickstock, *After Writing: On the Liturgical Consummation of Philosophy* (Oxford: Blackwell, 1998), 273. See also Josef Pieper, *In Search of the Sacred* (San Francisco: Ignatius Press, 1991); Aidan Nicholas, *Looking at the Liturgy: A Critical View of Its Contemporary Form* (San Francisco: Ignatius Press, 1996); Robert Sokolowski, *Eucharistic Presence: A Study in the Theology of Disclosure* (Washington, D.C.: Catholic University of America Press, 1995); Dietrich von Hildbrand, *Liturgy and Personality* (Manchester, N.H.: Sophia Institute Press, 1992); Joseph Cardinal Ratzinger, *The Spirit of the Liturgy* (San Francisco: Ignatius Press, 2000).

5. John Paul II, "*Fides et Ratio:* On the Relation between Faith and Reason," September 14, 1998, *The Pope Speaks* 44 no. 1, (1999): 1.

6. Leo Strauss, *Natural Right and History* (Chicago: University of Chicago Press, 1950), 163–64.

~

Thirty-Three Summary
and Concluding Maxims, Principles,
and Aphorisms Concerning
Roman Catholic Political Philosophy

1) "Could Socrates have been a corrupter of youth after all? And have deserved his hemlock?—But the struggle against Plato, or to express it more plainly and 'for the people,' the struggle against the Christian-ecclesiastical pressure of millennia—for Christianity is Platonism for 'the people'—has created in Europe a magnificent tension of the spirit such as never existed on earth before"[1] (Nietzsche).
2) "Whoever does not appreciate the fact that Catholic political philosophy lives in the cosmos—this is its true meaning—of Catholic Christian life, will easily come to strange conclusions" (Rommen).
3) "And many have imagined republics and principalities that have never been seen or known to be in truth; because there is such a distance between how one lives and how one should live that he who lets go that which is done for that which ought to be done learns his ruin rather than his preservation" (Machiavelli).
4) "To do wrong is in every sense bad and dishonorable for the person who does it" (Socrates).
5) "Many would go so far as to hold that statesmen have got to do things that virtuous persons hate to do, so that power should better be in the hands of men not too particular about the morality of their means. This goes directly against the doctrine of the Greek philosophers who founded political science and philosophy" (Simon).
6) "Render to Caesar the things that are Caesar's and to God the things that are God's" (The Gospel of Matthew).

7) "Man transcends the city only by pursuing true happiness, not by pursuing happiness however understood"[2] (Strauss).

8) "The activity of making distinctions always has something contemplative about it" (Sokolowski).

9) "Everyone hates a lie in that place (the soul) most of all" (Plato).

10) "The experiences of reason and spirit agree in the point that man experiences himself as a being who does not exist from himself" (Voegelin).

11) *"Nulla est homini causa philosophandi, nisi ut beatus sit."* (Augustine).

12) "Man is not made for justice from his fellows, but for love, which is greater than justice and, by including, supercedes justice" (MacDonald).

13) "All that offends truth or love is evil. This is a true principle" (Pascal).

14) "The vividness of the sensual world presented to us by Shakespeare is a pallid thing compared to that other world which was his primary concern" (Bloom).

15) "We never understand more than half of the things when we neglect the science of Rome" (Manent).

16) "I don't think you should write something as long as a novel around anything that is not of the gravest concern to you and everybody else and for me this is always the conflict between an attraction for the Holy and the disbelief in it that we breathe in with the air of our times" (O'Connor).

17) "It is requisite for the good of the human community that there should be persons who devote themselves to the life of contemplation" (Pieper).

18) "It is not possible to motivate people to do the right thing and avoid the wrong thing, unless people are told, from childhood on, what the right things and the wrong things are" (Kristol).

19) "There are things and I know them" (Gilson).

20) "I read there (in the Platonists) that God the Word was born not of flesh, not of blood, nor of the will of man, nor of the will of the flesh, but of God. But there I did not read that 'the Word was made flesh, and dwelt amongst us'" (Augustine).

21) "It will be observed, that Johnson at all times made the just distinction between doctrine *contrary* to reason, and doctrine *above* reason" (Boswell).

22) *"Homo non proprie humanus sed superhumanus est"* (Aquinas).

23) "And whereas in Plato the body is ultimately left behind, in Christianity the body and spirit are sacrificed together in order that the spirit and body together might be received back again together on the eschatological morning" (Pickstock).

24) "I forgot where the Church is" (Charlie Brown).
25) "God has implanted in the human heart a desire to know the truth" (John Paul II).
26) "Therefore this science (metaphysics) is not a human possession. . . . Yet that very small part of it which he does have outweighs all the things known through the other sciences" (Aquinas).
27) "The Deity is the truly active source from which something happens to man" (Pieper).
28) "It is better to tell a man not to steal than to tell him the thousands of things he can do without stealing" (Chesterton).
29) *"Non est igitur in potestate mundana summum hominis bonum"* (Aquinas).
30) "If man were the highest being, politics would be the highest science" (Aristotle).
31) "A man should spend his whole life at 'play'—sacrificing, singing, dancing—so that he can win the favor of the gods" (Plato).
32) "What impressed (Russian diplomatic) onlookers about the (Byzantine) liturgy was precisely its utter lack of an ulterior purpose" (Ratzinger).
33) *Eo magis Christianus, quo magis philosophus.*

Notes

1. Friedrich Nietzsche, *Beyond Good and Evil* (Harmondsworth: Penguin [1885], 1976), preface, 14.

2. Leo Strauss, *The City and Man* (Chicago: University of Chicago Press, 1964), 49.

Bibliography

Acton, Lord. "Review of Sir Erskine May's *Democracy in Europe*" (1878). In Rufus Fears, ed. *Essays in the History of Liberty: Selected Essays of Lord Acton.* 3 vols. Indianapolis: Liberty Classics, 1985.

Adler, Mortimer. *The Difference of Man and the Difference It Makes.* New York: Holt, 1967.

———. *Ten Philosophic Mistakes.* New York: Macmillan, 1985.

Alvis, John, and Thomas G. West. *Shakespeare's as a Political Thinker.* Durham, N.C.: Carolina Academic Press, 1981.

Arendt, Hannah. *The Human Condition.* Garden City, N.Y.: Doubleday Anchor, 1959.

Aristotle. *The Basic Works of Aristotle.* Edited by R. McKeon. New York: Random House, 1941.

Arkes, Hadley. *Beyond the Constitution.* Princeton, N.J.: Princeton University Press, 1990.

———. *First Things: An Inquiry into the First Principles of Morality and Justice.* Princeton, N.J.: Princeton University Press, 1986.

———. *Natural Rights and the Right to Choose.* New York: Cambridge University Press, 2002.

Aron, Raymond. *The Opium of the Intellectuals.* Translated by T. Kilmartin. New York: Norton, 1961.

Augustine. *Basic Writings of St. Augustine.* 2 vols. Edited by W. Oates. New York: Random House, 1948.

Baumgarth, William P., and R. Regan, Editors. *St. Thomas Aquinas: On Law, Morality, and Politics.* Indianapolis: Hackett, 1988.

Behe, Michael J. *Darwin's Black Box: The Biochemical Challenge to Evolution*. New York: Simon & Schuster, 1996.

Berdyaev, Nicolas. *The Destiny of Man*. New York: Harper Torchbooks, 1960.

Bishirjian, Richard. *The Development of Political Theory: A Critical Analysis*. Dallas: The Society for the Study of Traditional Christian Culture, 1978.

Blamires, Harry. *The Christian Mind*. Ann Arbor, Mich.: Servant, 1963.

Bloom, Allan, and Harry Jaffa. *Shakespeare's Politics*. Chicago: University of Chicago Press, 1964.

Bochenski, J. M. *Philosophy—an Introduction*. New York: Harper Torchbooks, 1972.

Boswell, James. *Boswell's Life of Johnson*. 2 vols. London: Oxford, 1931.

Browning, Robert. *Poems of Robert Browning*. Edited by D. Smalley. Boston: Houghton Mifflin, 1956.

Buchanan, Patrick J. *The Death of the West*. New York: St. Martin's Press, 2002.

Budziszewski, J. *The Revenge of Conscience: Politics and the Fall of Man*. Dallas: Spence, 1999.

———. *Written on the Heart: The Case for Natural Law*. Downers Grove, Ill.: Inter-Varsity Press, 1997.

Butterfield, Herbert. *Christianity and History*. London: Collins/Fontana, 1957.

Caponigri, Robert, ed. *Modern Catholic Thinkers: The Church and the Political Order*. Vol. 2. New York: Harper Torchbooks, 1960.

Catechism of the Catholic Church. Vatican City: Libreria Editrice Vaticana, 1994.

Charles, Rodger. *The Social Teaching of Vatican II*. San Francisco: Ignatius Press, 1982.

Chenu, M. Dominique. *The Scope of the Summa*. Washington, D.C.: The Thomist Press, 1958.

Chesterton, G. K. *Heretics*. New York: John Lane [1905], 1914.

———. "Negative and Positive Morality." *The Illustrated London News*, January 3, 1920. In *Collected Works*. Vol. 32, 17–20. San Francisco: Ignatius Press, 1989.

———. *Orthodoxy*. Garden City, N.Y.: Doubleday Image [1908], 1959.

———. *St. Thomas Aquinas*. In *Collected Works*, Vol 3. San Francisco: Ignatius Press, 1986.

———. *What's Wrong with the World*. San Francisco: Ignatius Press [1910], 1994.

Cullmann, Oscar. *The State in the New Testament*. New York: Scribner's, 1956.

Davies, Brian. *The Thought of Thomas Aquinas*. Oxford: Clarendon, 1992.

Dawson, Christopher. *Beyond Politics*. London: Sheed & Ward, 1939.

———. *Enquiries into Religion and Culture*. New York: Sheed & Ward, 1933.

———. *The Historic Reality of Christian Culture*. New York: Harper Torchbooks, 1960.

———. *The Judgment of the Nations*. New York: Sheed & Ward, 1942.

———. *The Movements of World Revolution*. New York: Sheed & Ward, 1959.

———. *Religion and the Rise of Western Culture*. Garden City, N.Y.: Doubleday Anchor, 1958.

Deane, Herbert. *The Political and Social Ideas of St. Augustine*. New York: Columbia University Press, 1963.

de Koninck, Charles. "*On the Primacy of the Common Good*," (1–70). "*The Principles of the New Order*, (71–132). I. Th. Eschmann. "*In Defense of Jacques Maritain*" (133–70). De Koninck, Charles. "*In Defense of St. Thomas*" (171–349). In *The Aquinas Review* 4, no. 1 (1997).

de Lubac, Henri. *A Brief Catechesis on Nature & Grace*. Translated by R. Arnandez. San Francisco: Ignatius Press, 1984.

———. *The Drama of Atheist Humanism*. Translated by E. Riley. Cleveland: Meridian [1950], 1963.

———. *The Christian Faith*. Translated by R. Arnandez. San Francisco: Ignatius Press [1969], 1986.

Dennehy, Raymond. "The Ontological Basis of Human Rights." *The Thomist* 42 (July 1978): 434–63.

Denziger, Henrich. *Enchiridion Symbolorum*. Friburg: Herder, 1955.

Derrick, Christopher. *Escape from Scepticism: Liberal Education as If Truth Mattered*. LaSalle, Ill.: Sherwood Sugden, 1977.

de Unamuno, Miguel. *The Agony of Christianity*. Translated by K. Reinhardt. New York: Ungar, 1960.

de Wulf, Maurice. *Philosophy and Civilization in the Middle Ages*. New York: Dover, 1953.

Documents of Vatican II. Edited by W. Abott. New York: Guild Press, 1966.

Dougherty, Jude P. *Western Creed, Western Identity: Essays in Legal and Social Philosophy*. Washington, D.C.: Catholic University of America Press, 2000.

Eliot, T. S. *Christianity and Culture: The Idea of a Christian Society and Notes towards a Definition of Culture*. New York: Harcourt, 1966.

Elshtain, Jean Bethke. *Augustine and the Limits of Politics*. Notre Dame, Ind.: University of Notre Dame Press, 1995.

Federici, Michael P. *Eric Voegelin: The Restoration of Order*. Wilmington, Del.: ISI Books, 2002.

Fendt, Gene, and David Rozema. *Plato's Errors: Plato, a Kind of Poet*. Westport, Conn.: Greenwood Press, 1998.

Finnis, John. *Aquinas: Moral, Political, and Legal Theory*. Oxford: Oxford University Press, 1998.

———. *Natural Law and Natural Rights*. Oxford: Clarendon, 1980.

Florovsky, Georges, "Empire and Desert: Antinomies of Christian History." *Cross Currents* 9 (summer 1959): 233–53.

Fortin, Ernest. *Collected Essays*. Vol. 1. *The Birth of Philosophic Christianity: Studies in Early Christian and Medieval Thought*. Vol. 2. *Classical Christianity and the Political Order: Reflections on the Theological-Political Problem*. Vol. 3. *Human Rights, Virtue, and the Common Good: Untimely Meditations on Religion and Politics*. Edited by B. Benestad. Lanham, Md.: Roman & Littlefield, 1996.

———. *Political Idealism and Christianity in the Thought of St. Augustine*. Villanova, Penn.: Villanova University Press, 1972.

———. "St. Thomas Aquinas." In Leo Strauss and Joseph Cropsey, editors, 248–75. *History of Political Philosophy*. 3rd Edition; Chicago: University of Chicago Press, 1987.

Fukyama, Francis. *The End of History and the Last Man.* New York: The Free Press, 1992.

Gadamer, Hans-Georg. "Aristotle and the Ethic of Imperatives." In R. Bartlett and S. Collins, eds. *Action and Contemplation.* Albany: State University of New York Press, 1999.

George, Robert P. *In Defense of Natural Law.* Oxford: Oxford University Press, 1999.

Gilby, Thomas. *Between Community and Society: A Philosophy and Theology of the State.* London: Longmans, 1953.

Gilson, Étienne. *A Gilson Reader.* Edited by Anton Pegis. Garden City, N.Y.: Doubleday Image, 1957.

——. *Letters of Étienne Gilson to Henri de Lubac.* Translated by M. Hamilton. San Francisco: Ignatius Press, 1988.

——. *Reason and Revelation in the Middle Ages.* New York: Scribner's, 1938.

——. *The Spirit of Thomism.* New York: Kennedy, 1964.

——. *The Unity of Philosophical Experience.* San Francisco: Ignatius Press [1937], 1999.

Glendon, Mary Ann. *Rights Talk: The Impoverishment of Political Discourse.* New York: The Free Press, 1991.

Glynn, Patrick. *God: The Evidence: The Reconciliation of Faith and Reason in a Post-Secular World.* Rocklin, Calif.: Prima Publishers, 1997.

Goerner, E. A. *Peter and Caesar: Political Authority and the Catholic Church.* New York: Herder & Herder, 1965.

Grisez, Germain G. "The 'Four Meanings' of Christian Philosophy." *Journal of Religion* 42 (April 1962): 103–18.

Guardini, Romano. *The End of the Modern World.* Wilmington, Del.: ISI Books [1950], 1998.

Heckel, Roger. *General Aspects of the Social Catechesis of John Paul II: The Use of the Expression 'Social Doctrine' of the Church.* Vatican City: Pontifical Commission on Justice and Peace, 1980.

Hittinger, John P. *Liberty, Wisdom, and Grace: Thomism and Democratic Political Theory.* Lanham, Md.: Lexington Books, 2003.

Hittinger, Russell. *A Critique of the New Natural Law Theory.* Notre Dame, Ind.: University of Notre Dame Press, 1987.

——. *The First Grace: Rediscovering the Natural Law in a Post-Christian World.* Wilmington, Del.: ISI Books, 2003.

Hodgson, P. E. "The Freedom of Scientific Research." ΕΛΛΗΝΙΚΗ ΛΝΘΡΩΙΙΣ-ΤΙΚΗ ΕΤΑΙΙΙΕΙΑ

Huizinga, Johan. *Homo Ludens: A Study of the Play Element in Culture.* Boston: The Beacon Press, 1950.

Jaffa, Harry. "Leo Strauss, 1889-1973." *The Conditions of Freedom: Essays in Political Philosophy.* Baltimore: The Johns Hopkins University Press, 1975.

Jaki, Stanley. *The Absolute and the Relative and Other Essays.* Lanham, Md: University Press of America, 1988.

——. *Catholic Essays.* Front Royal, Va.: Christendom Press, 1990.

——. *Chance or Reality and Other Essays*. Lanham, Md.: University Press of America, 1984.

——. *The Gist of Catholicism and Other Essays*. Pinckney, Mich.: Real View Books, 2001.

——. *Jesus, Islam, Science*. Pinckney, Mich.: Real View Books, 2001.

——. *The Road of Science and the Ways to God*. Chicago: University of Chicago Press, 1978.

John Paul II (Karol Wojtyla). "Catechetics and the Defense of Life." *The Pope Speaks* 36 (January/February 1993): 51–57.

——. *Crossing the Threshold of Hope*. Edited by V. Messori. New York: Knopf, 1994.

——. "Ecclesia de Eucharistia." *L'Osservatore Romano*. English edition. April 23, 2003.

——. "The Gospel of Life (*Evangelium Vitae*)." *The Pope Speaks* 40, no. 4 (1995): 199–281.

——. "On Faith and Reason (*Fides et Ratio*)." *The Pope Speaks* 44, no. 1 (1999): 1–63.

——. *On the Hundredth Anniversary of Rerum Novarum* (*Centesimus Annus*). Boston: St. Paul Editions, 1991.

——. *Person and Community: Selected Essays*. Translated by T. Sandok. New York: Peter Lang, 1993.

——. *Towards a Philosophy of Praxis*. Edited by A. Bloch and G. Czuczka. New York: Crossroads, 1981.

——. *The Whole Truth about Man: John Paul II to University Faculties and Students*. Boston: St. Paul Editions, 1981.

Johnson, Paul. *The Intellectuals*. New York: Harper, 1988.

——. *Modern Times*. New York: Harper, 1985.

——. "Is Totalitarianism Dead?" *Crisis* 7 (February 1989): 9–17.

Jones, E. Michael. *Degenerate Moderns*. San Francisco: Ignatius Press, 1993.

Kass, Leon. *The Hungry Soul: Eating and the Perfection of Our Nature*. New York: The Free Press, 1994.

——. *Toward a More Natural Science: Biology and Human Affairs*. New York: The Free Press, 1985.

King, Ross. *Ex Libris, a Novel*. New York: Penguin, 1998.

Knox, Ronald. *Enthusiasm: A Chapter in the History of Religion*. Westminster, Md.: Christian Classics [1950], 1983.

Kossel, Clifford. "The Moral Views of Thomas Aquinas." In V. Ferm, ed. *Encyclopedia of Morals*, 11–22. New York: Philosophical Library, n. d.

Kraynak, Robert P. *Christian Faith and Modern Democracy: God and Politics in the Fallen World*. Notre Dame, Ind.: University of Notre Dame Press, 2001.

Kreeft, Peter. *Back to Virtue*. San Francisco: Ignatius Press, 1986.

——. *Christianity for Modern Pagans: Pascal's Pensées*. San Francisco: Ignatius Press, 1993.

——. *C. S. Lewis for the Third Millennium*. San Francisco: Ignatius Press, 1994.

Kristol, Irving. "The Coming Conservative Century." *Wall Street Journal*, February 1, 1993.

Langan, Thomas. *The Catholic Tradition*. Columbia: University of Missouri Press, 1998.

Lawler, Peter Augustine. *Aliens in America: The Strange Truth about Our Souls*. Wilmington, Del.: ISI Books, 2002.

Lerner, R., and M Mahdi. *Medieval Political Philosophy*. Ithaca, N.Y.: Cornell University Press, 1978.

Levinas, Emmanuel. *Of God Who Comes to Mind*. Translated by B. Bergo. Stanford, Calif.: Stanford University Press, 1998.

———. *Proper Names*. Translated by M. Smith. Stanford, Calif.: Stanford University Press, 1996.

Lewis, C. S. *The Abolition of Man*. New York: Collier, 1962.

———. *God in the Dock: Essays in Theology and Ethics*. Grand Rapids, Mich.: Eerdmans, 1970.

———. *Mere Christianity*. New York: Macmillan [1943], 1975.

———. *Miracles: How God Intervenes in Natural and Human Affairs*. New York: Macmillan, 1960.

———. *The Screwtape Letters*. New York: Macmillan, 1977.

———. *Till We Have Faces*. Grand Rapids, Mich.: Eerdmans [1956], 1970.

———. *The Weight of Glory and Other Addresses*. New York: Macmillan [1949], 1980.

Lord, Carens. *Education and Culture in the Political Thought of Aristotle*. Ithaca, N.Y.: Cornell University Press, 1982.

MacDonald, George. *George MacDonald—an Anthology*. Edited by C. S. Lewis. New York: Macmillan [1947], 1974.

MacIntyre, Alasdair. *After Virtue*. Notre Dame, Ind.: University of Notre Dame Press, 1981.

Machiavelli, Niccolò. *The Prince*. Translated by L. De Alvarez. Irving, Tex.: University of Dallas Press, 1980.

Mahoney, Daniel J. *Aleksandr Solzhenitsyn: The Ascent from Ideology*. Lanham, Md.: Rowman & Littlefield, 2002.

———. *De Gaulle: Statesmanship, Grandeur, and Modern Democracy*. Westport, Conn.: Praeger, 1996.

Manent, Pierre. *The City of Man*. Translated by M. LePain. Princeton, N.J.: Princeton University Press, 1998.

———. *Modern Liberty and Its Discontents*. Edited by D. Mahoney. Lanham, Md.: Rowman & Littlefield, 1998.

Marcel, Gabriel. *The Mystery of Being*. 2 vols. Translated by G. Fraser. Chicago: Gateway, 1950.

Maritain, Jacques. *Christianity and Democracy* [1943] and *The Rights of Man and Natural Law*. Translated by D. Anson [1942]. San Francisco: Ignatius Press, 1986.

———. *Integral Humanism: Temporal and Spiritual Problems of a New Christendom*. Translated by J. Evans. Notre Dame, Ind. : University of Notre Dame Press [1936], 1973.

———. *Man and the State*. Chicago: University of Chicago Press, 1951.

———. In W. Sweet, ed. *Natural Law: Reflections on Theory & Practice*. South Bend, Ind.: St. Augustine's Press, 2001.

———. *The Peasant of the Garonne: An Old Layman Questions Himself about the Present Time*. New York: Holt, 1968.

———. *The Range of Reason*. New York: Scribe's, 1952.

———. *Reflections on America*. New York: Scribner's, 1958.

———. "Relation of Philosophy to Theology." In H. Klocker, ed. *Thomism and Modern Thought*, 305–6. New York: Appleton-Century-Crofts, 1962.

———. *Scholasticism and Politics*. Garden City, N.Y.: Doubleday Image [1940], 1960.

———. *The Social and Political Philosophy of Jacques Maritain*. Edited by J. Evans and L. Ward. Notre Dame, Ind.: University of Notre Dame Press, 1976.

Marshall, Paul. *Their Blood Cries Out*. Dallas: Word, 1997.

Martin, Thomas S. "Eulogy for Richard Alan Wood." Epiphany Episcopal Church. Flagstaff, Arizona, June 19, 1999.

Mascall, E. L. *The Christian Universe*. London: Dalton, Longmans & Todd, 1966.

McCool, Gerald A. *From Unity to Pluralism: The Internal Evolution of Thomism*. New York: Fordham University Press, 1989.

McCoy, Charles N. R. *On the Intelligibility of Political Philosophy: Essays of Charles N. R. McCoy*. Edited by James V. Schall and John Schrems. Washington, D.C.: Catholic University of America Press, 1989.

———. "St. Augustine." In Leo Strauss and Joseph Cropsey, editors. *History of Political Philosophy*, 151–59. 1st ed. Chicago: Rand-McNally, 1963.

———. *The Structure of Political Thought*. New York: McGraw-Hill, 1963.

McInerny, Ralph. "John Paul II and Christian Philosophy." In K. Whitehead, ed. *John Paul II—Witness to Truth*, 113–25. South Bend, Ind.: St. Augustine's Press, 2001.

———. *St. Thomas Aquinas*. Notre Dame, Ind.: University of Notre Dame Press, 1977.

———. *Thomism in an Age of Renewal*. Notre Dame, Ind.: University of Notre Dame Press, 1966.

McIntire, C., ed. *Herbert Butterfield: Writings on Christianity & History*. New York: Oxford, 1979.

McLean, Edward B., ed. *Common Truths: New Perspectives on Natural Law*. Wilmington, Del.: ISI Books, 2000.

Midgley, E. B. F. "Concerning the Modernist Subversion of Political Philosophy." *New Scholasticism* 53 (spring 1979): 168–90.

———. *The Ideology of Max Weber: A Thomist Critique*. Aldershot, Hants.: Gower, 1983.

———. *The Natural Law Tradition and the Theory of International Relations*. London: Paul Elek, 1975.

———. "On 'Substitute Intelligences' in the Formation of Atheistic Ideology." *Laval théologique et philosophique* 36 (October 1980): 239–53.

Milbank, John, and Catherine Pickstock. *Truth in Aquinas*. London: Routledge, 2001.

Milbank, John, Catherine Pickstock, and Graham Ward, eds. *Radical Orthodoxy: A New Theology*. London: Routledge, 1999.

Molnar, Thomas. *Politics and the State: The Catholic View.* Chicago: Franciscan Herald, 1980.

———. *Twin Towers: Politics and the Sacred.* Grand Rapids, Mich.: Eerdmans, 1988.

Montgomery, Marion. *The Men I Have Chosen for Fathers: Literary and Philosophical Passages.* Columbia: University of Missouri Press, 1990.

Morse, Jennifer Roback. *Love & Economics.* Dallas: Spence, 2001.

Mucci, Giandominico. "Le Gnosi Moderna." *La Civiltà Cattolica* 143 (January 4, 1992): 14–22.

Muggeridge, Malcolm. *The End of Christendom.* Grand Rapids, Mich.: Eerdmans, 1980.

Muncy, Mitchell, ed. *The End of Democracy? Judicial Usurpation in Politics.* Dallas: Spence, 1997.

Newman, John Henry. *The Idea of a University.* Garden City, N.Y.: Doubleday Image, 1959.

Nichols, Aidan. *Christendom Awake: On Reenergizing the Church in Culture.* Grand Rapids, Mich.: Eerdmans, 1999.

———. *Looking at the Liturgy: A Critical View of Its Contemporary Form.* San Francisco: Ignatius Press, 1996.

Niebuhr, Reinhold. *Moral Man and Immoral Society: A Study in Ethics and Politics.* New York: Scribner's [1932], 1969.

Niemeyer, Gerhart. "A Symposium on Gerhart Niemeyer." *Political Science Reviewer* 31 (2002): 29–282.

Nietzsche, Friedrich. *Beyond Good and Evil: Prelude to a Philosophy of the Future.* Translated by R. Holllingdale. Harmondsworth: Penguin, 1973.

———. *Ecce Homo.* Translated by W. Kaufmann. New York: Vintage, 1969.

———. *Twilight of the Idols,* in *The Portable Nietzsche.* Translated by W. Kaufmann. Harmondsworth: Penguin, 1959.

O'Connor, Flannery. *Letters of Flannery O'Connor: The Habit of Being.* Edited by S. Fitzgerald. New York: Vintage, 1979.

O'Connor, R. Eric, ed. *Conversations with Eric Voegelin.* No. 76. Montreal: Thomas More Institute Papers, 1980.

O'Donovan, Oliver. "Behold the Lamb." *Studies in Christian Ethics* 11 (1998): 91–110.

One Hundred Years of Thomism. Edited by V. Brezik. Houston: Center for Thomistic Studies, 1981.

Orr, Susan. *Jerusalem and Athens: Reason and Revelation in the Work of Leo Strauss.* Lanham, Md.: Rowman & Littlefield, 1995.

Owens, Joseph. *Human Destiny: Some Problems in Catholic Philosophy.* Washington, D.C.: Catholic University of America Press, 1985.

Pangle, T. *The Rebirth of Classical Political Rationalism: An Introduction to the Thought of Leo Strauss.* Chicago: University of Chicago Press, 1989.

———. *Studies in Platonic Political Philosophy.* Chicago: University of Chicago Press, 1983.

Papini, Roberto. *The Christian Democrat International.* Translated by R. Royal. Lanham, Md.: Rowman & Littlefield, 1997.

Pascal, Blaise. *Pensées*. Translated by W. Trotter. New York: Modern Library, 1941.

Pickstock, Catherine. *After Writing: The Liturgical Consummation of Philosophy*. Oxford: Blackwell, 1998.

Pieper, Josef. *The Concept of Sin*. Translated by E. Oakes. South Bend, Ind.: St. Augustine's Press [1977], 2001.

——. *Enthusiasm and the Divine Madness: On the Platonic Dialogue Phaedrus*." Translated by R. Winston and C. Winston. New York: Harcourt, 1964.

——. *Faith, Hope, Love*. San Francisco: Ignatius Press [1986], 1997.

——. *Guide to Thomas Aquinas*. Translated by R. Winston and C. Winston. San Francisco: Ignatius Press [1962], 1991.

——. *Happiness and Contemplation*. Translated by R. Winston and C. Winston. New York: Pantheon, 1958.

——. *In Defense of Philosophy*. Translated by L. Krauth. San Francisco: Ignatius Press [1960], 1992.

——. *In Search of the Sacred*. Translated by L. Krauth. San Francisco: Ignatius Press [1988], 1991.

——. *In Tune with the World: A Theory of Festivity*. Chicago: Franciscan Herald, 1971.

——. *Josef Pieper—an Anthology*. San Francisco: Ignatius Press [1981], 1989.

——. *Leisure: The Basis of Culture*. New York: Mentor, 1952.

——. *Living the Truth (The Truth of All Things and Reality and the Good)*. San Francisco: Ignatius Press [1966], 1989.

——. *Problems of Modern Faith: Essays and Addresses*. Translated by J. Van Heurch. Chicago: Franciscan Herald [1974], 1984.

——. *Scholasticism: Personalities and Problems of Medieval Philosophy*. Translated by R. Winston and C. Winston. New York: McGraw-Hill, 1964.

——. *The Silence of St. Thomas*. Chicago: Gateway, 1957.

Plato. *Complete Works*. Edited by J. Cooper. Indianapolis: Hackett, 1997.

Purcell, Brendan M. *The Drama of Humanity: Toward a Philosophy of Humanity in History*. Frankfurt: Peter Lang, 1996.

Quinn, Dennis. *Iris Exiled: A Synoptic History of Wonder*. Lanham, Md.: University Press of America, 2002.

Ratzinger, Josef. *Introduction to Christianity*. Translated by J. Foster. New York: Herder & Herder, 1973.

——. "Ratzinger on the Eucharist." *Inside the Vatican*. January 1998.

——. *The Spirit of the Liturgy*. Translated by J. Saward. San Francisco: Ignatius Press, 2000.

Redpath, Peter. *Masquerade of the Dream Walkers: Prophetic Theology from the Cartesians to Hegel*. Atlanta: Rodopi, 1994.

——. *Wisdom's Odyssey: From Philosophy to Transcendental Sophistry*. Atlanta: Rodopi, 1997.

Reinhardt, Kurt F. *A Realistic Philosophy: The Perennial Principles of Thought and Action in a Changing World*. New York: Ungar, 1962.

Rhodes, James. "Christian Faith, Jesus Christ, and History." In "Eric Voegelin's *The Ecumenic Age—a Symposium.*" *Political Science Reviewer* 27 (1998): 44–67.

———. "Philosophy, Revelation, and Political Theory: Leo Strauss and Eric Voegelin." *The Journal of Politics* 49 (1987): 1036–60.

Rice, Charles. *Fifty Questions on the Natural Law.* San Francisco: Ignatius Press, 1993.

Rommen, Heinrich, A. *The Natural Law: A Study in Legal and Social History and Philosophy.* Translated by T. R. Hanley. Indianapolis: Liberty Fund [1936], 1998.

———. *The State in Catholic Thought: A Treatise in Political Philosophy.* St. Louis: B. Herder, 1945.

Rougemont, Denis de. *Love in the Western World.* Translated by M. Belgion. New York: Schocken [1940], 1983.

Rousseau, Jean-Jacques. *On the Social Contract.* Translated by D. Cress. Indianapolis: Hackett, 1983.

Rowland, Tracey. *Culture and the Thomist Tradition.* London: Routledge, 2003.

Royal, Robert. *The Catholic Martyrs of the Twentieth Century: A Comprehensive World History* New York: Crossroad, 2000.

———. *The Virgin and the Dynamo: Use and Abuse of Religion in the Environmental Debates.* Washington, D.C.: Ethics and Public Policy, 1999.

Ryn, Claes G. "Universality and History: The Concrete as Normative." *Humanitas* 6 (fall 1992/winter 1993).

Sandoz, Ellis. *The Politics of Truth and Other Untimely Essays: The Crisis of Civic Consciousness.* Columbia: University of Missouri Press, 1999.

San Tommaso d'Aquino: Doctor Humanitatis (Atti del IX Congresso Tomistica Internazionale). Rome: Libreria Editrice Vaticana, 1991.

Sayers, Dorothy, *The Whimsical Christian.* New York: Macmillan, 1978.

Schall, James V. "A Latitude for Statesmanship?: Strauss on St. Thomas." *Review of Politics* 53 (winter 1991): 126–47.

———. "A Meditation on Evil," *The Aquinas Review* 7, no. 1 (2000): 25–42.

———. "A Reflection n the Classical Tractate on Tyranny: The Problem of Democratic Tyranny." *American Journal of Jurisprudence* 41 (1996): 1–20.

———. "Aristotle on Friendship." *The Classical Bulletin* 65, nos. 3 and 4 (1989): 83–88.

———. *At the Limits of Political Philosophy: From "Brilliant Errors" to Things of Uncommon Importance.* Washington D.C.: Catholic University of America Press, 1996.

———. "The Best Form of Government." *Review of Politics* 40 (January 1978): 97–123.

———. "The Death of Plato." *The American Scholar* 65 (summer 1996): 401–16.

———. *Far Too Easily Pleased: A Theology of Play, Contemplation, and Festivity.* Los Angeles: Benziger/Macmillan, 1976.

———. "Human Rights as an Ideological Project." *American Journal of Jurisprudence* 32 (1987): 47–61.

———. *Liberation Theology.* San Francisco: Ignatius Press, 1982.

———. "'Man for Himself': On the Ironic Unities of Political Philosophy (Charles N. R. McCoy)." *Political Science Reviewer* 15 (fall 1985): 67–108.

———. "Natural Law Bibliography." *The American Journal of Jurisprudence.* 40 (1995): 157–98.

———. "The Natural Restoration of Fallen Angels in the Depths of Evil." In A. Ramos and M. Geroge, eds. *Faith, Scholarship, and the Culture in the 21st Century* 252–68. Washington, D.C.: Catholic University of America Press/American Maritain Society, 2002.

———. "On Forgiveness." *Crisis* 17 (January 1999): 59.

———. "On the Place of Augustine in Political Philosophy: A Second Look at Some Augustinian Literature." *Political Science Reviewer* 23 (1994): 128–65.

———. "On the Point of Medieval Political Philosophy." *Perspectives on Political Science* 28 (fall 1999): 189–93.

———. "On the Relation between Political Philosophy and Science." *Gregorianum* 69, 70. no. 2, (1988): 205–23.

———. "On the Sum Total of Human Happiness." *The New Blackfriars* 83 (May 2002): 232–41.

———. "On the Uniqueness of Catholicism and the Diversity of Religions." *Homiletic and Pastoral Review* 97 (January 1997): 13–21.

———. *On the Unseriousness of Human Affairs: Teaching, Writing, Playing, Believing, Lecturing, Philosophizing, Singing, Dancing.* Wilmington, Del.: ISI Books, 2001.

———. *The Politics of Heaven and Hell: Christian Themes from Classical, Medieval, and Modern Political Philosophy.* Lanham, Md.: University Press of America, 1984.

———. "Possessed of Both a Reason and a Revelation." In Peter Redpath, ed. *A Thomistic Tapestry: Essays in Memory of Étienne Gilson,* 177–91. New York: Rodopi, 2003.

———. "The Problem of Philosophic Learning." *Logos* 5 (winter 2002): 103–19.

———. "Reason, Revelation, and Politics: Catholic Reflections on Strauss." *Gregorianum* 62, no. 2 and 3 (1981): 349–66 and 467–98.

———. *Reason, Revelation, and the Foundations of Political Philosophy.* Baton Rouge: Louisiana State University Press, 1987.

———. *Redeeming the Time.* New York: Sheed & Ward, 1968.

———. *Religion, Wealth, and Poverty.* Vancouver: The Fraser Institute, 1990.

———. "The Right Order of Polity and Economy: Reflections on St. Thomas and the 'Old Law.'" *Cultural Dynamics* 7 (November 1995): 427–40.

———. "Transcendent Man in the Limited City: The Political Philosophy of Charles N. R. McCoy." *The Thomist* 57 (January 1993): 63–95.

———. "Truth and the Open Society." In G. Carey and J. Schall, eds. *Order, Freedom, and the Polity: Critical Essays on the Open Society,* 71–90. Lanham, Md.: University Press of America, 1986.

———. "The Uniqueness of the Political Philosophy of Thomas Aquinas." *Perspectives in Political Science* 26 (Spring 1997): 85–91.

———. "What Is Medieval Political Philosophy?" *Faith & Reason* 16 (spring 1990): 53–62.

Schlier, Heinrich. *The Relevance of the New Testament*. New York: Herder & Herder, 1968.

Schulz, Charles. *And the Beagles and the Bunnies Shall Lie Down Together*. New York: Holt, 1984.

———. *Dogs Don't Eat Dessert*. New York: Topper Books, 1987.

———. *Here Comes Charlie Brown!* New York: Fawcett, 1958.

Schumacher, E. F. *A Guide for the Perplexed*. New York: Harper Colophon, 1977.

Scruton, Roger. *The West and the Rest*. Wilmington, Del.: ISI Books, 2002.

Senior, John. *The Death of Western Culture*. New Rochelle, N.Y.: Arlington House, 1978.

Short, Robert. *The Parables of Peanuts*. New York: Harper, 1968.

Simon, Yves R. *A General Theory of Authority*. Notre Dame, Ind.: University of Notre Dame Press, 1980.

———. *Philosophy of Democratic Government*. Chicago: University of Chicago Press, 1951.

———. *The Tradition of Natural Law: A Philosopher's Reflection*. New York: Fordham University Press, 1992.

Sirico, R., ed. *The Social Agenda: A Collection of Magisterial Texts*. Vatican City: Pontifical Commission on Justice and Peace, Liberia Editrice Vaticana, 2000.

Smith, Janet. *Humanae Vitae: A Generation Later*. Washington, D.C.: Catholic University of America Press, 1991.

Sobran, Joseph. "Happy at Home" (Political Thought of C. S. Lewis), 156–89. In *Single Issues: Essays on the Crucial Social Questions*. New York: Human Life Press, 1983.

Sokolowski, Robert. *Eucharistic Presence: A Study in the Theology of Disclosure*. Washington, D.C.: Catholic University of America Press, 1993.

———. *The God of Faith and Reason: Foundations of Catholic Theology*. Washington, D.C.: Catholic University of America Press, 1991.

———. *Introduction to Phenomenology*. Cambridge: Cambridge University Press, 2000.

———. "The Method of Philosophy: The Making of Distinctions." *Review of Metaphysics* 51 (March 1998): 515–32.

Song, Robert. *Christianity and Liberal Society*. Oxford: Clarendon, 1997.

Spitzer, Robert J. *Healing the Culture*. San Francisco: Ignatius Press, 2000.

Steiner, George. *Real Presences*. Chicago: University of Chicago Press, 1989.

Strauss, Leo. *The City and Man*. Chicago: University of Chicago Press, 1964.

———. *Natural Right and History*. Chicago: University of Chicago Press, 1953.

———. "On the Mutual Influence of Theology and Philosophy." *Independent Journal of Philosophy* 3 (1979): 111–18.

———. *Persecution and the Art of Writing*. Westport, Conn.: Greenwood, 1952.

———. *Studies in Platonic Political Philosophy*. Edited by T. Pangle. Chicago: University of Chicago Press, 1983.

———. *Thoughts on Machiavelli*. Glencoe, Ill.: The Free Press, 1958.

———. *What Is Political Philosophy? and Other Studies*. Glencoe, Ill.: The Free Press, 1959.

Taylor, Charles. "The Sources of Authenticity." *Canadian Forum*. January/February, 1992.

Thomas Aquinas. *Commentary on Aristotle's Nicomachean Ethics*. Translated by C. Litzinger. Notre Dame, Ind.: Dumb Ox Press, 1993.

———. *Expositio Politicorum Aristotles*. Quebec: 1940.

———. *Summa contra Gentiles*. Romae: Apud Sedem Commissionis Leoninae, 1931.

———. *Summa Theologiae*. Ottawa: Garden City Press, MDCCCXLI.

Tinder, Glenn. *The Political Meaning of Christianity: An Interpretation*. San Francisco: Harper, 1991.

Torre, Michael D., ed. *Freedom in the Modern World: Jacques Maritain, Yves R. Simon, Mortimer J. Adler*. Notre Dame, Ind.: University of Notre Dame Press/ American Maritain Society, 1989.

Veatch, Henry B. *Aristotle: A Contemporary Appreciation*. Bloomington: Indiana University Press, 1974.

———. *Human Rights: Fact or Fancy?* Baton Rouge: Louisiana State University Press, 1985.

———. *Swimming against the Current in Contemporary Philosophy: Occasional Essays and Papers*. Washington, D.C.: Catholic University of America Press, 1990.

Voegelin, Eric. *Hitler and the Germans*. Columbia: University of Missouri Press, 1999. Vol. 31 in *The Collected Works of Eric Voegelin*.

———. *The New Science of Politics*. Chicago: University of Chicago Press, 1952.

———. *Order and History*. 5 vols. Baton Rouge: Louisiana State University Press, 1956–87.

———. "Political Science and the Intellectuals." Paper presented at the 48th Annual Meeting of the American Political Science Association. August 26–28, 1952.

———. *Science, Politics, and Gnosticism*. Chicago: Regnery, 1968.

Von Balthasar, Hans Urs. *The Fullness of Faith: On the Centrality of the Distinctively Catholic*. Translated by G. Harrison. San Francisco: Ignatius Press, 1975.

Von Hildebrand, Dietrich. *Liturgy and Personality*. Manchester, N.H.: Sophia Institute Press, 1993.

Wallace, William, A. *The Elements of Philosophy: A Compendium for Philosophers and Theologians*. Staten Island, N.Y.: Alba House, 1977.

———. *The Modeling of Nature: Philosophy of Science and the Philosophy of Nature in Synthesis*. Washington, D.C.: Catholic University of America Press, 1996.

Walsh, David. *After Ideology: Recovering the Spiritual Foundations of Freedom*. San Francisco: Harper, 1990.

———. *The Growth of the Liberal State*. Columbia: University of Missouri Press, 1977.

———. *Guarded by Mystery: Meaning in a Post-Modern Age*. Washington, D.C.: Catholic University of America Press, 1999.

———. *The Third Millennium: Reflections on Faith and Reason*. Washington, D.C.: Georgetown University Press, 1999.

Waugh, Evelyn. *A Little Learning: An Autobiography*. Boston: Little, Brown, 1964.

Weigel, George. *The Courage to Be Catholic*. New York: Basic Books, 2002.

————. *The Final Revolution: The Resistance Church and the Collapse of Communism.* Washington, D.C.: Ethics and Public Policy Center, 1992.

————. *Witness to Hope: The Biography of Pope John Paul II.* New York: Cliff Street Books, 1999.

Weigel, George, and Robert Royal, eds. *A Century of Catholic Social Thought: Essays on Rerum Novarum and Nine Other Key Documents.* Washington, D.C.: Ethics and Public Policy, 1991.

Weisheipl, James A. *Friar Thomas D'Aquino: His Life, Thought, & Works.* Washington, D.C.: Catholic University of America Press, 1983.

Wilhelmsen, Frederick. *Christianity and Political Philosophy.* Athens: University of Georgia Press, 1978.

————. "Faith and Reason." *The Modern Age* 13 (winter 1969): 25–32.

Williams, George Hunston. *The Mind of John Paul II: Origins of His Thought and Action.* New York: Seabury, 1981.

Wippel, John. *Metaphysical Themes in Thomas Aquinas.* Washington, D.C.: Catholic University of America Press, 1984.

Wiser, James. *Political Theory: A Thematic Inquiry.* Chicago: Nelson-Hall, 1986.

Woznicki, Andrew N. *Karol Wojtyla's Existential Personalism.* New Britain, Conn.: Mariel, 1980.

Index

~

About the Author

James V. Schall was born in Pocahontas, Iowa, in 1928. He was educated in public schools in Iowa. His family moved to California in 1945, where he attended the University of Santa Clara. He served in the United States Army from 1946 to 1947, after which he returned to Santa Clara. He entered the Society of Jesus in 1948 and was ordained a Roman Catholic priest in 1963. He received B.A. and M.A. degrees in philosophy from Gonzaga University in 1954 and 1955. He received a Ph.D. degree from Georgetown University in 1960, where he wrote his thesis in political philosophy under Professor Heinrich Rommen. After a year of studies in Ghent, Belgium, he taught at the Gregorian University in Rome from 1964 to 1977. From 1969 to 1977, he taught one semester each year at the University of San Francisco. In 1978, he joined the Government Department at Georgetown University, where he continues to serve as a full professor. He served one term on the Pontifical Commission on Justice and Peace and one term on the National Endowment for the Humanities. The complete listing of his publications—books, academic and popular essays, and columns—can be found at www.moreC.com/schall or www.georgetown.edu/schall. His books include: *Redeeming the Time; Reason, Revelation, and the Foundations of Political Philosophy; Another Sort of Learning; Jacques Maritain: The Philosopher in Society; On the Unseriousness of Human Affairs; At the Limits of Political Philosophy; What Is God Like?; Schall on Chesterton; Idylls and Rambles; Religion, Wealth, and Poverty; Human Dignity and Human Numbers; The Distinctiveness of Christianity; Does Catholicism Still Exist?; The Praise of 'Sons of Bitches,'* and others. He writes regular columns in *Crisis, Gilbert!, Saint Austin Review, Excelsis,* and *The University Bookman.*